BASIC TEACHINGS OF THE BIBLE

Questions Christians
Ask—Biblical Answers
VOLUME 1

Edward D.
Andrews

BASIC TEACHINGS OF THE BIBLE

Questions Christians Ask—Biblical Answers

VOLUME 1

Edward D. Andrews

ISBN-13: **978-0615931203**

ISBN-10: **0615931200**

Christian Publishing House

Cambridge, Ohio

BASIC TEACHINGS OF THE BIBLE Life Questions Christians Ask Themselves

support@christianpublishers.org

Write to: Christian Publishing House, P.O. Box 382, Cambridge, Ohio 43725

Edward D. Andrews is to be identified as the author of this work.

Editor: Dr. Thomas F. Marshall

Christian Publishing House
Professional Christian Publishing of the Good News

INTRODUCTION

Basic Teachings of the Bible is going to be a series of books that covers the Bible's position on the life questions that Christians and non-Christians ask themselves and others,

- Is it a Sin to Drink Alcoholic Beverages?

- Is it Wrong for Christians to Flirt?

- Are Women Allowed to Teach the Church?

- Should infants be baptized?

- Is hell a place of eternal torment?

- Do We Possess a Soul or Are We a Soul?

- Is Gambling a Sin?

- Why Does an All-Loving God Permit Pain, Suffering and Wickedness to Continue?

- Who Is the Avenging Messenger that Destroys the Wicked Ones?

- Does God Step in and Solve Our Every Problem, Because We are Faithful?

- If Homosexuals Are Born Genetically Predisposed, Is That Not of God?

- Is Anger Always Wrong?

- What About the Rod of Discipline of Proverbs 22:15?

- Has Fate Already Written Your Future?

- Who is the Antichrist?

These are the type of basic Bible questions that are discussed and debated, before and after church services, at Christian gatherings, and on the Internet. There are literally hundreds of them. These are questions that Bible critics might raise as well, which Christians have struggled to answer and now will have a simplified biblical response. The answers to these Bible questions are given from the Bible itself, as well as reasoning from the Scriptures. If the texts are straightforward, which answer the life question, the text alone will be used. However, if the text is difficult to understand, reasoning from the Scriptures will be used with the text. Some of the topics will be answered in just 2-3 pages, while some may take up to 15 pages or more. It is hoped that the reader will find the answers as additional evidence demonstrating that the Bible is the best source for guiding one's life. This publication is **volume 1** of numerous volumes to come.

BASIC TEACHING: Why Study the Bible?

2 Timothy 3:16 American Standard Version (ASV)

¹⁶ Every scripture inspired of God is also profitable for teaching, for reproof, for correction, for training in righteousness.

Today we have self-help books by the tens of thousands. We have magazines that offer advice on healthy living, fitness training, parenting, the family, men only, women only, and everything else imaginable. We have mental health doctors on television, offering counsel on everything from dieting, to bipolar disorder. We have Professional Counselors, covering a variety of walks of life, even Christian counselors. We also have the Social Worker, Psychologist, and Psychiatrist, to mention just a few. Nevertheless, tens of millions of people still look to a book, made up of sixty-six smaller books, which were written over a 1,600-year period, by forty different authors, who were inspired by the Creator of all things, THE BIBLE. Where do you go for guidance on the everyday decisions (where to eat), to the major decisions of life (which school to send your kids to)?

The Book of Truth

John 8:31-32 English Standard Version (ESV)

³¹ So Jesus said to the Jews who had believed him, "If you abide in my word, you are truly my disciples, ³² and you will know the truth, and the truth will set you free."

Only if we remain in the truth of God's Word, can we be freed from a false faith, false teachings, false relationships, false religion, and false righteousness. Those who are truly disciples of Jesus Christ, have the mind of Christ, which encompasses humility. As a Christian grows in knowledge and understanding of God's Word, there will be times that he or she will have to adjust conclusions that were based on a previous understanding. Yes, more knowledge, or accurate knowledge of what may have only been known partially, may mean that we will have to adjust our thinking, which requires humility. Those who are truly Jesus' disciples will remain in his word, and they will therefore be set free by the truth of that word.

One day, Jesus and his disciples were passing through Samaria, when they came to a town called Sychar, where the well of Jacob was. Tired from the journey, he decided this would be the place to rest. A woman from Samaria came to draw water, and a conversation ensued, which ended with Jesus saying, "God is spirit, and those who worship him must worship in spirit and truth." (John 4:24) We will take a deeper look at this verse in a moment, but for now, this is a clear indication that there is a form of worship, which is acceptable and there are forms of worship, which are unacceptable. Jesus made this all too clear when he said, "Not everyone who says to me, 'Lord, Lord,' will enter the kingdom of heaven, but the one who does the will of my Father who is in heaven. On that day many will say to me, 'Lord, Lord, did we not prophesy in your name, and cast out demons in your name, and do many mighty works in your name?' And then will I declare to them, 'I never knew you; depart from me, you workers of lawlessness.'" (Matthew 7:21-23) Toward the end of his life and ministry, Jesus prayed to the Father,

John 17:17 English Standard Version (ESV)

[17] Sanctify them in the truth; your word is truth.

If there is a form of worship that is acceptable, it must be in harmony with God's Word. God's Word contains the truth about him, his will and his purposes. "The realm in which the disciples' consecration is to be realized is the truth of God's word and of his name (see 17:11). This involves the work of both Son and Spirit; association with them, the one who in his person is the truth (14:6), and the one who is the "Spirit of truth" (14:17; 15:26; 16:13) who will lead believers into all truth (16:13), will so sanctify believers that they will be equipped for service of God. Critically, such service is ultimately grounded in divine revelation and predicated on an accurate understanding of and response to such revelation (Morris 1995: 647)."[1]

Psalm 119:142 English Standard Version (ESV)

[142] Your righteousness is righteous forever,
and your law is true.

2 Samuel 7:28 English Standard Version (ESV)

[28] And now, O Lord God, you are God, and your words are true, and you have promised this good thing to your servant.

Psalm 19:7 English Standard Version (ESV)

[7] The law of the LORD is perfect,
reviving the soul;

---

[1] Andreas J. Köstenberger, *John*, Baker Exegetical Commentary on the New Testament (Grand Rapids, MI: Baker Academic, 2004), 495–496.

the testimony of the LORD is sure,
  making wise the simple;

Proverbs 2:6 English Standard Version (ESV)

⁶ For the LORD gives wisdom;
  from his mouth come knowledge and understanding;

If it is the truth, which sets us free, how can we know what the truth is? The most basic rule of biblical interpretation in arriving at the correct meaning of a text is, it means what the author meant by the words he used, as should have been understood by his intended readers. While we will not take the time to be bogged down in how to correctly interpret God's Word, we will touch on it briefly, by first offering the Bible advice as to the level of effort needed, and recommending the best book for learning the truly conservative evangelical way of interpreting Scripture. The grammatical-historical method of biblical interpretation, which is found in Roy B. Zuck's BASIC BIBLE INTERPRETATION: A Practical Guide to Discovering Biblical Truth (1991).

Proverbs 2:1-5 English Standard Version (ESV)

¹ My son, **if you** receive my words
  and treasure up my commandments with **you**,
² making **your** ear attentive to wisdom
  and inclining **your** heart to understanding;
³ yes, **if you** call out for insight
  and raise **your** voice for understanding,
⁴ **if you** seek it like silver
  and search for it as for hidden treasures,
⁵ then **you** will understand the fear of the LORD
  and find the **knowledge of God**.

Basics in Biblical Interpretation

Step 1: What is the historical setting and background for the author of the book and his audience? Who wrote the book? When and under what circumstances was the book written? Where was the book written? Who were the recipients of the book? Was there anything noteworthy about the place of the recipients? What is the theme of the book? What was the purpose for writing the book?

Step 2a: What would this text have meant to the original audience? (The meaning of a text is what the author meant by the words that he used, as should have been understood by his readers.)

Step 2b: If there are any words in your section that you do not understand, or that stand out as interesting words that may shed some insight on the meaning, look them up in a word dictionary.

Step 2c: After reading your section from the three Bible translations, doing a word study, write down what you think the author meant. Then, pick up a trustworthy commentary, like Holmen Old or New Testament commentary volume, and see if you have it correct.

Step 3: Explain the original meaning down into one or two sentences, preferably one. Then, take the sentence or two; place it in a short phrase.

Step 4: Now, consider their circumstances, the reason for it being written, what it meant to them, and consider examples from our day that would be similar to theirs, which would fit the pattern of meaning. What **implications** can be drawn from the original meaning?

Step 5: Find the pattern of meaning, the "thing like these," and consider how it could apply in our modern day life. How should individual Christians today live out the implications and principles?

You know that Scripture makes it all too clear that there is only one acceptable way of worshiping God, the way outlined in God's Word. Everything that we believe and do needs to be based on that Word, and our understanding of that Word needs to be accurate. There are 41,000 different Christian denominations, and clearly not all are on the path of doing the will of the Father as outlined in the Bible, for Jesus said, in that day he will say to some, "depart from me, you workers of lawlessness." (Matt 7:23) We can either place our trust in man, who bickers and argues over what the Word of God means, or we can take the Bible's point of view itself. After all, it is the inspired Word of God, which is profitable for teaching, for reproof, for correction, and for training in righteousness, so that the man of God may be complete, equipped for every good work." (2 Tim 3:16-17)

Proverbs 3:5-6 English Standard Version (ESV)

5 Trust in the LORD with all your heart,
    and do not lean on your own understanding.
6 In all your ways acknowledge him,
    and he will make straight your paths.

Milton H. Terry wrote, "It is an old and oft-repeated hermeneutical principle that words should be understood in their literal sense unless such literal interpretation involves a manifest contradiction or absurdity."[2] Robert L. Towns writes, "The Bible is the

---

[2] Robert L. Thomas. *Evangelical Hermeneutics: The New Versus the Old* (p. 280). Kindle Edition.

best interpreter of itself. As we study the Bible, we should learn to compare the Scriptures we are studying with other relevant passages of Scripture to interpret the Bible."[3] These are a couple of the principles, which this series of books will live by, so that you can trust that these Basic Bible Teachings are from the Word of God, not the Word of man. Moreover, what is offered herein will live by the rules below. Lastly, you can take advantage of the book we recommended by Roy B. Zuck, Basic Bible Interpretation, so that you are not entirely dependent on the interpretation of others. In other words, you will be able to do as the Bereans did with the Apostle Paul, and for which he commended them,

Acts 17:10-11 English Standard Version (ESV)

Paul and Silas in Berea

[10] The brothers immediately sent Paul and Silas away by night to Berea, and when they arrived they went into the Jewish synagogue. [11] Now these Jews were more noble than those in Thessalonica; they received the word with all eagerness, examining the Scriptures daily to see if these things were so.

Note that they **(1)** "received the word with all eagerness," and then went about **(2)** "examining the Scriptures daily to see if these things were so." If the apostle Paul was to be examined to see if what he said was so, surely uninspired commentators must be examined as well.

---

[3] Towns, *AMG Concise Bible Doctrines* (AMG Concise Series) (Kindle Locations 1011-1012). AMG Publishers. Kindle Edition.

Live by the Rules

The Rule is to Remember Context

As you know, the context is the surrounding verses and chapters, to the text under consideration, as well as the book, and the entire Word of God. Is the interpretation you have come away with, in harmony with the context? Does this interpretation fit the **pattern of meaning** (see Image 1, below), of the historical setting? For example, Psalm 1:1-3 tells us that if we do not walk in the counsel of the wicked, or stand in the path of sinner, nor sit in the seat with scoffers, but delight in the Word of God, 'whatever he does, he will prosper.' Is that how we are to understand this, WHATEVER we do, we will prosper, if we only follow that counsel? No. In psalms, proverbs and other genre, there is an invisible "generally" before these absolute statements. In other words, 'generally speaking, whatever we do, we will prosper, if we follow the counsel correctly.'

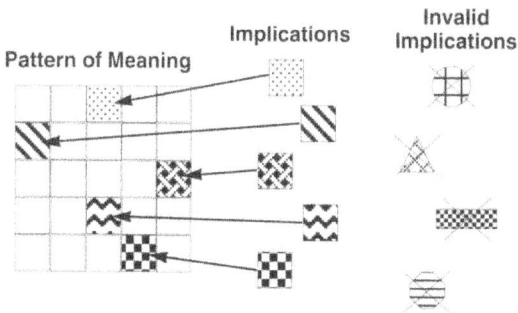

Image 1 Stein, p. 39

The Rule is Know the Whole of the Word of God

One needs to be familiar with the whole of the Word of God, to not be misled when someone presents you with Scriptures that are out of context. Too many people take a verse by what it says, without looking at what comes before or after it. For example, Jesus said at John 15:7, "ask whatever you wish, and it will be done for you." This brings up to immediate questions: (1) can we simply ask for anything and God will give it to us, (2) and even if it is according to His will and purposes, are we guaranteed of getting it? First, the context of the first part of that verse qualifies what is being talked about here, as Jesus said, "If you abide in me, and my words abide in you . . ." Thus, you must be doing **A** to get **B**. Second, this is not an absolute, which has the invisible "generally speaking" before it. In other words, "generally speaking," if you are abiding in Jesus and his words, the Father will answer your prayer if it is in harmony with His will and purposes.

The Rule is to Remember that Scripture Will Never Contradict Itself

If something is said in one place in Scripture that is at odds with another text in Scripture, it is being misinterpreted, or the context is being violated or misunderstood. There are verses that say the earth will be here forever, and then 2 Peter 3:7 says "the heavens and earth that now exist are stored up for fire." This would seem like a contradiction to the many other verses that say the earth will be here forever. However, if you look at the second half of that verse, it lets you know who is going to be destroyed, "destruction of the ungodly."

The Rule is to Not Hang Your Doctrinal Beliefs on Texts that are Hard to Understand

Do not be ashamed of struggling with passages that are hard to understand, because the apostle Peter even felt this way about some of the Apostle Paul's letters. ". . . Our beloved brother Paul also wrote to you according to the wisdom given him, as he does in all his letters when he speaks in them of these matters. There are some things in them that are hard to understand, which the ignorant and unstable twist to their own destruction, as they do the other Scriptures." (2 Pet 3:15-16)

The Rule is Literal Interpretation

The Bible is to be interpreted literally, in accordance with what it meant to the original audience at the time of its being written. We are to seek the obvious meaning of the words that the author used, and in the context, he used them, as well as the language he used. This rule does not mean that we are to be ignorant regarding idiomatic,[4] hyperbolic,[5] symbolic[6] or figurative[7] language, where Jesus says he is a door, and Jehovah says he is a rock. Herein, we still take it literally, as to what the figurative language means. In other words, we get a correct understanding of the idiomatic, hyperbolic, symbolic or figurative words, and this is what we take literally. For example, if Jesus meant that he is the way, it is through him that we receive life, we take that message literally, not that we actually believe he is literally some

---

[4] "Flowing with milk and honey" (Exodus 3:8)

[5] "You blind guides, who strain out a gnat and swallow a camel!" (Matt. 23:24)

[6] "… Israel committed adultery …" (Jer 3:8-9) How does a nation commit adultery? Adultery is symbolic of idolatry.

[7] Jesus said to his disciples, "You are the light of the world." (Matt. 5:14)

movable barrier used to open and close the entrance to a building, room, closet.

The Rule is what the Author Meant by the Words He Used

This rule will be stressed throughout this book. The meaning is what the author meant by the words that he used, as should have been understood by his readers, at the time of writing. We must understand that descriptive history to move the text along is not necessarily prescribing what we should do. For example, in Judges Chapter 6, Gideon, desiring evidence that God was with him, requested that a fleece be exposed at night on the threshing floor and be wet with dew the next morning but that the floor be dry. This does not mean that we follow this as an example, to see if God wants us to do something. This was descriptive not prescriptive.

The Rule is that Not All Commentaries are Created Equal

Sadly, not all commentaries are equal. Sadly, theological bias affects us all, some more than others do. Therefore, it is good to find a few dependable companies and rely on them, until you discover others just as dependable.

Walk by Spirit and Truth

John 4:24 Lexham English Bible (LEB)

24 God is spirit, and the ones who worship him must worship in spirit and truth."

What does it mean to worship in spirit? In spirit is not a reference to the Holy Spirit, but more of an attitude, a mental disposition, a way of thinking, or a mindset. We worship in "spirit" when we following our hearts, which are filled with faith and love of God and his Word. We worship in "spirit" when the inspired Word of God, trains our Christian conscience, the inner law that helps us to determine what is right, and leads us to recognize what is wrong. We worship in "spirit" when our worship is pure, based on an accurate knowledge of God's Word, having grateful hearts. We worship in "spirit" when we apply God's Word in our lives, having our spirit; mental disposition in harmony with the Holy Spirit's leading.

What does it mean to worship in truth? It means honestly, biblically, centered on the Word of God. In other words, we study the Word of God, having biblical truths revealed to us through the study, and then we worship according to that truth. In addition, it means that we are to be obedient to the truths revealed. This would include "truth of the gospel," which focuses on Jesus Christ and his efforts in the vindication of the sovereignty of his Father. (Galatians 2:14) God will allow a strong delusion to fall on those that "refuse to love the truth," 'condemning those who do not believe the truth.' (2 Thess. 2:9-12) Therefore, salvation only belongs to those, who upon hearing the Gospel, accept it as truth, and begin to walk in that truth. —2 Thessalonians 2:9-12; Ephesians 1:13, 14.

All true Christians should strive to be "fellow workers for the truth." They would certainly want to follow in the steps of John and Gaius as they defend the truth (Jude 1:3; 1 Pet 3:15), and like "children are walking in the truth." (3 John 3-8) They are doing so by going out into the community, proclaiming the Gospel, bringing people into the truth. They were to stay committed to the Gospel that they had heard in the beginning, when they were first brought into the truth.

Be Aware of Spiritual Needs

We need to strengthen ourselves spiritually, recognizing our spiritual needs. Our spiritual strength needs to grow stronger each day, because if we can be steadfast in the small trials, we will endure the more difficult that may lie in our path.

Imagine the faith it must have required for those Israelites, who celebrated the first Passover and then took some of the blood and smeared it on the sides and tops of the doorframes of the houses. (Exodus 12:1-28) Even after their firstborn sons surviving that night, many lost their faith shortly thereafter, when the Pharaoh's army was closing in on them at the Red Sea. (Exodus 14:9-12) However, after they walked the night through on the dry seabed to the other side of the Red Sea, then they looked back as the 80 feet walls of water fell in on the Egyptian army, killing them all. "Then they believed his words; they sang his praise." (Psa. 106:12) Yes, once again, they had faith. These Israelites were truly unsure about their relationship with God, whether he was really with them or not, which caused them to be unstable. Certainly, they could not have any peace of mind, as in one moment;

they would have a surge of hope, and in the next, a moment of despair.

James 1:6 English Standard Version (ESV)

6 But let him ask in faith, with no doubting, for the one who doubts is like a wave of the sea that is driven and tossed by the wind.

Questions to Ponder

• If only one form of worship is acceptable to God which one is it? --John 4:24; 8:31-32; 1:17.

• Who is the one responsible for you to ascertain the wisdom of God? -- Proverbs 2:1-4.

• The Bible is the source of practical guidance, but for whom? -- Hebrews 5:14.

BASIC TEACHING: Why is Life So Unfair!

On December 14, 2012, 20-year-old Adam Lanza fatally shot twenty children and six adult staff members in a mass murder at Sandy Hook Elementary School, in the village of Sandy Hook in Newtown, Connecticut. Before driving to the school, Lanza shot and killed his mother Nancy at their Newtown home. As first responders arrived, he committed suicide by shooting himself in the head.[8]

Parents, who sent their children to school that morning, never expected that by the end of the day, Adam Lanza would have murdered them. Worse still, there were signs that, if paid attention to, things may have not turned out the way they did. These parents are certainly what comes to mind when we think of life being unfair.

Unfairness the World Over

The world is full of these type of accounts the world over. We have social depravities everywhere we look. In the United States, there are hundreds of thousands living in homeless shelters, under bridges, eating at soup kitchens, and many have young children with them as well. On the other hand, the United States throws away more food than any other country. Sadly, the hungry in the United States, while truly unfair, rates very low when one considers the inhumane conditions of other

---

[8] http://en.wikipedia.org/wiki/Sandy_Hook_Elementary_School_shooting

countries. In some countries, like Mexico, you have a millionaire living in a mansion, with a poor person living in a shack next door, and a person living in a car, living next door to him. Almost two billion people live in such hopeless poverty and inhuman conditions that those in the Western part of the world could never relate.

A slum is a run-down area of a city. It can also be called shantytown, favela, skid row, barrio and ghetto.

Slums are characterized by urban decay, unemployment and high rates of poverty.

A slum in India.

Poverty is defined as a state of want; lacking means; inadequacy. Poverty "brings hunger, disease, high infant mortality, homelessness, and even war." Poverty "falls on the more vulnerable groups in society, such as women, the elderly, minority groups, and children." About 1 billion people around the world live on less than $1 a day.[9]

---

[9] http://prezi.com/8duqy_es2rmu/inadequate-living-conditions-around-the-world/

Some pictures of the slums

God's View of Fairness[10]

Leviticus 19:15 English Standard Version (ESV)

[15] "You shall do no injustice in court. You shall not be partial to the poor or defer to the great, but in righteousness shall you judge your neighbor.

Deuteronomy 32:4 English Standard Version (ESV)

[4] "The Rock, his work is perfect,
    for all his ways are justice.
A God of faithfulness and without iniquity,
    just and upright is he.

Acts 10:34-35 English Standard Version (ESV)

[34] So Peter opened his mouth and said: "Truly I understand that God shows no partiality, [35] but in every

---

[10] See Basic Teaching below, Why has God Permitted Wickedness and Suffering?

nation anyone who fears him and does what is right is acceptable to him.

From Where Does Unfairness Stem?

Genesis 2:17 Updated American Standard Version (UASV)

17 "but from the tree of the knowledge of good and evil you shall not eat, for in the day that you eat from it you shall surely die."

Genesis 3:4-5 Updated American Standard Version (UASV)

4 And the serpent **[Satan the Devil]** said to the woman, "You shall not surely die. **5** For God knows that when you eat of it your eyes will be opened, and you will be like God, knowing good and evil." knowing good and evil.

6 So when the woman saw that the tree was good for food, and that it was a delight to the eyes, and that the tree was to be desirable to make one wise, and she took of its fruit and ate, then she also gave some to her husband when with her, and he ate.

Genesis 3:24 Updated American Standard Version (UASV)

24 So he drove the man out, and at the east of the garden of Eden he placed the cherubim and a flaming sword that turned every way to guard the way to the tree of life.

John 8:44 English Standard Version (ESV)

44 You are of your father the devil, and your will is to do your father's desires. He was a murderer from the beginning, and does not stand in the truth, because there is no truth in him. When he lies, he speaks out of his own character, for he is a liar and the father of lies.

Revelation 12:9, 12 English Standard Version (ESV)

⁹ And the great dragon was thrown down, that ancient serpent, who is called the devil and Satan, the deceiver of the whole world, he was thrown down to the earth, and his angels were thrown down with him.

Unfairness in the Last Days

Revelation 12:12 English Standard Version (ESV)

¹² Therefore, rejoice, O heavens and you who dwell in them! But woe to you, O earth and sea, for the devil has come down to you in great wrath, because he knows that his time is short!"

Daniel 12:4 English Standard Version (ESV)

⁴ But you, Daniel, shut up the words and seal the book, until the time of the end. Many shall run to and fro, and knowledge shall increase."

2 Timothy 3:1-5 English Standard Version (ESV)

¹ But understand this, that in the last days there will come times of difficulty. ² For people will be lovers of self, lovers of money, proud, arrogant, abusive, disobedient to their parents, ungrateful, unholy, ³ heartless, unappeasable, slanderous, without self-control, brutal, not loving good, ⁴ treacherous, reckless, swollen with conceit, lovers of pleasure rather than lovers of God, ⁵ having the appearance of godliness, but denying its power. Avoid such people.

Unfairness Removed

Romans 16:20 English Standard Version (ESV)

20 The God of peace will soon crush Satan under your feet. The grace of our Lord Jesus Christ be with you.

1 John 2:15-17 English Standard Version (ESV)

Do Not Love the World

15 Do not love the world or the things in the world. If anyone loves the world, the love of the Father is not in him. **16** For all that is in the world, the desires of the flesh and the desires of the eyes and pride of life, is not from the Father but is from the world. **17** And the world is passing away along with its desires, but whoever does the will of God abides forever.

Matthew 24:3 English Standard Version (ESV)

Signs of the End of the Age

3 As he sat on the Mount of Olives, the disciples came to him privately, saying, "Tell us, when will these things be, and what will be the sign of your coming and of the end of the age?"

Matthew 24:36 English Standard Version (ESV)

No One Knows That Day and Hour

36 "But concerning that day and hour no one knows, not even the angels of heaven, nor the Son, but the Father only.

Fairness Restored

Isaiah 2:1-4 English Standard Version (ESV)

[1] The word that Isaiah the son of Amoz saw concerning Judah and Jerusalem.

[2] It shall come to pass in the latter days
    that the mountain of the house of the LORD
shall be established as the highest of the mountains,
    and shall be lifted up above the hills;
and all the nations shall flow to it,
[3]   and many peoples shall come, and say:
"Come, let us go up to the mountain of the LORD,
    to the house of the God of Jacob,
that he may teach us his ways
    and that we may walk in his paths."
For out of Zion shall go the law,
    and the word of the LORD from Jerusalem.
[4] He shall judge between the nations,
    and shall decide disputes for many peoples;
and they shall beat their swords into plowshares,
    and their spears into pruning hooks;
nation shall not lift up sword against nation,
    neither shall they learn war anymore.

Isaiah 11:3-4 English Standard Version (ESV)

[3] And his delight shall be in the fear of the LORD.
He shall not judge by what his eyes see,
    or decide disputes by what his ears hear,
[4] but with righteousness he shall judge the poor,
    and decide with equity for the meek of the earth;

and he shall strike the earth with the rod of his mouth,
   and with the breath of his lips he shall kill the wicked.

Isaiah 42:1 English Standard Version (ESV)

42 Behold my servant, whom I uphold,
   my chosen, in whom my soul delights;
I have put my Spirit upon him;
   he will bring forth justice to the nations.

Isaiah 35:5-6 English Standard Version (ESV)

5 Then the eyes of the blind shall be opened,
   and the ears of the deaf unstopped;
6 then shall the lame man leap like a deer,
   and the tongue of the mute sing for joy.
For waters break forth in the wilderness,
   and streams in the desert;

Isaiah 65:21-23 English Standard Version (ESV)

21 They shall build houses and inhabit them;
   they shall plant vineyards and eat their fruit.
22 They shall not build and another inhabit;
   they shall not plant and another eat;
for like the days of a tree shall the days of my people be,
   and my chosen shall long enjoy the work of their
hands.
23 They shall not labor in vain
   or bear children for calamity,
for they shall be the offspring of the blessed of the LORD,
   and their descendants with them.

Psalm 37:9-10 English Standard Version (ESV)

9 For the evildoers shall be cut off,
   but those who wait for the LORD shall inherit the land.

¹⁰ In just a little while, the wicked will be no more;
though you look carefully at his place, he will not be there.

Revelation 21:3-4 English Standard Version (ESV)

³ And I heard a loud voice from the throne saying, "Behold, the dwelling place of God is with man. He will dwell with them, and they will be his people, and God himself will be with them as their God.⁴ He will wipe away every tear from their eyes, and death shall be no more, neither shall there be mourning, nor crying, nor pain anymore, for the former things have passed away."

John 5:28-29 English Standard Version (ESV)

²⁸ Do not marvel at this, for an hour is coming when all who are in the tombs will hear his voice ²⁹ and come out, those who have done good to the resurrection of life, and those who have done evil to the resurrection of judgment.

BASIC TEACHING: Is Anger Always Wrong?

"Holding on to anger is like grasping a hot coal with the intent of throwing it at someone else; you are the one who gets burned." -- **Buddha**

"Anger is an acid that can do more harm to the vessel in which it is stored than to anything on which it is poured." -- **Mark Twain**

"Anybody can become angry - that is easy, but to be angry with the right person and to the right degree and at the right time and for the right purpose, and in the right way - that is not within everybody's power and is not easy." -- **Aristotle**

"Anger dwells only in the bosom of fools." -- Albert Einstein

"Whatever is begun in anger ends in shame. Anger is never without a reason, but seldom with a good one." -- **Benjamin Franklin**

Many humanly wise persons have offered their thoughts on anger. What has the Bible to say on the subject of anger and is it ever justified?

The Psalmist David says,

Psalm 37:8 English Standard Version (ESV)

[8] Refrain from anger, and forsake wrath!
Fret not yourself; it tends only to evil.

The apostle Paul says,

Ephesians 4:31 English Standard Version (ESV)

[31] Let all bitterness and wrath and anger and clamor and slander be put away from you, along with all malice.

The righteousness that God expects from his servants are "the wisdom from above is first pure, then peaceable, gentle, open to reason, full of mercy and good fruits, impartial and sincere." (Jam 3:17) If we "frequently react in an angry way to life's many annoyances, if we are substantially more irritable than the average person is," we cannot have the godly qualities of being "peaceable, gentle, open to reason, full of mercy and good fruits." Proverbs 29:22 warns us "an angry man stirs up strife, and a wrathful man abounds in transgression." This means that Christians, who suffer from anger issues, will want to get control over their vessel.

Yes, God desires that his servants also be slow about anger and wrath. Our anger is brought on by our perception of the situation. For example, if you spill coffee on your work shirt while driving to work or your car is stuck in the mud, making you late for work, or you lose an important business call when your cellphone drops the call, and on and on. This means that our anger over the situation is brought about without a justifiable cause. Our view of the situation is distorted, biased, or simply mistaken. We can distort a situation by making a molehill into a mountain, as the saying goes. We may say things to ourselves, like "life is just against me!" "These kinds of things only happen to me!" It can be biased, in that we consider only one side of a matter while ignoring other aspects of it. This could be the case with when we get all red lights on the way to driving to work, and we blame the city for not setting the lights, so we can catch more green lights. What we do not do is consider the fact that we procrastinated at home, which made us run late; otherwise, the red lights would have not mattered.

Christians are likely well aware that they have an anger issue, or they would not have bought this book. It is likely our greatest desire to overcome the anger issues, to be slow about anger, as we are very concerned about our relationship with God, as well as family and friends. We know that God is righteous in everything that he does, so any anger on his part would be completely justified. Our anger though, it is generally unjustified, which means that we live in a world of regretful comments and actions because we are quick to anger. "A man of quick temper acts foolishly." (Pro.14:17) Because of this, we have taken the first step, by investing the time, in covering material that will help us overcome our quickness to anger, because we are distraught over our hurting others.

Reasoning from the Scriptures

The Bible never contradicts itself, so one has to slow down when Paul also says to the Ephesians, "Be angry and do not sin; do not let the sun go down on your anger." (4:26) This verse would seem to be at odds with his above statement, and other biblical verses.

R. C. H. Lenski correctly commented on Ephesians 4:26, "The ethics which forbids all anger and demands unruffled calmness in every situation is Stoic and not Christian." Professor William Barclay similarly noted, "There must be anger in the Christian life, but it must be the right kind of anger." However, the question that begs to be asked is what is "the right kind of anger"?

Righteous Anger

It should be understood that anger is not a sin or sinful, if it is unselfish, righteous indignation. This righteous anger is a controlled reaction to the injustices within this fallen world. Jesus had an encounter with the Jewish religious leaders in the Synagogue over a man with a withered hand, "he looked around at them **with anger**, grieved at their hardness of heart, and said to the man, 'Stretch out your hand.' He stretched it out, and his hand was restored." (Mark 3:1-5) In addition, we find the following situation on the Gospel of John.

John 2:14-17 English Standard Version (ESV)

14 In the temple he found those who were selling oxen and sheep and pigeons, and the moneychangers sitting there. **15** And **making a whip of cords, he drove them all out of the temple**, with the sheep and oxen. And he poured out the coins of the moneychangers and overturned their tables. **16** And he told those who sold the pigeons, "Take these things away; do not make my Father's house a house of trade." **17** His disciples remembered that it was written, "**Zeal** for your house will consume me."

Jesus had righteous anger over the injustices he saw, but he also controlled that anger. In the account in John, Jesus could rightly take it to the level he did, because he was in his Father's house, and he needed to make certain points that would be recorded for generations to come. This does not mean that we can overturn some tables at a restaurant, because the management mistreated us. Therefore, righteous indignation for us is going to be different from some of the actions Jesus took. We have to deal with imperfections that he did not understand. We do not know the thinking of others, while he did. We do not know the heart condition of others, while he did. We tend to misunderstand, while Jesus did not. Our perception of a situation can be distorted, biased, or mistaken, while his was not. Jesus' anger was always based on truth and righteousness. Here is an account from Mark where Jesus was anointed at Bethany, and human imperfection, contributed to **un**righteous indignation.

Mark 14:3-9 English Standard Version (ESV)

3 And while he was at Bethany in the house of Simon the leper, as he was reclining at table, a woman came with an alabaster flask of ointment of pure nard, very costly, and she broke the flask and poured it over his head. **4** There were some who said to themselves indignantly, "Why was the ointment wasted like that? **5** For this ointment could have been sold for more than three hundred denarii and given to the poor." And they scolded her. **6** But Jesus said, "Leave her alone. Why do you trouble her? She has done a beautiful thing to me.

The imperfect humans were indignant by their perception of the situation, as well as by their selfishness, because the money from selling the ointment would have went in their moneybox for them. Jesus stops them, and explains why their indignation was actually **un**righteous indignation.

Mark 14:7-9 English Standard Version (ESV)

7 For you always have the poor with you, and whenever you want, you can do good for them. But you will not always have me. **8** She has done what she could; she has anointed my body beforehand for burial. **9** And truly, I say to you, wherever the gospel is proclaimed in the whole world, what she has done will be told in memory of her."

We are imperfect and cannot perceive situations, as Jesus can. Therefore, we need to dismiss any irrational thinking, until all the facts are in, and fully understood. This way we can make a rational decision.

Ephesians 2:3 English Standard Version (ESV)

3 among whom we all once lived in the passions of our flesh, carrying out the desires of the body and the mind, and were by nature children of wrath, like the rest of mankind.

Colossians 3:8 English Standard Version (ESV)

8 But now you must put them all away: anger, wrath, malice, slander, and obscene talk from your mouth.

Handling Anger Appropriately

Ephesians 4:22-24 tells us that we are to **put off your old self**, which belongs to your former manner of life and is corrupt through deceitful desires, and to be **renewed in the spirit of your minds**, and to **put on the new self**, created after the likeness of God in true righteousness and holiness." Colossians 3:9-10 informs us that we are to "**put off the old self** with its **practices** and have **put on the new self**, which is **being renewed** in **knowledge** after the image of its creator."

Chapter 4, verse 24 of Ephesians means that we allow our new Christian person to lead us in all that we do in our lives. In other words, whether we are at a Christian meeting, at work, at home, in school, or at recreation, we are to start living the life that follows in Christ Jesus' steps, as he set the example for us. (1 Pet 2:21) This putting on the new person is not some miraculous switch that is flipped on and the old person is immediate removed. No, the new person in Christ is developed over time, as we mature in our Christian walk.

We are "renewed in knowledge" by 'getting to know the only true God, and Jesus Christ whom had sent.' (John 17:3) Yes, as one starts their study of and application of God's Word, they will begin to develop a relationship with the Father and the Son. The former worldly desires, as well as anger issues, speaking ill of others, will fade away, and the new spiritual desires, long suffering personality, building up of others, will emerge.

Yes, again, it is a correct knowledge of the whole of Scripture, which gives us our new person, our being renewed. This is not some fake self, placed over an inner self that has not changed. No, the mind needs to be renewed by the Spirit of God. There is no hypocrisy, deceit, or duplicity associated with the "new self." We are sincerely to be a new person, not some masquerade.

The Mind of Christ

1 Corinthians 2:16 asks us who has 'known the mind of the Lord;[11] who has advised him?" But we have the mind of Christ.'

The Christian mind is influenced by the Spirit, in that they accept the Word of God as "breathed out by God and profitable for teaching, for reproof, for correction, and for training in righteousness that the man of God may be complete, equipped for every good work" (2 Tim 3:16), enabling him to take on the mind of Christ.

---

[11] A quotation from Isaiah 40:13, "Who has directed the Spirit of Jehovah, or being his counselor has taught him?" (ASV)

In other words, the thought processes of the Christian mind are Jesus' thoughts; their view of life is through his eyes. If the Christian has a correct mental grasp of scripture, they are not a victim of fleshly wisdom, which only leads to destruction. Those who truly reflect the Word of God in what they say, in deed, or in mind or heart attitude, will not be led astray by fleshly reasoning.

Some in the world have a measure of success in dealing with our imperfections, by the use of behavioral-cognitive therapy. However, the secular counselors are not as effective, as the Christian counselors are. The secular do not value or accept the spiritual aspect. They do not see the applying of the Bible as beneficial, for them, it is just the word of man. They do not understand the power of God's Spirit. While the world can affect personality changes, God can remove the old person, and replace it with a new person. However, like anything else, God expects us to apply the things that he teaches us, so we must take the wisdom of God, and apply it in our life, because that wisdom has become our wisdom.

We may have been living with our anger for so long, it seems that it just is part of us, and we have come to believe change is impossible. Let us look at Ephesians 4:31 again, "Let all bitterness and wrath and anger and clamor and slander be put away from you, along with all malice." We should note that Paul makes no exceptions for any Christian. We all are able to overcome our anger issues by means of the Holy Spirit, and the application of Scripture. Millions of Christians have removed character flaws from themselves. Therefore, you too can be slow about anger. God's Word does not speak of the impossibility of change, but of change as a fact.

Overcoming Should Statements

We need to come to the realization that nothing or no one is responsible for our anger issues. It is we and we alone. It is common by those that suffer from unrighteous anger to believe, it is the conditions, which *cause* the outbursts. The truth is nothing can *cause* us to get angry. However, the events or situations can contribute to our getting angry, if we feed them with irrational thinking. When an unpleasant situation falls upon us, we can feel the physical effects of a racing heart, tension in our muscles, the grinding of our teeth, and so on. These physical signs mean that we are dialoguing with ourselves either consciously or subconsciously. Yes, these thoughts can be present in the mind without our awareness of it. It is the physical signs that must wake us up to hidden thoughts.

If you are aware of what you are thinking, because you are saying it aloud, even if it is mumbling under your breath, or you have hidden comments that you are unaware of, you have signs to let you know. You need to be the one to reverse course. You must ask yourself, "What am I saying." Get a grasp of the thoughts that are racing through your mind. Maybe the events are with your spouse. First, we set ourselves up for failure, because the dating stage of a relationship is unrealistic. During this stage, both parties do their best to present nothing but the best side of themselves. After the honeymoon, a few months down the road, both begin to get comfortable and let their guard down, and show they flawed qualities. It can be a rude awakening, even more so if either of the spouses felt that marriage was going to be some perfect storybook life, with a happy ending.

If he says she *should* be like this, or he *should* be like that, this is another unrealistic aspect. We will get angry if we are caught up in the syndrome of *should*. A Christian marriage *should* be this way. Life *should* be list this, or

41

that. We must realize that we can even do this with ourselves as well. "I should do this, or I should do that." When someone or we do not live up to our expectation, this can contribute to frustration. "I should have been paying closer attention." "He should have been more considerate." Generally, we are making these should statement before we are even aware of all of the facts.

This should syndrome will affect our life far more than we may ever imagine, contributing to a life of tumult. When we go around setting standards of perfection for others, and ourselves (meaning mistake free), when humankind is imperfect, we are just setting ourselves up for a life of disappointment. We are going to fall short of our own standards that we have set, every day, as an imperfect person. Everyone is going to fall short of our standard setting of what we believe he or she should be like. We expect them to act a certain way in certain circumstances. We expect them to talk a certain way, drive a certain way, react a certain way, live a certain way, believe a certain way, and so on.

When we do not live up to our *should* standards of being mistake free, falling short daily, our statements of "I *should*" are going to contribute to intense-dislike of self, unworthiness and embarrassment, faultfinding, and frustration. When the rest of humanity does not live up to our *should* standards of them, namely being mistake free, we will become hostile toward them, have a self-righteous attitude that they should have done better. Imagine, we are only addressing one word, which possess so much power, and by changing it, we can free ourselves of constant let downs.

Christians, sad to say, are more susceptible to these *should* statements. Because we are involved in a biblical worldview that revolves around the moral values of

God, we tend to begin thinking more of ourselves than we ought to, when we become more successful at our spiritual lives. When we take a pause to notice our should statements, we will see that the vast majority revolve around morality, standards of conduct that are generally accepted as right or wrong. "He should have done a better job in mowing the lawn, because I pay him more than enough!" The rational side of that is that there are no rules that the lawn company has to go above the standards for us; he need not take extra pride in his work, just because we think he should. It is perfectly fine to do a standard job, as long as it is not substandard. Another should statement might be, "He should have thought to call, if he knew he was going to be late, because it is the descent thing to do!" He probably feels that he should have remembered as well, but he is imperfect, and so is his memory, especially when he is deeply involved in his job.

Our should statements assume that we are entitled to error free people, including ourselves. If we have been "wronged" because of human imperfection, make allowances, forgive them as God forgives us every day. If we have been wronged because of substandard behavior, take care of it in a rational manner. If we deal with it through anger, we will not get the desired outcome. Rather we will only end up with a defensive person, be it a family member, a friend, or another, who may have not had bad intentions to start with, but now he is being pushed into a corner. Think of the folly of this statement, "I was nice to the people at that table, being a good waitress; they *should* have given me a tip." We cannot be the controller over someone else's free will, their right to live life the way they believe to be correct. As much as we may desire that they live by our standards, our wanting it will not bring it about.

In fact, if we react inappropriately to what we believe they should or should not do, it will only create bitterness in our stomach, and distance them from us. We certainly detest the idea of anyone taking control of the way we do things, and this is the case with all free willed people. Once we realize that there is no such thing as absolute fairness among imperfect humanity, as it is relative to the one carrying out the actions. What we see as fair biblically, the world sees as unfair. There is absolute fairness with God, as well as his Word the Bible, but at present, the world of mankind alienated from God, does not live by that fairness. Being that Christians live among 41,000 different denominations of other Christians, who believe differently, it might be best not to assume the same fairness with Christians we meet.

Spend each day watching for the word should. The moment we are aware of something, we will notice it far more often. Pick out a type of car or truck, watch for them on the road over the next week. They will be everywhere, as will our *should* statements.

Self-Amplifying Thinking

Small negative things, events happen to each of us every day, but these are amplified to unrealistic measures by our overactive thinking, which leads to frustration, followed by an angry outburst eventually. This section is self-explanatory. If we are wronged or we perceive that we are wronged, to amplify the situation will only contribute to more frustration, as well as holding onto the negative emotions for far longer. Suppose that we are going for an interview, or some test, for a company that we want to hire us, and we enter it thinking, "This is impossible, I can't do this!" Well, that is certainly an overreaction, an amplification of the situation. This will only bring about a self-prophecy. We see interviews or tests as ending negatively, so we end up fulfilling our own negative thinking.

Self-Psychic Thinking

We make judgments about others, **ir**rationalizing their behavior. We assume that someone is thinking badly of us or talking badly about us without any evidence. We assume that bad things just always happen to us, which leads to frustration, followed by an angry outburst eventually. In this, we tell ourselves what we want to hear, and we could care less if it is rational or not, because we know it must be true. I we were to just stop for a moment and listen to ourselves, we would discover that our thinking is mistaken.

An example of this is, when someone commits a perceived wrong against us, we make a judgment call (labeling) about them, "He **is** just a hothead." "She **is** dumb." These kids **are** evil." "She **is** one-sided." A person is never to be evaluated by to be verb, like "is," and "are." When we say someone "is" something, this means that she is 100 percent whatever label we gave her, it is who she is, her essence. If we say, "She **is** a bad mother," this means that she is a bad mother 100 percent of the time. No one is that bad of a mother.

When we generate irrational belief, because we misjudge intentions, like "he loves that television more than me," or "he loves his friends more than me," we are not only misdiagnosing the problem, but we create an atmosphere that will build up inside you until it reaches explosive proportions. If we entertain these irrational thoughts, they will actually look worse than they actually are. If the spouse has done or is doing something that is distressing, do not overreact with condemnation of labeling them as "unloving," or foolish." It is best to approach them with a question than a statement. The wife might ask, "I do not understand, can you please explain ..." As they explain, we need to listen, with understanding, trying to wrap or mind around how they view things. Take notice the warning of Proverbs 18:13: "If one gives an answer before he hears, it is his folly and shame." No one likes to be labeled, judged, or evaluated unfairly. Therefore, instead of reacting to quickly to irrational thoughts, we should take a moment to gather ourselves with a prayer. Then, we need to attempt to determine the thinking, purpose or motive behind the situation. We do well to follow the counsel of Proverbs 20:5, "Counsel in a man's heart is deep water; but a man of understanding draws it out."

We have already discussed that anger is not a sin, and that there is righteous anger and unrighteous anger. Moreover, we can use our anger to our benefit under the right circumstances. We need to learn how to determine when our anger is beneficial and when it is harmful.

Proverbs 14:29 English Standard Version (ESV)

²⁹ Whoever is slow to anger has great understanding,
but he who has a hasty temper exalts folly.

Proverbs 29:11 English Standard Version (ESV)

¹¹ A fool gives full vent to his spirit,
but a wise man quietly holds it back.

If we are one, who has real issues with anger and rage, our first line of defense is to flee the area that has contributed to an oncoming episode. This is for those that verbally or even physically abuse others when angry. In the beginning of dealing with your anger, you will want to remove yourself from the situation the very moment that you feel an onset of anger. Beforehand, you need to set the spouse or child down, whomever is the victim of your anger, tell them that you love them, and you are working on your anger. Tell them that the beginning stages are to leave the scene before you hurt the ones you love. This is not a solution, just a protection for the victims.

Proverbs 17:14 English Standard Version (ESV)

[14] The beginning of strife is like letting out water,
   so quit before the quarrel breaks out.

Each of us are responsible for what we do when a case of anger or rage sets in, and we do harm to others, or property. It is our thinking that leads to the outburst.

Psalm 37:8 English Standard Version (ESV)

[8] Refrain from anger, and forsake wrath!
   Fret not yourself; it tends only to evil.

Proverbs 15:1 English Standard Version (ESV)

[1] A soft answer turns away wrath,
   but a harsh word stirs up anger.

Proverbs 29:22 English Standard Version (ESV)

[22] A man of wrath stirs up strife,
   and one given to anger causes much transgression.

Righteous anger is toward anyone who has set out to hurt us willfully and purposely, deliberately, and needlessly. We have to contemplate how we are going to deal with anger when we are not in the throes of our rage. When we feel that we have been treated unjustly, no matter how slight, our moral emotions can consume us, if we are not prepared. What we want to do is start with the small things, because we are at a low level of anger. Here we are looking at times when someone cuts us off in traffic, someone cuts in front of us at the checkout line at the store, a waitress fails to care for our needs, someone makes fun of you in public, we are on the phone with customer service and she can barely speak English, and so on. Our goal is to internally dialogue in our head as we feel the onset of anger. Below, follow the progress from A – D.

(A) SITUATON (Outside your control): A waitress fails to serve you as she should have, and was distant toward you	**(B) YOUR THINKING** (inside your control): "What!" "You stupid fool!" "What an idiot!" "She is a … jerk!" "What a loser!"
(C) BEHAVIOR: You tell her off, and do not leave a tip. On the other hand, you daydream about telling her off. You very loudly tell the cashier when you pay as you head out.	**(D) EMOTIONS**: frustration, anger, even guilt over your thoughts

On your way out to the car, you run the situation through your mind, as though it were a movie, repeatedly. You go through how it happened, what you did, or what you would have like to have said and did. Each time you play it through, you get even angrier. You slam your car door, drive recklessly out of the parking lot, and speed back to work, going through it over and over again. You get to work, and tell your coworkers or anyone who will listen. It has warped you and has stolen your desire and energy, which means you have a bad day. Once you are home, you take it out on your wife, as you loudly tell the story again, and explain how this waitress ruined your day. Throughout the night, you are rude and disrespectful with your wife and children, as you will not let go of the mood.

Here is the irony; you have done the same thing to other people, including your family, throughout your day, which you felt the waitress had done to you. Moreover, you were not aware of why the waitress failed to do a good job in serving you, and was distant toward you. She has to work because every penny counts, but she has a husband who verbally or physically abuses her, or maybe her teenager ran away again, or she found drugs in their room, or the electricity is about to get shut off, or she can't afford to go to the doctor, and is in serious pain. Anyone of these or other reasons could be why she was distant. Most self-righteous people would say, "Well, she *should* not have taken her problems to work with her!" First, there is that *should* statement again. Moreover, what did you do? You took one tiny incident in your day back to work and home to your family. Is a distant waitress who affected you so badly anywhere near the problems she may have been having?

Change the Internal Dialogue

You may or may not have noticed, but I started this chapter with first person plural pronouns or first person plural possessive adjective (we, us, our), and I am now moving to second person pronouns (you), because I want to speak to you the reader directly. Your anger is built up like in the above, because of the conscious or subconscious dialogue going on in your head. It results from the things that you are telling yourself. If you are going to overcome this, you must dialogue back, and put out the fire. First, whether people deserve it or not, you need to **make allowances for them**, as God makes allowances for you each and every day.

Romans 5:10 Lexham English Bible (LEB)

10 For if, *while we* were enemies, we were reconciled to God through the death of his Son, by much more, having been reconciled, we will be saved by his life.

Since the sinful rebellion of Adam, we have all inherited sin and death, meaning that no father can pass on perfection, everlasting life, to their child. (1 Tim. 6:19) When Adam and Eve rebelled in the Garden of Eden, we immediately lost our status as sons and daughters of God. This created a rift in our relationship with our loving heavenly Father. (Deut. 32:5) From the moment that the first human couple was expelled from Eden, the human family that was to come would be outsiders to the created family of Jehovah God, which included spirit persons as well. We, by way of our forefather, Adam, placed ourselves in an alienated position with our heavenly Father.

However, we as imperfect humans can be accredited a righteous standing before God, being accepted back into the family of God. **He makes allowances** for our imperfection.

Psalm 103:9-12 Lexham English Bible (LEB)

9 He does not dispute continually,
nor keep *his anger* forever.
10 He has not dealt with us according to our sins,
nor repaid us according to our iniquities.
11 For as *the* heavens are high above the earth,
so his loyal love prevails over those who fear him.
12 As far as east *is* from west,
so he has removed far from us *the guilt of* our transgressions.

Isaiah 38:17 Lexham English Bible (LEB)

[17] Look! Bitterness was bitter to me for peace.
And you were the one who loved my life from *the* pit of destruction,
    for you have cast all my sins behind your back.

Micah 7:18-19 Lexham English Bible (LEB)

[18] Who *is* a God like you, forgiving sin
    and passing over rebellion for the remnant of his inheritance?
He does not retain his anger forever,
    for he delights in loyal love.
[19] *He will again have compassion* on us;
    he will trample our iniquities.
And you will hurl all their sins
    in the depths of the sea.

You will notice in Psalm 103:12, that God removes the sins of the repentant one as far as the east is from the west. The picture being painted is, to the human mind that is the farthest you can remove something, as there is no greater distance. In Isaiah 38, we are given another visual, God throwing our sins behind his back, meaning he can no longer see them, as they are out of sight, thus out of mind. In Micah, our last example, we see that God hurls all of the sins of a repentant person into the depths of the sea. In the setting of the ancient person, this meant that retrieving them was literally impossible. In other words, God has removed them, to never be retrieved or brought to mind ever again. This was the viewpoint that he had before Jesus ever even offered himself as a ransom sacrifice.

Now, your first step in internally dialoguing with yourself is to make allowances for the things that are happening. Just like the reasons of why the waitress in the above may have been distant, you need to make allowances of what might be why. You need to remove the alleged or real injustice to you, as far as the east is from the west, by placing them behind your back (out of sight), or throwing them in the sea (incapable of recovery). You say these things to yourself. Remind yourself that God forgives you daily, all day for your transgression in just this way.

Now,

(1) you immediately make various allowances as to why the events are the way they are,

(2) you remind yourself of how God views your transgressions (say a short prayer of thanks),

(3) you tell yourself the repercussions of what anger will do (result of anger),

(4) you take notice of the *should* thoughts that would have come to you, and

(5) you revise those should thoughts.

Someone commits a transgression against you, and you feel your jaw tightening, as well as your body getting warm, so **(1)** you tell yourself she or he is this way because ... **(2)** You tell yourself that God has overlooked my transgressions, setting them aside because he is making allowances for my imperfection. You now feel less tense, but **(3)** you still tell yourself that if I had gotten angry, I would have ruined the rest of my day, been in a foul mood, would have taken it out on all who I met, as well as my loved ones. I would have normally said something like, **(4)** "I treated him well; he **should** have treated me good as well. This is a *should* statement, an unrealistic expectation." Rather, **(5)** "the reality is, it would be great if he treated me well, but it is not realistic that all people will do so. Sometimes, things are affecting them.

This may seem like a lot initially, but this can be said internally, within just a couple minutes. At first, you may want to make a laminated card that has the above 1 – 5 on it, to carry it with you wherever you go, until you have memorized the steps. Every single thought, whether it is conscious or subconscious makes an electrical path through the white matter of our brain, with a record of the thought and event. This holds true with our actions as well. If it is a repeated way of thinking or acting, it has no need to form a new path; it only digs a deeper, engrained, established path. This would explain how a factory worker who has been on the job for some time, gives little thought as they perform their repetitive functions each day, it becomes unthinking, automatic, mechanical. These repeated actions become habitual. There is yet another facet to considered; the habits, repeated thoughts and actions become simple and effortless to repeat. Any new thoughts and actions are more difficult to perform, as there needs to be new pathways opened up. These five steps to a new way of thinking will have to be practiced daily, until they become your new way of thinking.

BASIC TEACHING: What About the Rod of Discipline of Proverbs 22:15?

Proverbs 22:15 English Standard Version (ESV)

15 Folly is bound up in the heart of a child, but the rod of discipline drives it far from him.

It is paramount that you not live any portion of the Bible that you have not established to be the correct interpretation, as shortcuts can result in mistakes. There are many who have applied God's Word without a correct understanding. Not all cases can be as extreme as the one I am listing here, but it should bring home the point that the Bible needs to be fully understood [a correct mental grasp] before applying.

Wisconsin Church Members Charged With Abusing Infants. Pastor Philip Caminiti, 53, and his brother, John Caminiti, 45, were charged with a dozen counts of child abuse last week and also pleaded innocent. The victims included 12 children ranging in age from infancy to 6 years old, according to the sheriff's office. "During interviews with detectives, Phil expressed his belief that the Bible dictates the use of a rod over a hand to punish children. He stated that children only a few months old are 'worthy' of the rod and that by 'one and a half months,' a child is old enough to be spanked," according to the sheriff's office release. "Throughout the investigation, the church members were open with detectives about their 'Spare the rod, spoil the child' philosophy. They described using wooden dowels and wooden spoons on the bare skin of children, starting as young as 2 months old," the sheriff's office said.[12]

Proverbs 13:24 (English Standard Version)

[24] Whoever spares the rod hates his son, but he who loves him is diligent to discipline him

Proverbs 22:15 (English Standard Version)

[15]Folly is bound up in the heart of a child, but the rod of discipline drives it far from him.

Proverbs 23:13 (English Standard Version)

[13]Do not withhold discipline from a child; if you strike him with a rod, he will not die.

How are we to understand these verses? Are we to take them literally, and beat our children with rods? In this context, the rod is representative of authority in the Bible, and stands for parental authority, correction, whatsoever form it may take. In Bible times, the Hebrew word for "rod" stood for a stick or a staff, such as the one a shepherd used to guide his sheep. (Psalm 23:4) Can you picture a shepherd beating his sheep with his rod or staff? Hardly! Therefore, "the rod" of parental authority advocates loving guidance, not harsh or brutal punishment. It does not mean beating a child, but spanking is permissible, depending on the age and to the extent that it is, a corrective measure, not to punish, hurt or harm. Many times, a simple rebuke will be the corrective measure that gets the desired results.

U.S.News & World Report, August 7, 1989, correctly states, "Parents who are not harshly punitive, but who set firm boundaries and stick to them, are significantly more

---

[12] http://www.aolnews.com/2011/03/26/members-of-aleitheia-bible-church-in-wisconsin-charged-with-abus/

likely to produce children who are high achievers and who get along well with others." In its conclusion, the article stated, "Perhaps the most striking theme to emerge from all the scientific data is that establishing a pattern of love and trust and acceptable limits within each family is what really counts, and not lots of technical details. The true aim of discipline, a word that has the same Latin root as disciple, is not to punish unruly children but to teach and guide them and help instill inner controls."

Many people read the Bible and immediately understand it in the context of their own expectations. They do not look for the context of the Bible and find a like context in their life. It is like the Bible study that Dr. Stein shared at the outset of this book, A Guide to Interpreting the Bible, where the person said, "this means . . . to me." As you work your way around the group, each person offers their individual stamp on what the text under consideration means to them. They are not considering what the text meant to the initial readers, just what it means to them.

The Bible' View

Would you say the following counsel is better than the Bible's advice?

• "don't exasperate your children by coming down hard on them. Take them by the hand and lead them."

• "don't come down too hard on your children or you'll crush their spirits."

Some will be quick to say, 'this is far better than the Bible's advice. However, this *is* the advice from the Bible. It can be found at Ephesians 6:4 and Colossians 3:21. I simply took it from a paraphrase, (*The Message* (MSG)) so that it would not be easily known that it was from the Bible.

The Bible is very balanced in its counsel on how to correct a child. It suggests other measures to be just as effective and even more effective than physical punishment. In the Bible, physical punishment is the last measure taken, and it is corrective, not punitive, to be applied modestly.

Proverbs 8:33 English Standard Version (ESV)

³³ Hear instruction and be wise,
and do not neglect it.

Proverbs 17:10 English Standard Version (ESV)

¹⁰ A rebuke goes deeper into a man of understanding
than a hundred blows into a fool.

Deuteronomy 11:19 English Standard Version (ESV)

¹⁹ You shall teach them to your children, talking of them when you are sitting in your house, and when you are walking by the way, and when you lie down, and when you rise.

How Should You Discipline Your Child?

While this text is not applied to parenting children, but everyone, certainly includes your children,

2 Timothy 2:24-25 English Standard Version (ESV)

²⁴ And the Lord's servant must not be quarrelsome but kind to everyone, able to teach, patiently enduring evil, ²⁵ correcting his opponents with gentleness. God may perhaps grant them repentance leading to a knowledge of the truth,

Discipline is not something that we carry out in the heat of our emotions, as we are to offer corrective counsel. The object is to teach the child the errors of his or her ways. If this is done when angry, you will over discipline, sending the wrong lesson to the child. How did God discipline his children, the Israelite people?

Jeremiah 46:28 English Standard Version (ESV)

²⁸ Fear not, O Jacob my servant,
declares the LORD,
   for I am with you.
I will make a full end of all the nations
   to which I have driven you,
   but of you I will not make a full end.
I will discipline you in **just measure**,
   and I will by no means leave you unpunished."

While good parenting is not allowing a child to go unpunished, it needs to be accomplished in a just measure, proportionate to the wrong committed. There is no wrong that a child can commit, even if it is horrific, as we have seen in the news of late, which necessitates child abuse, going beyond the just measure. Paul says that we are to "return evil for evil to no one," which would include our children. (Rom 12:17) Spanking is child abuse when it is done in anger. Spanking is meant to get their attention, so they pay attention to counsel, not punish them corporally.

BASIC TEACHING: Is It Wrong for Christians to Flirt?

Flirting comments, "I'm not flirting. I'm just being extra nice to someone who is extra attractive." "It's called flirting when you are in a relationship but it is called being friendly when you are single." "I've found this new disease, it's called LOVE. I know it's contagious 'cause you gave it to me." "If you got any hotter this whole world would catch fire." "I was so enchanted by your beauty that I ran into that wall over there. So I am going to need your name and number for insurance purposes." "If I stole your heart, and you stole mine, wouldn't it be the perfect crime?"

What is flirtation? The Encarta dictionary says, "a short playful interaction based on lighthearted feeling, especially one that suggests sexual interest." What is the Bible's viewpoint on flirting? There are no black and white verses, which explicitly state whether flirting as right or wrong. Nevertheless, we can ascertain the Bible's view by looking at the principles behind some texts that do touch on the matter, while also keeping our definition in mind, "**especially** one that suggests sexual interest."

Married Couples

Certainly, none would disagree that flirting between married couples is perfectly fine, and expected. However, outside of the marriage, this is never just harmless fun. Should a husband or a wife flirt with someone outside of his or her marriage, just to try and make the other jealous, thinking that will reignite interest?

Genesis 2:24 English Standard Version (ESV)

[24] Therefore a man shall leave his father and his mother and hold fast to his wife, and they shall become one flesh.

Ephesians 5:31, 33

English Standard Version (ESV)

[31] "Therefore a man shall leave his father and mother and hold fast to his wife, and the two shall become one flesh." [33] ... let each one of you love his wife as himself, and let the wife see that she respects her husband.

While most would believe that a little harmless flirting would never go anywhere, far too often it actually leads to adultery.

Proverbs 6:25-26 Lexham English Bible (LEB)

25 Do not desire her beauty in your heart;
may she not capture you with her eyelashes.
26 [Although the price of a prostitute may be as much as a
loaf of bread,
another man's wife hunts the precious life.][13]

Exodus 20:14, "You shall not commit adultery,"
which means that we need to value the sanctity of
marriage, to remain faithful at times of temptation. In
Matthew 5:28 Jesus states, "But I say to you that
everyone who looks at a woman with lustful intent has
already committed adultery with her in his heart." (ESV)
Jesus identified the preliminaries, which was a sin in and
of itself, that lead up to the sinful act of adultery, as
"lustful intent." Focus on the word "intent." This is not a
man walking along who catches sight of a beautiful
woman, and has an indecent thought, which he then
dismisses (that is not lusting). It is not even a man in the
same situation that has an indecent thought, who goes on
to entertain and cultivate that thought (this is lusting, and
is a sin). No, this is a man that is staring, gazing at a
woman with the intent of lusting, and is looking at the
woman, with the intention of peaking her interest and
desire, to get her to lust.

Verse 25 of chapter 26 in Proverbs warns the son
against just that, do not get "lustful intent" in your heart
because of her beauty. Yes, even when the evil woman is
seeking to flame such desires. Aside from the fact that it
violates God's Law, for mere moments of immediate
gratification at a very inexpensive price, you are risking

---

[13] Duane A. Garrett, vol. 14, Proverbs, Ecclesiastes, Song of Songs,
The New American Commentary, 100 (Nashville: Broadman & Holman
Publishers, 1993).

your life on a wife, who has a husband that will take your precious life.

James 1:14-15 Lexham English Bible (LEB)

¹⁴ But each one is tempted *when he* is dragged away and enticed by his own desires. ¹⁵ Then desire, *after it* has conceived, gives birth to sin, and sin, *when it* is brought to completion, gives birth to death.

We resist the devil by immediately dismissing any thought that is contrary to God's values found in his Word, which enters our mind, we do not entertain it for a moment, nor do we cultivate it, causing it to grow. We then offer rational prayers in our head, or better yet, aloud, so we can defeat fleshly irrational thinking with rational biblical thinking.

Proverbs 5:21 Updated American Standard Version (UASV)

²¹ For the ways of man are before the eyes of Jehovah;
And he makes level all his paths.

Solomon began Proverbs chapter 5, by looking at the consequences of immoral behavior. The reality is that our actions, even our desires that are not immediately dismissed, are "before the eyes of Jehovah." Regardless of how well we might believe that we are hiding inappropriate sexual desires, or worse still acting on those sexual inappropriate desires, it will ruin our relationship with God, as he sees all things. Is some brief immediate gratification worth losing the most precious relationship we can have with God? Moreover, nothing stays hidden forever, and the wife will eventually discover this dirty secret sinful life.

Proverbs 6:27-29 Lexham English Bible (LEB)

²⁷ Can a man carry fire in his lap,
and his clothes not burn?
²⁸ If a man walks upon the hot coals,
will his feet not be burned?
²⁹ Thus, he who goes to the wife of his neighbor,
any who touches her shall not go unpunished.

This pictorial message is all too clear, as there is no way of committing adultery, and not suffering the consequences in some fashion. The picture that these two questions paint is that most generally, it is not some mild pain, but something that will bring about agonizing, unbearable pain, which will scar you for life.

Matthew 5:27-28 English Standard Version (ESV)

²⁷ "You have heard that it was said, 'You shall not commit adultery.' **²⁸** But I say to you that everyone who looks at a woman with **lustful intent** has already committed adultery with her in his heart.

In verse 28 of Matthew chapter 5, you will notice the phrase "**lustful intent**," keying in on the word "intent." This is not a man walking along who catches sight of a beautiful woman, and has an indecent thought, which he then dismisses. It is not even a man in the same situation that has an indecent thought, who goes on to entertain and cultivate that thought. No, this is a man that is staring, gazing at a woman with the intent of lusting, and is looking at the woman, with the intention of peaking her interest and desire, to get her to lust.

Those Who Are Unmarried

Flirting should be within the confines of a couple, who intend to getting married. However, remember our definition made it clear, "a short playful interaction based on lighthearted feeling, **especially one that suggests sexual interest**." Being that you are still unmarried, just dating, or even engaged, the fear of committing fornication should restrict any flirtation, to be very small, and done where it cannot be acted upon, if at all. Is a little pleasure from flirting, with the pent up sexual desire that cannot be acted on until marriage, really worth the stress, not to mention the risk. Rather than flirt, simple ways of showing romantic interest in each other is best.

What though are the dangers of single people flirting with others just for mere entertainment, believing it to be harmless? What does the Bible say?

Proverbs 13:12 English Standard Version (ESV)

¹² Hope deferred makes the heart sick,
   but a desire fulfilled is a tree of life.

The appropriate use of this verse is that one gains renewed strength through the fulfillment of a long-awaited desire. However, when the long-awaited desires are never fulfilled, these will likely lead to pent-up sexual desires, which will possible overpower the person, causing him or her to act on them. Even if both persons, who are being flirtatious say they would never act on them, how do they really know the heart's desire of the other, when the Bible tells us we cannot even know our own heart,

Jeremiah 17:9 English Standard Version (ESV)

⁹ The heart is deceitful above all things,
   and desperately sick;
   who can understand it?

Consider some other texts that we can draw on, to ascertain how God feels.

Colossians 3:5 English Standard Version (ESV)

5 Put to death therefore what is earthly in you: sexual immorality, impurity, passion, evil desire, and covetousness, which is idolatry.

1 Thessalonians 4:3-5 English Standard Version (ESV)

3 For this is the will of God, your sanctification: that you abstain from sexual immorality; **4** that each one of you know how to control his own body in holiness and honor, **5** not in the passion of lust like the Gentiles who do not know God;

Ephesians 5:3

English Standard Version (ESV)

3 But sexual immorality and all impurity or covetousness must not even be named among you, as is proper among saints.

1 Timothy 2:9-10 English Standard Version (ESV)

9 likewise also that women should adorn themselves in respectable apparel, with modesty and self-control, not with braided hair and gold or pearls or costly attire, **10** but with what is proper for women who profess godliness, with good works.

1 Timothy 5:1-2 English Standard Version (ESV)

1 Do not rebuke an older man but encourage him as you would a father, younger men as brothers, **2** older women as mothers, younger women as sisters, in all purity.

BASIC TEACHING: Has Fate Already Written Your Future?

On December 14, 2012, 20-year-old Adam Lanza fatally shot twenty children and six adult staff members in a mass murder at Sandy Hook Elementary School, in the village of Sandy Hook in Newtown, Connecticut. Before driving to the school, Lanza shot and killed his mother Nancy at their Newtown home. As first responders arrived, he committed suicide by shooting himself in the head.[14]

There are hundreds of millions of people, who view such events as the above, as an act of fate. Fate is the force or principle believed to predetermine events. You hear people say things like, "It was fate," "it was his time to go," or "if it is your time, there is nothing you can do about it." Some will say, "It was written." What is your thought on some force that predetermines your life? Was fate responsible for the above slaughter of twenty children and six adult staff members? Has fate already written your future?

What do you believe? Was fate responsible? Does fate shape our future?

Does Fate Write Our Future?

Fatalism is a philosophical doctrine stressing the subjugation of all events or actions to fate. Fatalism generally refers to any of the following ideas:

14

http://en.wikipedia.org/wiki/Sandy_Hook_Elementary_School_shooting

(1)   The view that we are powerless to do anything other than what we actually do.[15] Included in this is that man has no power to influence the future, or indeed, his own actions.[16] This belief is very similar to predeterminism.

(2)   An attitude of resignation in the face of some future event or events, which are thought to be inevitable. Friedrich Nietzsche named this idea with "Turkish fatalism"[17] in his book *The Wanderer and His Shadow*.[18]

(3)   That action is free, but nevertheless work toward an inevitable end.[19] This belief is very similar to compatibilist predestination.

(4)   That acceptance is appropriate, rather than resistance against inevitability. This belief is very similar to defeatism.

While the terms are often used interchangeably, fatalism, determinism, and predeterminism are discrete in stressing different aspects of the futility of human will or the foreordination of destiny. However, all these doctrines share common ground.

Determinists generally agree that human actions affect the future but that human action is itself determined by a causal chain of prior events. Their view does not accentuate a "submission" to fate or destiny, whereas fatalists stress an acceptance of future events as inevitable. Determinists believe the future is

---

[15]   Hugh   Rice   (October   11,   2010). "Fatalism". *Stanford Encyclopedia of Philosophy]*. Retrieved December 2, 2010.

[16]   Richard Taylor (January 1962). "Fatalism". *The Philosophical Review* (Duke University Press) **71** (1): 56–66. JSTOR 2183681

[17]   Metheus

[18]   Friedrich Nietzsche, The Wanderer and His Shadow, 1880, Türkenfatalismus

[19]   Catholic Encyclopedia

fixed specifically due to causality; fatalists and Predeterminists believe that some or all aspects of the future are inescapable, but not necessarily due to causality.

Fatalism is a looser term than determinism. The presence of historical "indeterminisms" or chances, i.e. events that could not be predicted by sole knowledge of other events, is any idea still compatible with fatalism. Necessity (such as a law of nature) will happen just as inevitably as a chance. Both can be imagined as sovereign.

Likewise, determinism is a broader term than predeterminism. Predeterminists, as a specific type of determinists, believe that an uninterrupted chain of events that goes back to the origin of the universe causes every single event or effect. Determinists, holding a more generic view, meanwhile, believe that each event is at least caused by recent prior events, if not also by such far-extending and unbroken events as those going back in time to the universe's very origins.

Both fatalism and predeterminism, by referring to the personal "fate" or to "predetermined events" strongly imply the existence of a someone or something that has done the "predetermining." This is usually interpreted to mean a conscious, omniscient being or force who has personally planned, and therefore knows at all times, the exact succession of every event in the past, present, and future, none of which can be altered. One of the most famous theological interpretations of this idea is the Calvinist Christian notion of predestination, in which God has already willed all occurring events at the beginning of the universe. Contrarily, determinism does not usually imply the existence of such a supernatural being;

many determinist models fall under scientific rather than religious or mystical philosophies.[20]

"The OT speaks of death as the common fate of humankind (Pss. 49:12; 81:15; Eccles. 2:14; 3:19; 9:2–3). The OT similarly speaks of violent death as the destiny of the wicked (Job 15:22; Isa. 65:12; Hos. 9:13)."[21] While this is true, notice that this is a predestination of groups, but not the destiny of individuals. What you have when you look at the context of the Scriptures is not some blind fatalism, but rather it is what commonly happens to all humans, as well as the fate which humanity brings on themselves. For example, see,

Numbers 16:29 Revised Standard Version (RSV)

29 If these men die the common death of all men, or if they are visited by the fate of all men, then the Lord has not sent me.

A Time for Everything

Ecclesiastes 3:1-2 English Standard Version (ESV)

3 For everything there is a season, and a time for every matter under heaven: **2** a time to be born, and a time to die; a time to plant, and a time to pluck up what is planted

When Solomon says that "a time to die," he is not suggesting that every individual has a fixed, predestined time to die, but generically in this time of imperfection, each of us are born, and each of us will die. If we look at

---

[20] http://en.wikipedia.org/wiki/Fatalism

[21] Chad Brand, Charles Draper, et al., eds., "Fate," *Holman Illustrated Bible Dictionary* (Nashville, TN: Holman Bible Publishers, 2003), 560.

what Solomon writes a few chapters later, this is made clear, "Be not overly wicked, neither be a fool. Why should you die before your time?" (Ecclesiastes 7:17) This clearly shows that a person's death in not written in stone (i.e., predetermined). In fact, Solomon writes in another book "The fear of Jehovah prolongs days, but the years of the wicked shall be shortened." (Proverbs 10:27) King David writes in Psalm 55:23, "But you, O God, will cast them down into the pit of destruction; men of blood and treachery shall not live out half their days. But I will trust in you." When we look at the context of Ecclesiastes 3:11-12, as well as the rest of Scripture, the Bible is simply discussing the conditions of imperfect humanity, and the fact that we are all born, and that we all die. This does not mean that God intended it this way, or that it will remain this way.

Even those who claim that fatalism is their belief, believing that they will not die until their time is up, yet their actions usually belie that belief. Why would they eat healthy? Why do they wear seatbelts? Why avoid neighborhood where there are continuous drive-by-shootings? Why avoid smoking for fear of cancer? Why worry if they live in a war zone? Why wear a bulletproof vest if they are an officer of the law? Why see a doctor for regular physicals? Why wear a parachute if they are skydiving? Why wear a Life preserver when on a fishing boat? Clearly, one's life can end in many different ways, if safety measures are not taken.

Galatians 6:7 English Standard Version (ESV)

⁷ Do not be deceived: God is not mocked, for whatever one sows, that will he also reap.

Notice from the above text that there is not thought of some blind fate, but rather a cause and effect relationship. It is a truism that if you commit certain actions (drinking and driving), there will be greater result or likelihood (a car wreck), than if they had taken another action, driving sober. Thus, humans reap what they sow, which means, outcomes are our responsibility by way of the actions that we take. Fate does not fix and predestine a time for everything that happens in life.

The Freedom to Choose

Deuteronomy 30:19-20 American Standard Version (ASV)

[19] I call heaven and earth to witness against you this day that I have set before thee life and death, the blessing and the curse. Therefore choose life, that you may live, you and your offspring; [20] to love Jehovah your God, to obey his voice, and to cleave to him; for he is your life, and the length of your days; that you may dwell in the land which Jehovah swore to thy fathers, to Abraham, to Isaac, and to Jacob, to give them.

Clearly, here, God is giving the Israelites and us by extension, the choice of life (obedience through love) or death (disobedience). If there was no freedom to choose, why does God offer us one? Moreover, why does Jesus say that our path to life is based on our 'striving to enter through the narrow door"? (Lu 13:24) Moreover, why would say, "The one who endures to the end will be saved." (Matt 24:13) A spiritually sluggish person has no reason to strive to enter through the narrow door, if from eternity past; he was predetermined to receive the gift of everlasting life.

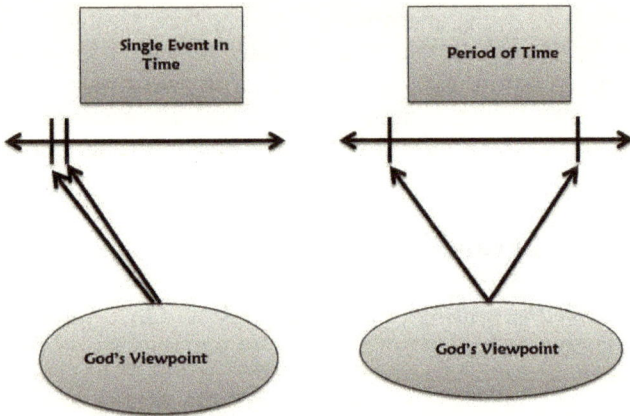

Figure 2 - God outside Time/Space Continuum

Before God carried out his very first creative act, there was no time, as we humans know it. Once the universe(s) were created, the sun and the moon have served humans as a timepiece for determining the seasons, days, and years. (Gen 1:14-18) Before the creation, there was no time for God to be outside of, as time did not exist. After creation God was still outside of the universe(s), his creation, in his heavenly home, meaning that, in essence, he was/is still outside of time. However, he is very much involved in his creations and is quite aware of everything that happens within his creation, as he personally involves himself, even directly at times. (1Ki 18:18-29) While God is clearly aware of future decision we have freely made, we must still make them. If three years from now, you the reader are to evangelize an atheist, who eventually accepts Christ, and enters the path of salvation, God knows that you are going to do this, but it is not an act of fate, as you have yet to freely choose to do so.

How do we correctly understand our freedom as it relates to God's foreknowledge? Because God has the power to exercise his foreknowledge of everything in advance, some have suggested that everything is fated to occur.

For example, if God knows that 20 years from now, you will have pizza for dinner, does it not seem that it is a necessity that you must have pizza 20 years from now, because God's knowledge is infallible. Thus, how could you do anything else? If God can know, and it is written; then, how do you do it freely? Is that not incompatible with your free will? Thus, does not God's foreknowledge of the future, not destroy the whole concept of human freedom? Because of these questions, some theologians have equated that because God foreknows these future events, God, in effect foreordains them. What follows is adopted from a lecture that William Lane Craig gave on his book, *The Compatibility of Divine Foreknowledge & Human Freedom*. (Jan 2000)

Just because something will happen, this does mean that it was foreordained to happen. If this were true, human freedom would be nonexistent. If the foreknowledge of God equaled foreordination, this would mean that God foreordained the sin of Adam and Eve, and they never really had the free will to eat or not eat of the tree of knowledge. Therefore, the misunderstanding is equating God's foreknowledge with equating foreordination.

Therefore, our best way of understanding God's foreknowledge and our freewill is to say that foreknowledge does not equal foreordination.

FOREKNOWLEDGE

Does **Not =**

FOREORDINATION

Remember, God is outside of time. He can see the past, the present and the future, and is aware of what freely happens in the future. He can see what you will freely choose to do ten years from now, and is aware of it now, and was aware of it in the past as well, even before you were born. It is your freely made decisions that are made in the future, which give God the foreknowledge that he has of them.

It is not

FOREKNOWLEDGE

Determine

FREE DECISIONS

Rather it is

FREE DECISIONS

Determine

FOREKNOWLEDGE

God's foreknowledge does not determine the decisions that you will freely make in the future, but rather the free decisions that you will make in the future will determine his foreknowledge. In this, we can make a distinction between what Dr. Craig calls **Chronological priority** and **logical priority**. Below we quote extensively,

> Chronological priority would mean that Event "A" [God's knowledge], as it relates to time, would come before Event "B" [the event God foreknows]. Thus, God's knowledge is chronologically prior to the event that he

foreknows. However, logically speaking, the event is prior to God's foreknowledge.

In other words, the event does not happen because God foreknows it, but God foreknows the event because it will happen. The event is logically prior to the foreknowledge, so he foreknows it because it will happen, even though the foreknowledge is chronologically prior to the event.

We can see foreknowledge on this, as the foreshadowing of something. When you see the shadow of someone coming around the corner of the building, you see his or her shadow on the ground before you see the person. You know that person is about to come around the corner because of their shadow but the shadow does not determine the person, the person determines the shadow.

God's foreknowledge is like the foreshadow of a future event. By seeing this foreshadowing, you know the events will happen, But the shadow does not determine the reality, the reality determines the shadow. Therefore, we should think of God's foreknowledge as the foreshadowing of things to come. Therefore, just because God will know something will happen, this does not prejudice or remove the freedom of that happening.

It is better to understand it that God knows in advance what choice people will freely make. It is the free decisions of human beings that determine what foreknowledge God has of them, as opposed to the reverse.

In fact, if the events were to happen differently, God's foreknowledge would be different as well. An illustration of this is, like an infallible barometer of the weather. Whatever the barometer says, because it is infallible, you know what the weather will be like. However, the barometer does not determine the weather; the weather determines the barometer's findings. Thus, God's foreknowledge is like an infallible barometer of the future. It lets him know what the future is going to be, but it does not constrain the future in any way. The future is going to happen anyway the free moral agent wants it to happen. However, the barometer is going to track whatever direction the future will take.

Thus, those that believe that God's foreknowledge removes the freedom of the person are mistaken. They posit a constraint upon human choices, which is really quite unintelligible. Let us use another illustration.

Suppose this is the **timeline** . . .

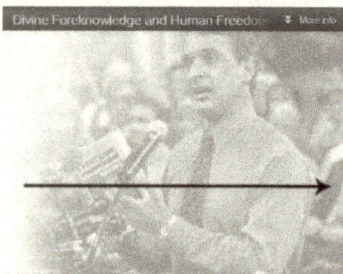

Let us place an event **"E"** on the timeline.

Let us
suppose God is back here in time and by his
foreknowledge (the dotted line); he knows that
"E" will happen. How does God's knowing
about "E" constrain "E" from happening. How
can God's knowing "E" will occur, make "E"
occur.

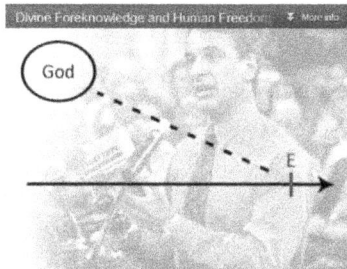

If you
were to erase the line, and say God does not
have foreknowledge of the future, how has
anything changed? How would "E" be affected
if you erased God's foreknowledge of it? "E"
would occur just the same, it would not affect
anything at all.

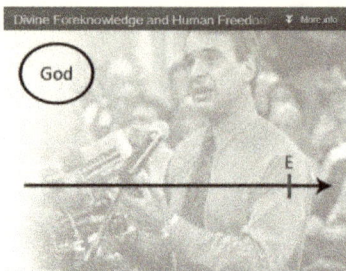

So, the presence of God's foreknowledge really does not prejudice anything about whether "E" will occur or not. Therefore, those that think that foreknowledge is incompatible with freedom are simply quite mistaken. What we need to understand is this, if "E" were not to occur

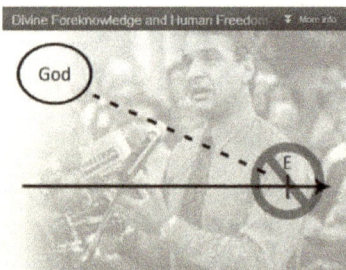

Then God would not have foreknown "E". And as long as that statement is true, "E" being able to occur and not occur, God's foreknowledge does not prejudice anything with respect to "E's" occurrence.[22]

In the end, the Bible does not teach that we are fated to a life that is without free will and the freedom to choose, but that God can see down the timeline, to what

---

[22] We have quoted at length from a transcript that we made of Dr. William Lane Craig's lecture on foreknowledge.
http://www.youtube.com/watch?v=mXUMhSmeivE

we will choose. Some may ponder, why do bad things happen to good people, is this not fate. We live in an imperfect world, because of the inherited sin of Adam.

Romans 5:12 English Standard Version (ESV)

Death in Adam, Life in Christ

[12] Therefore, just as sin came into the world through one man, and death through sin, and so death spread to all men because all sinned

Because humanity has entered this era of imperfection, we are subject to the wickedness of human imperfection, as well as the fact that we cannot generate perfection on our own; we were not designed to walk alone outside of God's sovereignty. (Jer. 10:23) Therefore, the actions of imperfect humans are subject to error and defect. This would also include anything that we build or manufacture at this time. You couple an imperfectly manufactured car, with imperfect road, and an imperfect human that has chosen to drink alcoholic beverage and drive; it is likely to end in tragedy. Imperfect man with his imperfectly manufactured things is adversely affected when one fails to heed safety warnings. Then, there are those that may start out with good intentions, but are affected by their greed, all stemming from his imperfect nature. Therefore, it is not fate, which brings bad things on good people, it is

Ecclesiastes 9:11 English Standard Version (ESV)

[11] Again I saw that under the sun the race is not to the swift, nor the battle to the strong, nor bread to the wise, nor riches to the intelligent, nor favor to those with knowledge, but time and chance [unexpected events] happen to them all.

Rest assured it is not fate, which determines the course of anyone's lives. Therefore, you can freely choose what lies ahead. Listen to the words of Joshua,

Joshua 24:15 American Standard Version (ASV)

¹⁵ And if it seems evil to you to serve Jehovah, choose for yourself this day whom you will serve: whether the gods which your fathers served that were beyond the River, or the gods of the Amorites in whose land you dwell; but as for me and my house, we will serve Jehovah.

BASIC TEACHING: Why has God Permitted Wickedness and Suffering?

The big issue that drove me to Agnostcism [Dr. Bart D. Ehrman is now an Atheist] has to do not with the Bible, but with the pain and suffering in the world. I eventually found it impossible to explain the evil so rampant among us—whether in terms of genocides (which continue), unspeakable human cruelty, war disease, hurricanes, tsunamis, mudslides, the starvation of millions of inocent children, you name it—if there was a good and loving God who was actively involved in this world.
Misquoting Jesus (p. 248)

As you will see with this chapter and the next, Ehrman's issue is simply a matter of starting with the wrong premise. **Point One**: He starts with 'if God is a God of love, who has the power to fix anything, how can there have been such horrific pain and suffering in imperfection over the last 6,000 years?' **Point Two**: He also likely starts with the premise that 'God is responsible for everything that happens.' If one starts with the wrong premise, there is no doubt that he will reach the wrong conclusion(s). **Point One** is dealt with below, but let it be said that Ehrman is looking through the binoculars from the wrong end, the big side through the small. When you do that, you get a narrow, focused outlook. God looks through the binoculars the right way, and can see the big picture. Ehrman can only see but a fraction and a moment of time, 70 – 80 years, while God sees everything that has happen these past 6,000 plus years in the greatest of detail, and can see what the outcome would be if he had handled things in a variety of ways.

Point Two is certainly one reason suffering and evil is often misunderstood. God is responsible for everything, but not always directly. If he started the human race, and we end up with what we now have, in essence, he is responsible. Just as parents, who have a child are similarly responsible for the child committing murder 21 years into his life, because they procreated and gave birth to the child. The mother and father are **in**directly responsible. King David commits adultery with Bathsheba and has her husband Uriah killed to cover things up, and impregnates Bathsheba, but the adulterine child, who remains nameless, died. Is God responsible for the death of that child? We can answer yes and no to that question. He is responsible in two ways: **(1)** He created humankind, so there would have been no affair, murder, adulterine child if he had not. **(2)** He did not step in and save the child, when he had the power to do so. However, he is not directly responsible, because he did not make King David and Bathsheba commit the acts that led to the child being born, nor did he bring an illness on the adulterine child, he just did not step in to save the child, in a time that had a high rate of infant deaths.

The reason why people think that God does not care about us is the words of religious leaders, which have made them, feel this way. When a tragedy strikes, what do pastors and Bible scholars often say? When 9/11 took place, with thousands dying in the twin towers of New York, many ministers said: "It was God's will. God must have had some good reason for doing this." When religious leaders make such comments or similar ones, they are actually blaming God for the bad things that happen. Yet, the disciple James wrote, "Let no one say when he is tempted, 'I am being tempted by God,' for God cannot be tempted with evil, and he himself tempts no one." (James 1:13) God never directly causes what is bad. Indeed, "far be it from God that he should do wickedness, and from the Almighty that he should do wrong." Job 34:10.

The history of humans has been inundated with pain and suffering on an unprecedented scale, much of which they have brought on themselves. The question that has plagued many a person is, 'why if there is a loving God, would he allow it to start with, and worse still, why allow it to go on for over 6,000 years?' Many apologist scholars have struggled to answer this question, because they are over analyzing, as opposed to just looking for the answer in God's Word. Therefore, if we are to answer this question, we must go back to Adam and Eve at the time of the first sin. Many have read this account, but I will list the texts as a refresher.

Genesis 2:17 (English Standard Version)

¹⁷but of the tree of the knowledge of good and evil you shall not eat, for in the day that you eat of it <u>you shall surely die</u>."

As you can see, humankind's continued existence in a paradise, with perfection, was dependent upon obedience, his continued acceptance of God as his sovereign.

Genesis 3:1-5 (English Standard Version)

¹Now the serpent was more crafty than any other beast of the field that the LORD God had made. He said to the woman, "Did God actually say, 'You shall not eat of any tree in the garden'?" ²And the woman said to the serpent, "We may eat of the fruit of the trees in the garden, ³but God said, 'You shall not eat of the fruit of the tree that is in the midst of the garden, neither shall you touch it, lest you die.'" ⁴ But the serpent said to the woman, "<u>You will not surely die</u>. ⁵For God knows that when you eat of it your eyes will be opened, and you will be like God, knowing good and evil."

Later Bible texts establish Satan the Devil as the one using a serpent as his mouthpiece, like a ventriloquist would a dummy. Anyway, take note that Satan contradicts the clear statement made to Adam at Genesis 2:17, "you will not surely die." Backing up a little, we see Satan asking an inferential question, "Did God actually say, 'You shall not eat of any tree in the garden'?" First, he is overstating what he knows to be true, not "any tree," just one tree. Second, Satan is inferring, 'I can't believe that God would say . . . how dare he say such.' Notice too that Eve has been told so thoroughly about the tree that she even goes beyond what Adam told her, not just that you 'do not eat from it,' no, 'you do not even touch it!' Then, Satan out and out lied and slandered God as a liar, saying that 'they would not die.' To make matters much worse, he infers that God is withholding good from them, and by rebelling they would be better off, being like God, 'knowing good and bad.' This latter point is not knowledge of; it is the self-sovereignty of choosing good and bad for oneself, and created creatures acting in a rebellious manner. What was symbolized by the tree is well expressed in a footnote on Genesis 2:17, in The Jerusalem Bible (1966):

> This knowledge is a privilege which God reserves to himself and which man, by sinning, is to lay hands on, 3:5, 22. Hence it does not mean omniscience, which fallen man does not possess; nor is it moral discrimination, for unfallen man already had it and God could not refuse it to a rational being. It is the power of deciding for himself what is good and what is evil and of acting accordingly, a claim to complete moral independence by which man refuses to recognize his status as a created being. The first sin was an attack on God's sovereignty, a sin of pride.

The Issues at Hand

(1) Satan called God a liar and said he was not to be trusted, as to the life or death issue.

(2) Satan's challenge therefore took into question the right and legitimacy of God's rightful place as the Universal Sovereign.

(3) Satan also suggested that people would remain obedient to God only as long as their submission to God was to their benefit.

(4) Satan all but said that humankind was able to walk on its own, there being no need for dependence on God.

(5) Satan argued that man could be like God, choosing for himself what is right and wrong.

(6) Satan claimed that God's way of ruling was not in the best interests of humans, and they could do better without God.

Job 1:6-11 (English Standard Version)

⁶Now there was a day when the sons of God came to present themselves before the LORD, and Satan also came among them. ⁷The LORD said to Satan, "From where have you come?" Satan answered the LORD and said, "From⁽ᶜ⁾ going to and fro on the earth, and from walking up and down on it." ⁸And the LORD said to Satan, "Have you considered my servant Job, that there is none like him on the earth, a blameless and upright man, who fears God and turns away from evil?" ⁹Then Satan answered the LORD and said, "<u>Does Job fear God for no reason</u>? ¹⁰Have you not put a hedge around him and his house and all that he has, on every side? You have blessed the work of his hands, and his possessions have increased in the land. ¹¹But <u>stretch out your hand and touch all that he has, and he will curse you to your face</u>."

Job 2:4-5 (English Standard Version)

⁴Then Satan answered the LORD and said, "Skin for skin! All that <u>a man</u> has he will give for his life. ⁵But stretch out your hand and touch his bone and his flesh, and he will curse you to your face."

This general reference to "a man," as opposed to specifically naming Job, is suggesting that all men [and women] will only obey God when things are good, but when the slightest difficulty arises, he will not obey. If you were put to the test, would you prove your love for your heavenly Father and show that you preferred His rule to that of any other?

God Settles the Issues

There is one thing that Satan did not challenge, that is the power of God. Satan did not suggest that God was unable to destroy him as an accuser of God's creatures. However, he did challenge God's way of ruling, not His right to rule. Therefore, it is a moral issue that must be settled.

An illustration of how God chose to deal with the issue can be demonstrated in human terms. A neighbor down the street slandered a man, who had a son and a daughter. The slanderer said that he was not a good father, that he withheld good from his children, and was so overbearing, to the point of being abusive. The slanderer stated that the children would be better off without the father. He further argued that the children had no real love for their father, and only obeyed him because of the food and shelter. How should the father deal with these false and slanderous accusations? If he were to go down the street and pummel the slanderer, it would only validate the lies, making the neighbors believe he is telling the truth.

The answer lies within his family, they can serve only as his witnesses. (Pro 27:11; Isa 43:10) If the children stay obedient and grow to be successful adults, turning out to be loving, caring, honest people with spotless character, it proves the accusations were false. If the children accept the lies, and rebel, and grow up to be despicable people, it just further validates that they would have been better off by staying with the father. This is how God chose to deal with the issues. The issues that were raised must be settled beyond all reasonable doubt.

If God had destroyed the rebellious three: Satan, Adam and Eve; he would have not resolved the issues of whether man could walk on his own, if he would be better off without his Creator, if God's rulership was not best, and if God were hiding good from man. In addition, there was an audience of untold billions of angelic spirit creatures looking on. If God destroyed without settling things, these spirit persons would be following God out of dreadful fear, not love, fear of displeasing God. Moreover, say He did destroy them, and start over, and ten thousand years down the road (with billions of humans now on earth), the issues were raised again, He would have to destroy billions of people again, and again, and again all throughout time, until these issues were laid to rest.

What God has done is to allow time to pass, and the issues to be resolved. Man thought he was better off without God, and could walk on his own. In addition, man has attempted every kind of rulership imaginable, and one must ask, 'have they proven themselves better than rulership under the sovereignty of their Creator?' (Proverbs 1:30-33; Isaiah 59:4, 8) Sadly, the issues must be taken up to the brink of destroying man (Rev 11:18), otherwise, the argument would be that if given enough time, they could have turned things around. If man goes up to the point of destroying himself and Armageddon comes at the last minute, it will have set a case law, solved the issue, and the Bible can serve as the example forever. If the issues of God's sovereignty or the loyalty of His created creatures, angelic or human, is ever questioned again, we would have the Holy Bible that will serve as a law established based on previous verdicts of not guilty, please see below.

What Have the Results Been?

(1) God does not cause evil and suffering. He does not cause injustices. Romans 9:14.

(2) That fact that God has allowed evil, pain and suffering has proved that independence from God has not brought about a better world. Jeremiah 8:5, 6, 9.

(3) God's permission of evil, pain and suffering has also proved that Satan has not been able to turn all humans away from God. Exodus 9:16; 1 Samuel 12:22; Hebrews 12:1.

(4) The fact that God has permitted evil, pain and suffering to continue has provided proof that only God, the Creator, has the capability and the right to rule over humankind for their eternal blessing and happiness. Ecclesiastes 8:9.

(5) Satan has been the god of this world since the sin in Eden (over 6,000 years), and how has that worked out for man, and what has been the result of man's course of independence from God and his rule? Matthew 4:8-9; John 16:11; 2 Corinthians 4:3-4; 1 John 5:19; Psalm 127:1.

Satan's impact on the earth's activities has carried with it conflict, evil and death, and his rulership has been by means of deception, power and his own self-interest.

He has demonstrated himself an unfit ruler of everything. Therefore, God is now completely vindicated in putting an end to this corrupted rebel along with all who have shared in his evil deeds. (Romans 16:20)

God has tolerated evil, sickness, pain, suffering and death until our day in order to resolve all the issues raised by Satan. We are self-centered in thinking that this has only pained us. Imagine that you are holding a rope on a sinking ship that 20 other men, women and children are clinging to, when your child loses her grip and falls into the ocean. You can either hold the rope, saving 20 people, or you can let go and attempt to rescue your daughter. God has been watching the suffering of billions from the day of Adam and Eve's sin. Moreover, it has been His great love for us, which causes Him to cling to the rope of issues, saving us from a future of repeated issues. Nevertheless, he will not allow this evil to remain forever. He has set a fixed time (Acts 17.31) when He will end this wicked system of Satan's rule.

Daniel 11:27 (Holman Christian Standard Bible)

[27] The two kings, whose hearts are bent on evil, will speak lies at the same table but to no avail, for still the end will come <u>at the appointed time</u>.

Unlike what many people of the world may think (the world that lies in the hands of Satan), being obedient to God is not difficult. We simply must set our pride aside and accept that the wisdom of God is so far greater than our own, and accept that He has worked for the good of obedient humankind, as He loves each one of us.

Matthew 7:21 (Holman Christian Standard Bible)

[21] "Not everyone who says to Me, 'Lord, Lord!' will enter the kingdom of heaven, but [only] the one who does the will of My Father in heaven.

1 John 2:15-17 (Holman Christian Standard Bible)

[15] Do not love the world or the things that belong to the world. If anyone loves the world, love for the Father is not in him. Because everything that belongs to the world, [16]the lust of the flesh, the lust of the eyes, and the pride in one's lifestyle, is not from the Father, but is from the world. [17]And the world with its lust is passing away, but the one who does God's will remains forever.

As Christians, there is a love we must not have. We must 'not love the world or anything in it.' Instead, we need to keep from becoming infected by the corruption of unrighteous human society that is alienated from God and must not breathe in its mental disposition or be moved by its sinful dominant attitude. (Ephesians 2:1, 2; James 1:27) If we were to have the views of those in the world that are in opposition to God, "the love of the Father" would not be in us. (James 4:4)

BASIC TEACHING: Does God Step in and Solve Our Every Problem, Because We are Faithful?

As the deer pants
for streams of water,
so my soul pants for You, my God

My soul thirsts for God,
the living God.

Psalm 42:1-2

Psalm 42 depicts for us the circumstances of a Levite, one of the offspring of Korah, who found himself in exile. His inspired words can be very beneficial to us in preserving high thankfulness for friendship with fellow Christians and for continuing steadfastly while going through hostile conditions.

The psalmist stated,

Psalm 42:1-2 English Standard Version (ESV)

1 As a deer pants for flowing streams,
  so pants my soul for you, O God.
2 My soul thirsts for God,
   for the living God.
When shall I come and appear before God?

A female deer cannot survive long without water. If water is low, the deer will risk its life going out of cover to get at the lifesaving water, even though she knows that the prey could attack at any moment. Like the deer that longs for water because it is a matter of life or death, the psalmist longed for God. "The word pants in the Hebrew means "to have a keen, consuming desire for." His driving passion was not for people, possessions, or prosperity but for God."[23]

In the Bible lands of dry country, where the vegetation wastes away rapidly throughout the dry season, water is a very valuable commodity, as it is limited in the extreme. That is why the Psalmist says that he was a 'soul thirsting for God.' He had been going without his basic spiritual needs being satisfied, that is the freedom of going to the sanctuary; therefore, he asks when he might again "appear before God."

He had been confined because of persecution, which prevented him from having contact with his fellow believers, which can result in intense sadness, unhappiness and hopelessness, as verse three indicates.

Psalm 42:3 English Standard Version (ESV)

3 My tears have been my food
   day and night,

---

[23] Anders, Max; Lawson, Steven (2004-01-01). Holman Old Testament Commentary - Psalms: 11 (p. 224). B&H Publishing. Kindle Edition.

while they say to me all the day long,
   "Where is your God?"

   Because of this hostile situation, the Psalmist was depressed to point of being unable to eat. Therefore, his 'tears was as his food.' Yes, "day and night" tears would roll down his cheeks into his mouth. His isolation and distress was not enough, as his enemies aggravated his wounds by provoking, ridiculing, in a hurtful or mocking way, as they would say all day long, "Where is your God?" He needed to find a way to reassure himself during this time of difficulty, to not be overrun by sorrow and heartache.

Psalm 42:4-6 English Standard Version (ESV)

4 These things I remember,
   as I pour out my soul:
how I would go with the throng
   and lead them in procession to the house of God
with glad shouts and songs of praise,
   a multitude keeping festival.

5 Why are you cast down, O my soul,
   and why are you in turmoil within me?
Hope in God; for I shall again praise him,
   my salvation 6 and my God.

My soul is cast down within me;
   therefore I remember you
from the land of Jordan and of Hermon,
   from Mount Mizar.

   Here we find the Psalmist not living in the moment of suffering, but rather recalling a time before he was in exile. He 'pours out his soul,' reaching the depths of his inner self with such passion, as he reminisces within about the former days. The Levite is recalling in his mind what

94

life was like when he was in his land, as he lived and worshiped with his brother and sister Israelites, as they walked "to the house of God," to celebrate a festival. Initially, these memories did not bring joy, but the pain of knowing they were a thing of the past, deeply missed.

Then, he asked himself, "Why are you cast down, O my soul and why are you in turmoil within me"? At that moment, he realized that his hope of salvation was not in himself, but in God. Therefore, the sweet memories truly brought him relief! He knew that if he patiently waited, God would act in his behalf. He then knew that his unfavorable circumstances were not going to define his faith that, in time God would aid him in his time of need. When that moment would happen, he would "praise him" for 'his salvation' and being 'his God.' He might have been far removed from the sanctuary, but the Psalmist kept his God at the forefront of his mind.

If we ever find ourselves in difficult times, unrelenting times, we need to follow the pattern set by the Psalmist. We need to remember that God is well aware of our circumstances, and he will not forsake us. We must realize that the issues that were raised by Satan in the Garden of Eden, the sovereignty of God, the rightfulness of his rulership, and the issues raised by Satan to God in Job, the loyalty of God's creatures, are greater than we are.

Proverbs 3:25-26 Lexham English Bible (LEB)

25 Do not be afraid of sudden panic,
   or the storm of wickedness that will come.
26 [Jehovah] will be *your confidence*
   and guard your foot from capture.

Before delving into the rest of Psalm 42, let us take a moment to establish what these verses do not mean.

Should we understand these verses, or any other in Scripture teach that because we are wisely walking with God that he will miraculously step in to protect each servant personally from difficult times, diseases, mental disorders, injury or death? No. These sorts of miracles are the extreme exception to the rule. Of the 4,000 plus years of Bible history, from Adam to Jesus, with tens of millions of people living and dying, we have but a few dozen miracles that we know of in Scripture. Even in Bible times, miracles were not common, far from it. Hundreds of years may pass with no historical record of a miracle happening at all.

Walking With God

If we are wisely walking with God, we can be confident that bodily disease, mental disorders, injury or early death is far less likely than if we were not. Moreover, we can draw on the resurrection hope. Does God miraculously move events to save us out of difficult times or miraculously heal us? Yes, he certainly can, but it is an extreme exception to the rule. He miraculously heals those who are going to play a major role in his settling of the issues that were raised in the Garden of Eden.

What God's Word teaches us is this, if we walk by using biblical discernment and exercising biblically sound judgment, unless time and an unforeseen occurrence befall us, we can be confident that we will not stumble into the difficulties that the world of mankind alienated from God faces every day. Conversely, the wicked do not have this protection. In other words, Christians live by the moral values of Scripture, which gives them an advantage over those that do not. Therefore, God answers our prayers **by our faithfully acting** in behalf of those prayers, by applying Scripture in a balanced manner. If we have not taken in a deep knowledge of God's Word, how can we have the Spirit inspired wisdom, the very knowledge of God to guide and direct us in our ways? Just because we are not being rescued when we feel that we should, this does not mean that we have lost faith, or that God is displeased. Even though the Psalmist had no doubt that Jehovah God was coming to his aid, he still experienced grief.

Psalm 42:7 English Standard Version (ESV)

7 Deep calls to deep
    at the roar of your waterfalls;
all your breakers and your waves
    have gone over me.

Yes, the Psalmist's surroundings of his exile, were very beautiful; however, they brought him back to the reality of his difficulty! Verse 7 may very well be describing when the snow on Mount Hermon melts. Marvelous waterfalls are fashioned, which pour into the Jordan, causing it to increase in size. It is as though one wave is speaking to another wave. This extraordinary spectacle of power brought to the Psalmist's mind that he had been consumed by distress as if being overcome by a flood. Nevertheless, his faith in God does not waiver.

Psalm 42:8 English Standard Version (ESV)

8 By day [Jehovah][24] commands his steadfast love,
    and at night his song is with me,
    a prayer to the God of my life.

---

[24] Translations take liberties with God's personal name, by removing it and replacing it with the title LORD in all caps. There is no rational reason, or Scriptural grounds for doing so. In fact, Scripture shows just the opposite.—See the American Standard Version Isaiah 42:8; Malachi 3:16; Micah 4:5; Proverbs 18:10; Joel 2:32; Ezekiel 36:23; Exodus 9:16; Malachi 1:11; Psalm 8:1; 148:3.

There is no doubt in the Psalmist that Jehovah God will engulf him with his steadfast love, freeing him of anxiety. This will empower him to praise God in song and to offer a prayer of thanks 'to the God of his life.'

The Korahite Levite thinks,

Psalm 42:9-11 English Standard Version (ESV)

⁹ I say to God, my rock:
  "Why have you forgotten me?
Why do I go mourning
  because of the oppression of the enemy?"
¹⁰ As with a deadly wound in my bones,
  my adversaries taunt me,
while they say to me all the day long,
  "Where is your God?"

Then, it seems that the Psalmist slips, even though he views God as 'his rock,' a place of protection from one's enemies. Yes, he now asks, "Why have you forgotten me?" Yes, the Psalmist was allowed to remain in his circumstances of sadness, feeling depressed, as his enemies reveled in what appeared to be a victory. The psalmist speaks of himself as being criticized in an unbearable way. So malicious was the mockery and disdain that it could be likened 'as with a deadly wound in his bones.' However, the Levite again comes at himself with self-talk, challenging his irrational thinking with rational thinking.

Psalm 42:11 English Standard Version (ESV)

¹¹ Why are you cast down, O my soul,
  and why are you in turmoil within me?
Hope in God; for I shall again praise him,
  my salvation and my God.

It is not the troubles of the Psalmist, which actually caused him to feel bad. It is what he told himself that contributed to how he felt. Self-talk is what we tell ourselves in our thoughts. In fact, it is the words we tell ourselves about people, self, experiences, life in general, God, the future, the past, the present; it is specifically all the words we say to ourselves all the time. Destructive self-talk, even subconsciously, can be very harmful to our mood: mood slumps, our self-worth plummeting, our body feeling sluggish, our will to accomplish even the smallest of things is not to be realized and our actions defeat us.

Intense negative thinking of the Psalmist led to his feeling forsaken, resulting in painful emotions, and a depressive state. However, his thoughts based on a good mood were entirely different from those based on his being upset. Negative thoughts that flooded his mind were the actual contributors of his self-defeating emotions. These very thoughts were what kept the Psalmist sluggish and contributed to his feeling abandoned. Therefore, his thinking was also the key to his relief.

Every time the Psalmist felt down because of his irrational self-talk, he attempted to locate the corresponding negative thought he had to this feeling down. It was those thoughts that created his feelings of low self-worth. By offsetting them and replacing them with rational thoughts, he actually changed his mood. The negative thoughts that move through his mind, did so with no effort, and were the easiest course to follow, because imperfect human tendencies gave him that way of thinking, a pattern of thinking. However, the Psalmist challenged those irrational thoughts of being forsaken with rational ones, saying that he would hope in God, and that he would continue to praise him, as in the end God is his salvation, even if that salvation comes in the form of a resurrection.

The centerpiece to it all is the mind. Our moods, behaviors and body responses result from the way we view things. It is a proven fact that we cannot experience any event in any way, shape, or form unless we have processed it with our mind first. No event can depress us; it is your perception of that event that will. If we are only sad over an event, our thoughts will be rational; but if you are depressed or anxious over an event, our thinking will be bent and irrational, distorted and simply wrong.

If we are to keep rational in our thinking, we need to fully grasp the fact that God does not always step in when we believe he should, nor is he obligated to do so, as was stated earlier, he has greater issues that need resolving, which have eternal effects for the whole of humankind. There are far more times that God does not step in, meaning that our relief may come in the hope of a resurrection. However, for his servants that apply his Word in a balanced manner, to the fullest extent, God is acting in their best interest by way of his inspired inerrant Word.

BASIC TEACHING: Are Women Allowed to Teach the Church?

This chapter will be a careful discussion of the correct interpretation of 1 Timothy 11-15. Specifically, we will on 1 Timothy 2:12, where the natural reading of Paul is understood as instructing Timothy that women are not to teach or have authority over men in the Christian congregation.

There is little doubt as to why there are different conclusions as to the meaning of 1 Timothy 2:12. **(1)** The interpreter does not follow grammatical-historical principles of interpretation, but rather grammatical-critical-historical principles of interpretation. **(2)** In addition, the interpreter takes the passage out of context. **(3)** Moreover, the interpreter misinterprets historical-cultural background. **(4)** Furthermore, little or incorrect attention is given to lexical or grammatical matters.

---

1 Timothy 2:11 Updated American Standard Version (UASV)[25]

11 Let a woman learn in silence with all submissiveness.

---

11 Let a woman

Woman (Gr., *gune*), as it is used here in the singular, means women in general, not just wives,[26] as it has

---

[25] Unless otherwise indicated, Scripture quotations are from the Updated American Standard Version, 2016 (UASV).

throughout this section of text (8-15). In verse 9, Paul addresses how women are to carry themselves, namely, their dress and outward appearance. In verse 10, Paul speaks of what is proper for women, who profess godliness, which is that they should be helpful to others; in other words, good works.

learn (let her be learning) **(Why and How?)**[27]

The apostle Paul, as an inspired writer, had actually extended to women more consideration than they ever had in Judaism. Having the privilege and right to *Learn* (Gr., manthaneto), outside of the home, was not something Jewish women of the first century would have ever considered. Paul was not borrowing from Judaism of the time, who also did not allow women to speak, having to remain silent. Judaism could care less about women growing in knowledge of God's Word. Paul on the other hand had specifically said that they were to **learn** in silence, knowing that they were ministers of the good news as well, just not in the church, over the congregation of men, baptized brothers. —1 Corinthians 14:34; Genesis 2:18–25; 3:16

In silence

In silence (Gr., hesuchia) meant that the woman was 'to be quietness,' 'to be still.' In other words, she was to show respect for her head, man, especially the leadership of the congregation by not raising questions, attempting to teach. This was not a life of silence, just at the Christian congregation meetings. They were quietly to receive instruction at the meetings, and to ask their

---

[26] R. C. H. Lenski, The Interpretation of St. Paul's Epistles to the Colossians, to the Thessalonians, to Timothy, to Titus, and to Philemon (Columbus, Oh.: Wartburg, 1946), 562.

[27] In quietness, with all submissiveness

husbands questions in private, at home. Thus, in the public meeting, the woman was to learn by listening, not teaching through questions. —1 Corinthians 14:34-35.

with all submissiveness

Submissiveness (Gr., *hupotage*) means to be in "subjection, subordination, or submission," which is not being used in a negative sense. (2 Cor. 9:13; Gal. 2:5; 1 Tim. 2:11; 3:4) All Christians are to be submissive or in subjection to the Father, the Son, and superior authorities, which in no way detracts from their human equality to each other, male or female. In the same sense, women are to be submissive to their husband, man in general, and the men taking the lead in the Christian congregation.[28]

Here in verse 11, submissiveness is a reference to the relationship between women and men, especially men who hold a position of authority in the Christian congregation. Paul is very concerned that his words not be taken lightly, which stresses by his addition of "**in all** or **in entire** (NASB) or **in full** (NIV) submissiveness." (See 1 Tim. 4:9; 5:2) While Paul is informing the Christian congregations that women are to take in as much knowledge about God and his Word, as any man; this is not a means to their usurping man's position or authority within the congregation. In other words, the "all" is Paul stating emphatically that a woman's learning is not to be a pathway, to the role of authority over man, by way of teaching him. (See 1 Cor. 14:33-34) Yes, women are to learn in the Christian meetings, but it is being qualified in that it is to be (1) in silence and (2) in all submissiveness.

---

[28] (1 Cor. 14:34; Eph. 5:21-22, 24; Col. 3:18; 1 Pet. 3:1, 5; Heb. 12:9; Jas. 4:7; 1 Cor. 16:16; 1 Pet. 5:5; Rom. 13:1, 5; 1 Tim. 3:4; Tit. 2:9; 3:1; 1 Pet. 2:18; Tit. 2:5; 1 Cor. 11:3, 4, 5, 7, 10; Eph. 5:23)

Again, this subjection is to a position of authority, not as to person, as though women were/are inferior. Just as man is in subjection to Christ as their head, so too is woman to man, especially the husband.

---

1 Timothy 2:12 Updated American Standard Version (UASV)

[12] But I do not permit a woman to teach or to exercise authority over a man, but to be in quietness.

---

[12] But *I do not permit*

But (de), could be rendered "but," "and," "so," "rather," among other things. This Greek conjunction *de* (used to link sentences, clauses, phrases, or words), could be used to simply connect the previous verse ("and"); however, it is best to take it as a contrast here. Verse 11 is saying what a woman **can do**, namely learn, although the learning is qualified as to how. Now, verse 12, in contrast, a marked difference, Paul is stating what a woman **cannot do**. The woman may learn, but may not teach or have authority over a man.

If this were a *descriptive* present (as it is sometimes popularly taken), the idea *might* be that in the future the author would allow this: *I do not presently permit...* However, there are several arguments against this: (1) It is overly subtle. Without some temporal indicator, such as ἄρτι or perhaps νῦν, this view begs the question. (2) Were we to do this with other commands in the present tense, our resultant exegesis would be both capricious and ludicrous. Does μὴ μεθύσκεσθε οἴνῳ..., ἀλλὰ πληροῦσθε ἐν πνεύματι in Eph 5:18 mean "Do not *for the moment* be filled with wine, but be filled *at the present time* by the Spirit" with the implication that such a moral code might change in the future? The normal use of the present tense in didactic literature, especially when introducing an exhortation, is not descriptive, but a general precept that has gnomic[29] implications. (3) Grammatically, the present tense is used with a generic object (γυναικί), suggesting that it should be taken as a gnomic present. (4) Contextually, the exhortation seems to be rooted in creation (note v 13 and the introductory γάρ), rather than an address to a temporary situation.[30]

"I do not permit" is not Paul's personal opinion of things, this authority is Paul's apostolic author to convey the words of God, and not that he is making some personal rule because he fancies it, but that this has been the case since creation. (Vs. 13), In 1 Corinthians 14:34, Paul gives us the same prohibition based on the law, "the women should keep silent in the churches. For they are not permitted to speak, but should be in submission, as the Law also says." (Gen. 3:16) There, same subject matter, in verse 37 Paul tells us where he gets that authority, by stating, "The things I am writing to you are a command of the Lord." When it comes to 1 Timothy 2:11-12, and women not being permitted to teach, is this only applicable to the Ephesian and Corinthian Congregations, or the first century culture? George W. Knight addresses this partially in his commentary on 1 Timothy.

---

[29] Gnomic: containing proverbs or other short pithy sayings that express basic truths

[30] Daniel B. Wallace, Greek Grammar Beyond the Basics - Exegetical Syntax of the New Testament, 525 (Zondervan Publishing House and Galaxie Software, 1999).

It has also been suggested that the present indicative form of [epitrepo, "permitting"] indicates a temporal limitation and thus limits Paul's statement to the then and there of Ephesus. An examination of other occurrences of Paul's use of first person singular present indicative (Rom. 12:1, 3; 1 Cor. 4:16; 2 Cor. 5:20; Gal. 5:2, 3, Eph. 4:1; 1 Thes. 4:1; 5:14; 2 Thes. 3:6; 1 Tim. 2:1, 8) demonstrates that he uses it to give universal and authoritative instruction or exhortation (cf. especially Rom. 12:1; 1 Tim. 2:8).[31]

a woman to teach[32] (Why / in what sense?)

As is true in verses 9 and 11, "woman" (γυνή, gune), is a reference to all women, women as a whole, which is underscored by the anarthrous (without definite article) forms for both γυνή (a woman) and ἀνήρ (a man). In verse 11, it was women as a whole that were required to remain silent, and here it is women as a whole that are refrain from teaching or exercising authority over a man.

These two verses are drawing an ever-increasing amount of comment today, but Paul's injunctions in 1 Timothy 2:11–12 require no special historical insights to understand. He says that women are not called to serve in the office of teacher or of elder in the church. A crucial distinction to understand here is that between special and general office ministries. Ordained men are called to a special office by

---

[31] George W. Knight, The Pastoral Epistles: A Commentary on the Greek Text, New International Greek Testament Commentary, 140 (Grand Rapids, MI; Carlisle, England: W.B. Eerdmans; Paternoster Press, 1992).

[32] First qualifier as to "in silence"

Christ (e.g., Rom. 10:15; Eph. 4:11), while non-ordained men and all women in the church have a general office to serve the Lord in various capacities. If we did not have the chapter division between 1 Timothy 2:15 and 3:1 (which is a modern invention), this special office context of Paul's statements on women in 2:11–12 would be more obvious to us, since he proceeds directly to the requirements for male overseers of the church in 3:1–7.[33]

or to exercise authority over a man[34]

The Greek coordinating conjunction *oude* (and not, neither, cannot, either, even, neither, no, nor, nothing, or, then), plays more of an important role here than one might first imagine. Let us start with feminists, such as I. H. Marshall, who have argued that "authority" (Gr., *authentein*) has a negative connotation. In other words, they are arguing that Paul is not saying that women are not to teach, because they would have authority over men in the Christian congregation, but that Paul is only against their negative authority in the church. Looking at the lexical study first, we turn to H. S. Baldwin on the word *authentein*, "have or exercise authority," who demonstrated that the Greek word was very rare in the New Testament period, and it occurs only once in the New Testament, in 1 Timothy 2:12. Outside of that, it only occurred a couple times prior to 65 C.E.

We then look at the syntax, by turning to A. J. Köstenberger on the word *oude*, "or," joining the words

---

[33] Clinton E. Arnold, Zondervan Illustrated Bible Backgrounds Commentary Volume 3: Romans to Philemon., 457-58 (Grand Rapids, MI: Zondervan, 2002).

[34] Second qualifier as to "in silence"

"teach" and "have authority." Köstenberger carried out meticulous searches of the use of *oude* in the New Testament and in as well as biblical Greek literature outside of the Greek New Testament and he found over 100 parallels. His research showed that *oude* served as coordinating conjunction, which linked verbs of like meaning. It was also discovered that either bother were positive, or both were negative. An example can be found in Matthew 6:20 where Jesus said, "But lay up for yourselves treasures in heaven, where . . . thieves do not break in and (*oude*) steal." You immediate notice that "break in" and "steal" have a negative meaning. Therefore, if *didaskein* ("to teach") has a positive meaning and oude is only known to link verbs of like meaning, we are only left with the conclusion both reasonably and syntactically *authentein* ("authority") must have a positive meaning as well. This then, removes the argument by the feminist scholars, as Paul is not just prohibiting negative exercise of authority by women over men in the Christian congregation, but rather the exercise of authority period. Simply put, men alone are to serve as elders and overseers in the congregation. 1 Timothy 3:2

αὐθεντεῖν ... [*authentein*, "authority"], once thought to be unique to Christian literature (e.g., Thayer, *Lexicon*), occurs in the papyrus *BGU* 1208:38 (27 B.C.) and in Philodemus, *Rhetoric* 2 (first century B.C.; see BAGD for further documentation and later occurrences) and is referred to as Hellenistic (Ἑλληνικῶς) over against Attic αὐτοδικεῖν by the second-century A.D. Attic lexicographer Moeris (ed. J. Pierson [1759], 58; [43 in 1831 edition]; cf. also the account of the word and its meaning and that of related words, especially αὐθέντης, in MM; Deissmann, *Light*, 88f.; Robertson, IV, 570; MHT II, 278). Contrary to the suggestion of *KJV*'s "to usurp authority" and BAGD's alternative, "domineer" (so also *NEB*), the use of the word shows no inherent negative sense of grasping or usurping authority or of exercising it in a harsh or authoritative way, but simply means "to have or exercise authority" (BAGD; LSJM: "to have full power or authority over"; cf. Preisigke, *Wörterbuch* I, 235f., giving three nuances for four different papyri, all in the sphere of the above definition; cf. finally Lampe, *Lexicon*, whose four main meanings are in the same orbit; so *NASB*, *RSV*, *TEV*, *NIV*: "to have authority").

Paul refers, then, with αὐθεντεῖν [*authentein*, "authority"] to exercise of a leadership role or function in the church (the contextual setting), and thus by specific application the office of ἐπίσκοπος/πρεσβύτερος [episkopos overseer/presbuteros elder], since the names of these offices (especially ἐπίσκοπος) and the activities associated with them (cf., e.g., 3:4, 5; 5:17; Tit. 1:9ff.; Acts 20:17, 28ff.) indicate the exercise of authority. It is noteworthy, however, that Paul does not use "office" terminology here (bishop/presbyter) but functional terminology (teach/exercise authority). It is thus the activity that he prohibits, not just the office (cf. again 1 Cor. 14:34, 35).[35]

---

[35] George W. Knight, The Pastoral Epistles: A Commentary on the Greek Text, New International Greek Testament Commentary, 141-42

"Man" (Gr., *aner*) is referring to "a man," not the more confined sense of the "husband." As in verse 8, "man" is being used as a distinction from woman. That it is in the singular means that it is a reference to men in general, just as the singular γυνή *gune* ("woman") here and in verse 11 refers to women in general.

but to be in quietness

Thus far, it is all too clear that a woman may not teach on the Christian congregation, nor may she teach a man biblically, doctrinally. This is emphasized, "but to be in quietness." The *alla*, "but," is used here to mark a contrast to what came before, "not to teach or to exercise authority." For those that would argue that we are only talking about certain types of authoritative teaching, this exhortation to 'be in silence,' would negate that argument. Of course, this does not rule out conversations before and after meetings, commenting at Bible studies, and singing. It is dealing explicitly with teaching and the exercise of authority.

---

1 Timothy 2:13 Updated American Standard Version (UASV)

[13] For Adam was formed first, then Eve,

---

[13] For Adam was formed first, then Eve[36]

The conjunction "for" (Gr., γάρ, *gar*), signifies that we are about to get the first reason as to why for the command in the previous verse. We go again to Paul's

---

(Grand Rapids, MI; Carlisle, England: W.B. Eerdmans; Paternoster Press, 1992).

[36] Causal connection: First reason as to why women are to learn in silence (submission [vs. 11] rather than "teach" or have "authority" [vs. 12] since the beginning)

words to the Corinthians, because he offers the same reason there for man's headship over woman. "But I want you to understand that the head of every man is Christ, the head of a wife is her husband, and the head of Christ is God." (1 Cor. 11:3) Paul goes on to say, "For man was not made from woman, but woman from man. Neither was man created for woman, but woman for man." 1 Corinthians 11:8-9

The Hebrew and Greek word "Adam" is a transliteration and occurs as "man," "mankind," as well as the proper name of the first human male created by God. The use here is not a generic use like "mankind," but rather as the "male" was created "first" (Gr., πρῶτος, protos, predicate adjective), making the contrasting point that "Adam" or the "male" was created prior to the female and is the chronological priority over the female. In other words, Paul is making the point that because the male was created first, it carries with it the head, the leadership role. Not only did God create Adam, the male first, but also he created the female *from* Adam, *for* the sake of Adam, to serve as a helper or compliment to Adam. (Gen. 2:18–25; 1 Cor. 11:8-9)

Embedded within Adam was the natural inclination to take the lead, while Eve's natural inclination was to follow that lead. Her body was created from a piece of Adam's body, his name in Hebrew is *ish*, meaning "man," while hers was derived from his name, *ishah*, meaning "woman" (literally, a female man). As Paul makes all too clear, we do not sidestep the order of things, when it comes to our worship in the Christian congregation. We are given one time, where Eve took the lead, without consulting her head, resulting in her being deceived by the serpent (Satan, John 8:44; Rev. 12:9). Eve led the way into sin, and Adam followed. Since the feminist movement of the 1960's, the divorce rate has risen steeply. We have asked women to go against their natural inclination to follow or support the lead of their head, and it has resulted in fractured families and homes, as well as the partial reason for some of the fragmentation of the Christian congregation.

Head Covering Excursion

Many Christians understand this section as a cultural issue which had application in first-century society but which does not apply to today. They see it in much the same way as 1 Corinthians 11 which also uses the Genesis account as a basis for women covering their heads in public worship.[37]

This would be a mistaken notion. It is *not* culturally bound to the first-century C.E. that women are not to teach or exercise authority over a man and that women are to wear a head covering under certain circumstances. They are both permanent and are applicable today.

The wearing of a head covering has a spiritual import within the Christian congregation. Paul, whose written word is inspired of God, lays out the God-designated principle of how headship was/is to take place in the Christian congregation, saying, "I want you to understand that the head of every man is Christ, the head of a wife is her husband, and the head of Christ is God." Paul informs the Corinthians, and by extension, us that the head covering is "a symbol of authority" that women are required to wear that man is their head, when she "prays or prophesies." In other words, if a woman is

[37] Knute Larson, vol. 9, I & II Thessalonians, I & II Timothy, Titus, Philemon, Holman New Testament Commentary, 170-71 (Nashville, TN: Broadman & Holman Publishers, 2000).

called on to substitute for her husband or a man that relates to some form of worship, she should wear a head covering. —1Co 11:4-6, 10.

For example, all families should have their own family Bible studies within their home. If the husband is not present for any reason (deceased, separated, divorced, or called away), and the wife has to conduct the family study, she is not obligated to wear a head covering, because the husband is not present. The same would hold true for saying the family prayer at meals as well. If for some reason the husband is present, but is unable to speak (maybe throat issues), she would wear the head covering. The wife would not have to wear a head covering with the children, as the woman is divinely authorized to teach the children. —Proverbs 1:8; 6:20.

However, if the husband is not present, and one of the children is a son, an adult born again Christian, he would conduct the study. If the son were a younger born again Christian, she would then wear a head covering. (1 Timothy 2:12) Since the son is a Christian, he is to receive his instruction from other male Christians.

Again, if a woman is called on to substitute for her husband or a man that relates to some form of worship, she should wear a head covering. Within the congregation, woman may be called on to teach a Bible study group for women or children, because there are not enough men, which means she would have to wear a head covering. If the woman is in a Bible study group that is conducted by a male, she does not have to wear a head covering to participate. Outside of the Christian congregation, both men and women are obligated to preach and teach the unbeliever, meaning she does not have to wear a head covering. —Matthew 24:14; 28:19, 20.

> ### 1 Timothy 2:14 Updated American Standard Version (UASV)
>
> [14] and Adam was not deceived, but the woman was deceived and came to be in transgression.

Genesis 3:6 Excursion

Almost all translations translate Genesis 3:6 as follows.

Genesis 3:6	Genesis 3:6	Genesis 3:6	Genesis 3:6
English Standard Version (ESV)	**Lexham English Bible (LEB)**	**American Standard Version (ASV)**	**New American Standard Bible (NASB)**
[6] So when the woman saw that the tree was good for food, and that it was a delight to the eyes, and that the tree was to be desired to make one wise, **she took of its fruit and ate, and she also gave some to her husband**	[6] When the woman saw that the tree was good for food and that it was a delight to the eyes, and the tree was desirable to make one wise, then **she took from its fruit and she ate. And she gave it also to her husband with her,**	[6] And when the woman saw that the tree was good for food, and that it was a delight to the eyes, and that the tree was to be desired to make one wise, **she took of the fruit thereof, and did eat; and she gave also unto her husband with her,**	[6] When the woman saw that the tree was good for food, and that it was a delight to the eyes, and that the tree was desirable to make one wise, **she took from its fruit and ate; and she gave also to her husband** with her, and he ate.

114

who **was** **with** **her**, and he ate.	and he ate.	and he did eat.	

As you can see from these English translations, the plain sense of the text is, Adam was with her. This creates a real Bible difficulty. Before I delve into why, I will say that if almost all of the translations are in agreement, generally, this should be respected, and accepted. It is very unlikely that the very best Hebrew and Greek scholars of the past 100 years are all mistaken. Now, the difficulty arises because, if Eve and Adam are standing there before the tree of knowledge, as the serpent spoke to Eve, it means that Adam, the head, was very much involved in this process. Think as you read this commentary below, trying to rationalize how the situation played out, with the both being there.

Eve "was indeed deceived," but Adam "was not deceived." Of course, this cannot be taken absolutely. It must mean something on this order: Adam was not deceived in the manner in which Eve was deceived. See Gen. 3:4–6. She listened directly to Satan; he did not. She sinned before he did. She was the leader. He was the follower. She led when she should have followed; that is, she led in the way of sin, when she should have followed in the path of righteousness.[38]

The reason for the difficulty is this, they are taking it as though Adam and Eve are standing before the tree of knowledge of good and evil, and the serpent, Satan, starts to speak to Eve. They carry on a conversation, with Adam simply passively listening. Satan deceives Eve, but Adam is not deceived, yet he does not argue with the serpent, snatch the fruit from Eve, but rather just stands there letting Eve eat the fruit, knowing she will die. Really? I just cannot see how that can rationally be the case. I would argue that Eve was alone, before Adam joined her.

Was Adam standing beside Eve when she had the conversation with the serpent, was deceived and chose to rebel against God? The Bible shows no indication that this is the case. The translations above make it appear that way though, "she took of its fruit and ate, and she also **gave** some to **her husband who was with her**, and he ate."

The Hebrew verb translated as "gave" is in the imperfect waw consecutive, as a result, it points to a temporal or logical sequence (usually called an "imperfect sequential"). Hence, a Bible translator or committee can

---

[38] William Hendriksen and Simon J. Kistemaker, vol. 4, Exposition of the Pastoral Epistles, New Testament Commentary, 110 (Grand Rapids: Baker Book House, 1953-2001).

translate the several occurrences of the waw, which tie together the chain of events in verse 6, with "and" as well as other transitional words, such as "subsequently," "then," "after that," afterward," and "so."

Genesis 3:6 English Standard Version (ESV)	**Genesis 3:6 Updated American Standard Version (UASV)**
6 So when the woman saw that the tree was good for food, **and** that it was a delight to the eyes, **and** that the tree was to be desired to make one wise, she took of its fruit **and** ate, **and** she also gave some to her husband who was with her, **and** he ate.	**6** So when the woman saw that the tree was good for food, **and** that it was a delight to the eyes, **and** that the tree was to be desirable to make one wise, **and** she took of its fruit **and** ate, *then* she also gave some to her husband when with her, **and** he ate.

One has to ask themselves, would Adam had passively stood beside his wife Eve, listening to the conversation, between her and the serpent, as the serpent spewed forth lies and malicious talk of Satan through this serpent, especially, when Paul tells us explicitly that he was not deceived by the serpent? Adam just stood there and remained silent? Adam just chose not to interrupt the peddling of lies. Listen to the Bible scholar below, he sure thinks this is reasonable.

> Genesis 3:6 makes it clear that he was "with her" during the interchange with the serpent, but he remained silent. He should have interrupted. He should have chased the serpent off. And when it comes down to it, when he is offered the fruit himself, he eats it—no

questions asked, no protests given. Adam and Eve together rebelled against their Creator, so they both suffer the horrible consequences.[39]

The conversation with the serpent reveals that Adam had previously carried out his responsibilities as the head, informing her of the command not to eat from the tree. (Gen. 3:3) It seems far more likely that Satan, through the serpent ignored this headship, going after the newer person in the Garden of Eden, Eve, when she was alone. Eve later replied, "The serpent deceived me, and I ate."

Let us assume that I am simply mistaken, and it should be translated, "and she also gave some to her husband who was with her." Adam need not be clear on the other side of the Garden; he could have just been out of hearing range, and still have been with her. Suppose he was across the field, visually in sight, but still out of hearing range, it could still be said he was with her. Husbands have you ever been in a huge store with your wife, like Wal-Mart, and at the same time you are on one side of the store (lawn-garden or automotive), and she is on the other side of the store. If you were to say you were **with your wife** at Wal-Mart, would that mean that you were necessarily standing right beside her. Say an issue came up in the store, so you walked over. The Garden of Eden was no small place, like a city park, but more like the size of a state park, possibly 18,000 acres of land and 3,000 acres of water. If Adam were in eyesight but out of hearing range, it could still be said that he was with her. She could have called him over after her transgression, at which point, he demonstrated that his

---

[39] Longman III, Tremper (2005-05-12). How to Read Genesis (How to Read Series How to Read) (p. 111). Intervarsity Press - A. Kindle Edition.

love for her was greater than that of his Creator, and so he ate.

¹⁴ and Adam was not deceived

Adam was absolutely not deceived; he simply chose that his love was greater for Eve than it was for his Creator. Paul is not shifting the blame on Eve; it is Adam, who was responsible for sin old age and death entering the world of humankind. (Rom 5:12, 19; 1 Cor. 15:22) He unlike Eve was not deceived by the lie that they would not die, or that God was withholding good from them, such as special knowledge. Both Adam and Eve intentionally and willfully went in a course of self-resolve, rebellion against God. Adam's sin was far more grievous than Eve. Moreover, it is his status as the head of Eve and of the human race, which laid the full accountability at his feet.

but the woman was deceived

Genesis 3:13 has Eve herself stating, "The serpent deceived me, and I ate." Eve had been completely deceived by the serpent, consumed by the desire of the eyes, mind and heart for the prospects lay before her, having only to eat of the tree, and she transgressed the law of God. This tree of knowledge of good and evil looked no different from any other tree; it was a mere symbol of God's sovereignty. However, look again at Eve's words, after she succumbed to the serpent's deception, "So when the woman **saw that the tree** was good for food, and that it was **a delight to the eyes**, and that **the tree was to be desired** to make one wise."

Both Adam and Eve had a natural desire to do good. We in this imperfect age and flesh, have the natural desire to do bad. Listen to the words of one of the greatest Christians ever to walk this earth. "So I find it to be a law that when I want to do right, evil lies close at hand. For I delight in the law of God, in my inner being, but I see in my members another law waging war against the law of my mind and making me captive to the law of sin that dwells in my members. Wretched man that I am! Who will deliver me from this body of death?" (Rom. 7:21-24) However, Paul knew the real source of his strength in weakness, as he goes on to answer his own question, "Thanks be to God through Jesus Christ our Lord! So then, I myself serve the law of God with my mind, but with my flesh I serve the law of sin."

With Eve's natural desire to be toward good, it means that she really had to go against the grain, to violate her conscience. James gives us an answer, as to how that can happen, even to a perfect person, with the natural desire toward good. "Each person is tempted when he is lured and enticed by his own desire. Then desire when it has conceived gives birth to sin, and sin when it is fully grown brings forth death." (Jam 1:14-15) The human eye is a wonder of creation, but it is also a direct channel of communication to the mind, which in turn affects the emotions and actions, the figurative heart, the seat of motivation. Satan tempted Eve by having her look upon a tree that was no different, giving it a whole other look with the desire of the eyes. He did the same thing with Jesus, trying to persuade him to sin by reaching out inappropriately for things Jesus saw with his eyes. (Lu 4:5-7) The apostle John warns us,

1 John 2:16-17 English Standard Version (ESV)

¹⁶ For all that is in the world—the desires of the flesh and **the desires of the eyes** and pride of life—is not from the Father but is from the world. ¹⁷ And the world

is passing away along with its desires, but whoever does the will of God abides forever.

and came to be in transgression

Sin can be in the form of a "transgression." The Greek parabasis basically means "overstepping." It is an "act of deviating from an established boundary or norm,"[40] especially in relation to a law.

---

1 Timothy 2:15 Updated American Standard Version (UASV)

15 Yet she will be saved through childbearing, if they continue in faith and love and holiness, with soundness of mind.[41]

---

15 Yet she will be saved through childbearing

No one would reasonable believe women are saved by simply bearing children. This being "saved" is not meant as eternal salvation, but more of being kept safe. You may remember the woman, "who had suffered from a discharge of blood for twelve years came up behind him and touched the fringe of his garment," and was healed. Well, it literally says, "your faith has saved you." However, translations render it as "your faith has made you well." Jesus was not telling this woman that her faith gave her eternal salvation, but that she had been healed

---

[40] William Arndt, Frederick W. Danker and Walter Bauer, A Greek-English Lexicon of the New Testament and Other Early Christian Literature, 3rd ed., 758 (Chicago: University of Chicago Press, 2000).

[41] σώφρων, ον, **gen.** ονος strictly having a sound or healthy mind; as having ability to curb desires and impulses so as to produce a measured and orderly life self-controlled, sensible.—Timothy Friberg, Barbara Friberg and Neva F. Miller, vol. 4, Analytical Lexicon of the Greek New Testament, Baker's Greek New Testament Library, 373 (Grand Rapids, MI: Baker Books, 2000).

and made safe from this ongoing affliction by her faith. The same is true of what Paul is saying here, for women in the Christian congregation. Women have a role to play in the marriage arrangement, which is to bear children and raise them with the teachings of God. If you encompass that with the preaching and teaching work of the Great Commission, and congregation responsibilities, she will not have time to feed of the spirit of this world that encourages women to forgo a family for career, nor will she have time to desire the position of pastoring a congregation. Moreover her role in the family, will keep her safe from being an idle gossiper and interferer in other people's affairs. (1 Timothy 5:11-15) The context of 1 Timothy is 2:15 is verse 9 says that, "women should adorn themselves in respectable apparel, with modesty and self-control, not with braided hair and gold or pearls or costly attire." Paul's additional counsel, in chapter five has this to say about the unmarried women, that they are "idlers, going about from house to house, and not only idlers, but also gossips and busybodies, saying what they should not."

If they continue in faith and love and holiness, with soundness of mind.

Turning again to the fifth chapter of this first letter to Timothy, Paul goes over some of the stumbling blocks that women (unmarried) suffer from, "idlers, going about from house to house, and not only idlers, but also gossips and busybodies, saying what they should not." He then gives them the following advice, "I would have younger widows marry, bear children, manage their households, and give the adversary no occasion for slander." Many young women stumble out of the faith, "straying after Satan," because they are idle from their responsibilities that they were given by God.

To be "sound in mind" comprises displaying good sense, being able to judge between right and wrong, modest, sensible in our speech and actions. It also means that women and men are to let God's Word be the guide of our thinking and actions. Roman 12:2

In conclusion, the natural reading of 1 Timothy 2:12 is that Paul in his apostolic authority prohibits women from teaching and exercising authority over a man, which means that women cannot serve as pastors or elders in the Christian congregation. We are not to mold to the pressures of the modern day feminist movement, because this position goes back to before the fall, has always been applicable, and will always be applicable.

BASIC TEACHING: Does Satan the Devil Really Exist?

Certainly, the vast majority of humankind would respond in the affirmative that they want happiness. However, humans have experienced anything but. For those who accept the theory of evolution, they would expect humankind to go through a period of extreme struggle, with conflict, animosity, wars and even death. However, they would be hard-pressed to explain the cruelty that has existed in humans, while the animal kingdom, a lower evolutionary form, has nothing of that sort. Yes, animals kill, grow old and die, even eat their young for survival. However, never will you find them torturing, raping, and killing for the mere pleasure of it.

How would the evolutionist explain humans with bombs strapped to them, getting on buses with children, and blowing themselves up with a bus full off innocents, just to make a political point? How would the evolutionist explain a man who kidnaps three young girls, chaining them in his basement for 10-12-years, torturing and beating them, using them as sex slaves? How would the evolutionist explain the crusades of the Medieval times, slaughtering hundreds of thousands in the name of a god? How would the evolutionist explain the inquisitions of the reformation, where so-called holy men tortured and killed in the name of God? How would the evolutionist explain the biological chemical used in war, the concentration camps of the Second World War, the slaughtering of six million Jews? How would the evolutionist explain that these are not even closest to the cruelest things that humans have done to other humans that these lists could go on for thousands of pages?

124

While evolution would allow for some very terrible actions by the human race, how would they explain the wickedness of humankind that does not exist in the animal kingdom? Is there some outside force that has contributed to this heinous history? Is there some invisible power that has been influencing human history? As far as the Christian faith is concerned, we need not guess on the matter. Jesus Christ, the Son of God referred to this invisible force, as "the ruler of this world." (John 12:31; 14:30; 16:11) Who or what has this kind of power.

When Jesus began his ministry at the age of 30 in 29 C.E., his cousin John baptized him. Thereafter, he went out into the wilderness for 40 days. At the end of that period, an invisible spirit creature known in the Bible as Satan the Devil tempted him. In the Gospel of Matthew the third temptation on Jesus reads this way, "the devil took him to a very high mountain and showed him all the kingdoms of the world and their glory. And he said to him, 'All these I will give you, if you will fall down and worship me.'"—Matthew 4:8-9

This invisible spirit creature offered Jesus "all the kingdoms of the world." The question that comes to mind is, 'how can he do that if they belong to God?' Without getting bogged down in the history of how, suffice it to say that, the issues that were raised when Adam and Eve rebelled against God in the Garden of Eden, placed humankind under the influence of Satan until the issues were to be settled. Notice Jesus response in verse 10, "Then Jesus said to him, "Be gone, Satan! For it is written, "'You shall worship the Lord your God and him only shall you serve.'" Jesus did not deny that "all the kingdoms of the world" were not under the rulership of Satan, which he would have logically done, if they were not. The apostle John informs his readers "the whole world lies in the power of the evil one." (1 John

5:19) The apostle Paul says, "The god of this world has blinded the minds of the unbelievers, to keep them from seeing the light of the gospel of the glory of Christ, who is the image of God." (2 Cor. 4:4) This latter text explains why humans are not aware of who is behind the cruelty that exists.

The Beginning of the Battle

We must go back to the beginning, when this battle began with Adam and Eve. You likely remember that God laid only one restriction on the first human couple, "but of the tree of the knowledge of good and evil you shall not eat, for in the day that you eat of it you shall surely die." (Gen 2:17, ESV) Adam must have went over this restriction often and very well, as Eve had it memorized and took it more serious than is usually taught. Satan through the serpent hanging from the tree was very clever and ingenious in how he indirectly said, "Did God actually say, 'You shall not eat of any tree in the garden'?" (Gen. 3:1) The woman replied to the serpent, "We may eat of the fruit of the trees in the garden, but God said, 'You shall not eat of the fruit of the tree that is in the midst of the garden, neither shall you touch it, lest you die.'"—Genesis 3:2-3

Notice how Eve, not only responded with the correct answer, but she was also very emphatic, going beyond the actual command, saying that they were to not only **not eat** from the tree, but they were **not to even touch it**. "You can be sure that you will not die," the serpent said to the woman. "God knows that when you eat the fruit of that tree, you will know things you have never known before. You will be able to tell the difference between good and evil. You will be like God." (Gen 3:4-5) The woman made two mistakes in that

126

moment, (1) she did not consult her head Adam, and (2) she entertained, cultivated this misleading, slanderous information. "When the woman saw that the tree *was* good for food and that it *was* a delight to the eyes, and the tree was desirable to make *one* wise, then she took from its fruit and she ate. *Afterward*[42] she gave *it* also to her husband with her, and he ate."—Genesis 3:6

Here Eve was deceived because she looked at the tree differently than she had before. Eve lost the battle for her mind based on this supposedly new set of "truths," **(1)** she would not die, **(2)** the fruit of the tree would make her wise, **(3)** she would be like God, independent, able to determine for herself what is good and what is bad, setting her own standard. Now, this one tree looked no different from any of the other thousands of trees in the Garden of Eden. Yet Eve now says 'the fruit of the tree looked good, it was pleasing to look at.' The human eyes are a window to the human heart, the seat of motivation. Eve, even though she was perfect, meaning that her natural desire was to do good, stumbled based on the principle that James gave his readers. "Each person is tempted when he is lured and

---

[42] Some Bible translations give a different impression. The King James Version renders the text: "She took of the fruit thereof, and did eat, and gave also unto her husband with her; and he did eat." The Hebrew verb *wattitten* for "gave" is "with a prefixed pronoun SUBJECT and a sequential waw, hence signifying a time-based or logical sequence of the events." (A Systematic Glossary to the Andersen-Forbes Analysis of the Hebrew Bible) Are we to believe that Adam simply stood by, passively watching this conversation and events, without interjecting anything into it? German Bible scholar J. P. Lange comments on just that: "The presence of the man during the act of temptation, even his keeping quiet, is hardly imaginable." And in explaining the phrase "with her," Jewish commentator B. Jacob mentions that it does "not [mean] who was standing with her (during the previous act or while she ate)."

enticed by his own desire. Then desire when it has conceived gives birth to sin, and sin when it is fully grown brings forth death."—James 1:14-15

We notice too that Satan was so crafty that he was able to deceive another perfect creature to go against the grain of her perfected leanings, and violate God's one prohibition, even though it had been so deeply ingrained in her. Eve was misled by misinformation and lies that was ingenuously presented in a very subtle, indirect way. Notice Paul's words to the first-century Corinthian congregation, "But I am afraid lest somehow, as the serpent deceived Eve by his craftiness, your minds may be led astray from the sincerity and the purity of devotion to Christ." Yes, Satan has misled Eve by his craftiness, leading her mind astray from what she knew to be true, getting her to accept the lie.—2 Corinthians 11:3.

Who Is Satan?

Satan is a real person, not some evil that exists in humans. In fact, he is an invisible spirit person, a higher life form than humans are. Just as God is a spirit person, so is Satan. (Jn 4:24) God did not create Satan per se; he created a spirit creature, just as he created millions of other spirit creatures. (Job 38:7; Psalm 104:4; Hebrews 1:7, 13, 14) This spirit creature became Satan (meaning, 'resister, opposer') the Devil (meaning, 'slanderer'), when he chose to oppose God in the Garden of Eden, and slander his great name.

Satan Thrown Down to Earth

Revelation 12:9, 12 English Standard Version (ESV)

9 And the great dragon was thrown down, that ancient serpent, who is called the devil and Satan, the deceiver of the whole world—he was thrown down to the earth, and his angels were thrown down with him. **12** Therefore, rejoice, O heavens and you who dwell in them! But woe to you, O earth and sea, for the devil has come down to you in great wrath, because he knows that his time is short!"

We see here that Satan the Devil is thrown down, and his angels were thrown down with him from the heavens to the earth. The first question is, 'when did this take place?' First, let us deal with what is meant by "the heavens." The Bible talks about the heavens, and it is only by the context that one can truly determine what is meant. The heavens can be the **earth's atmosphere** where the birds fly. (Deut. 4:17; Pro 30:19; Matt 6:26) The heavens can be **outer space**, which is on the other side of the earth's atmosphere. (Deut. 4:19; Isa 13:10; 1 Cor. 15:40, 41; Heb. 11:12) The heavens can be **midheaven**, which is where the eagles fly; thus, within our atmosphere. (Re 8:13; 14:6; 19:17; De 4:11 [Heb., "heart of the heavens"]) Heaven can also be the **heaven of heavens** or highest heavens (Deut. 10:14; Neh. 9:6). "The Hebrew expression [heaven of the heavens], however, may be nothing more than poetic imagery."[43] This is an expression of completeness for the physical heavens, as they visually extended out from the earth in all directions as far as the eye could see.

Now that we have covered all of the aspects of the physical heavens, we can now turn our attention to the **spiritual heavens**. The spiritual heavens exist outside of

---

[43] , vol. 2, The International Standard Bible Encyclopedia, Revised, ed. Geoffrey W. Bromiley, 713 (Wm. B. Eerdmans, 1979–1988).

the physical heavens, and are the home of God and all other spirit creatures, like the angels, cherubs and seraphs. (Jude 6; Gen 28:12, 13; Matt 18:10; 24:36) The spiritual heavens would have a vastness, unlike anything we could possibly imagine. In other words, the spirit creatures, who share the spiritual heavens with God, do not have access to **his presence** at all times, beholding the face of the Father.

For example, consider our Milky Way galaxy. There could be as many as a trillion stars in our galaxy. If humans had a space ship that could travel at the speed of light, **186,282 miles per second**, it would take 100,000 years to cross it. This boggles the mind does it not? Now, there are about 100 billion galaxies in our universe. We are not finished yet, because there are approximately 125 billion universes. Now, this is almost impossible for our human mind to grasp. What a backyard for the human family. Whoever said that we would get bored if we lived for an eternity, likely never considered the vastness of it all? Moreover, the universe is continuously growing, as are the others. If this is what we have, one cannot really wrap their mind around the spiritual heavens.

Satan and his angels, had access to the spiritual heavens in the days of Noah, and centuries later in the time of Job. "Again it came to pass on the day when the sons of God came to present themselves before Jehovah that Satan came also among them to present himself before Jehovah." (Job 2:1) Even centuries later Jesus speaks prophetically of a future fall that Satan is to have, as a result of Jesus ransom sacrifice. Jesus said, "I saw Satan fall like lightning from heaven." He also said, "Now is the judgment of this world; now will the ruler of this world be cast out." (John 12:31) The time of this being cast down to earth from heaven is "at a time when Christian martyrs are being made (Rev 12:11). Further, it

130

is at a time very shortly before the end of the age, when "he knows that his time is short" (Rev 12:12). This, then, must be a final exclusion of the devil from access to God shortly before Christ's return."[44]

In dealing with Satan and his angels being kicked out of the spiritual heavens, and cast down to the earth says, Revelation 12:12 says, "O heavens and you who dwell in them! But woe to you, O earth and sea, for the devil has come down to you in great wrath, **because he knows that his time is short**!" We do not know if this has specifically happened as of yet, but we do know that a great wrath will go with it, which will last for a short time. What a short time is specifically we do not know either. To whom is that great wrath going to be directed toward? Certainly, Satan is not interested in the world of mankind, but only the chosen ones of God, and his sole efforts will be toward eradicating them, if he cannot turn them away. In the Gospel of Matthew, Jesus identifies the signs of Christ's presence, and the conclusion of the age, followed by talk of the Great Tribulation. It would seem very likely that Satan's being expelled from the spiritual heavens, having a great wrath for God's people, because he knows his time is short, could very well coincide with the Great Tribulation.

Matthew 24:21-22 English Standard Version (ESV)

21 For then there will be great tribulation, such as has not been from the beginning of the world until now, no, and never will be. **22** And if those days had not been cut

---

[44] Kendell H. Easley, vol. 12, Revelation, Holman New Testament Commentary, 211 (Nashville, TN: Broadman & Holman Publishers, 1998).

short, no human being would be saved. But for the sake of the elect **those days will be cut short**.

Satan knows that soon **his time will be short**! Therefore, his goal is no longer to disprove the rightfulness of God's sovereignty, but rather to take as many with him as he can. His end goal now is to decimate the affirmative answer to Jesus' question rose clear back in the first-century C.E. "when the Son of Man comes, will he find faith on earth?" Yes, Satan is trying to hold this back from becoming a reality. The apostle Peter warned,

1 Peter 5:8-9 English Standard Version (ESV)

8 Be sober-minded; be watchful. Your adversary the devil prowls around like a roaring lion, seeking someone to devour. **9** Resist him, firm in your faith, knowing that the same kinds of suffering are being experienced by your brotherhood throughout the world.

How Satan Deceives

The apostle Paul was encouraging the Corinthians to "not be outwitted by Satan; for we are not ignorant of his designs." (2 Cor. 2:11) Satan is crafty, and he has outwitted most of humankind for thousands of years now, not to mention a third of the angels. However, because of the Bible, Christians do not have to be ignorant of his designs. In fact, think about, most of the world today does not even believe he exists, for them he is just a myth in a book written by men. Even eighty percent of Christianity does not believe in his existence. Paul explains: "Satan disguises himself as an angel of light."—2 Corinthians 11:14

Accordingly, we can anticipate that Satan's cunning plan for deceiving the mass of humanity will look as if harmless, even advantageous. You will recall in the above that Satan came to Eve as some benefactor, who was helping her overcome the trickery of her Creator, who was trying to hide freedom from her. (Gen. 3:4-6) This is the same today, the desire for absolute freedom (something that is unattainable), keeps most humans from accepting the sovereignty of God. They are so blinded that they fail to see the real source of peace and security. —Isaiah 9:6; Matthew 6:9, 10

The apostle James admonished:

James 4:7 English Standard Version (ESV)

7 Submit yourselves therefore to God. Resist the devil, and he will flee from you.

Let us take a moment to revisit Jesus' temptations by Satan. If we follow James' advice above, and live by the example set by Jesus, we will survive the onslaught of Satan's attacks on our Christian faith.

Jesus' First Temptation

Jesus after his baptism by John the Baptist went out into the wilderness for forty days and forty nights, which left him weak and hungry. It was **then** that Satan chose to tempt Jesus, waiting until he was in a weakened condition. Read carefully as Satan offers the first temptation to Jesus:

Luke 4:3 English Standard Version (ESV)

3 The devil said to him, "**If** you are the Son of God, command this stone to become bread."

First, Satan played on Jesus' natural desire for food, as he deliberately waited until Jesus was in a weakened state from fasting. In addition, Satan knew that Jesus was the Son of God, as he had been in heaven with him. Notice how he is attempting to attack Jesus hunger, by starting his accusation with "if," to get Jesus to use his powers for selfish gain. In other words, he wanted Jesus to be annoyed and say, 'You know I am the Son of God, so watch as I turn these stones into bread!' Was Jesus tempted into a selfish act, a needful feeling of proving himself right? No, Jesus did not permit Satan to bait him into rebellion.

Luke 4:4 English Standard Version (ESV)

[4] And Jesus answered him, "It is written, 'Man shall not live by bread alone.'"

Jesus' Second Temptation

Luke 4:6-7 English Standard Version (ESV)

[6] and said to him, "**To you** I will give all this authority and their glory, for it has been delivered to me, and I give it to whom I will. [7] If you, then, will worship me, it will all be yours."

One way of being emphatic in Greek is to front word(s) before others, and in this case, the second person pronoun (soi, "to you") was fronted to the beginning of the Greek sentence by Luke to show just how important this question was. The English is not able to bring this out well, but the Greek makes it all too clear. What Satan was saying, is a bit like what a car salesperson might say,[45] 'look, this deal is for you and you alone!.' Did Jesus even slightly consider Satan's offer? No, he responds,

Luke 4:8 English Standard Version (ESV)

8 And Jesus answered him, "It is written,

"'You shall worship the Lord your God,
 and him only shall you serve.'"

Jesus' Third Temptation,

Luke 4:9-10 English Standard Version (ESV)

9 And he took him to Jerusalem and set him on the pinnacle of the temple and said to him, "If you are the Son of God, throw yourself down from here, **10 for it is written**,

"'He will command his angels concerning you,
 to guard you,'

Notice that Satan even quotes Scripture, but of course twists it to suit his misleading purposes. This temptation is much more subtle than one might think. Satan wanted Jesus to get caught up in himself, and take the easy way out, as opposed to the humble three and half year ministry that lie ahead. If Jesus had stood on the top of the pinnacle of the temple, at a time of the day when everyone was out, with all gathered to see him there; it would have made his ministry easier. Because if he leaped in front of thousands of onlookers, and angels came to rescue him before he hit the ground, many would have had faith in him, based on his showmanship. However, Jesus knew his Father's will was for him to

---

[45] I borrowed the car salesperson analogy from Dr. Darrell Bock, with some revision.

have an education ministry of three and a half years, a ministry of humility. Moreover, how did Jesus feel about doing the will of the Father? Here are his own words, "My food is to do the will of him who sent me and to accomplish his work." (John 4:34)

Matthew 4:7 English Standard Version (ESV)

[7] Jesus said to him, "Again it is written, 'You shall not put the Lord your God to the test.'"

On many other occasions, Jesus used the Scriptures to help unsuspecting ones escape Satan's influences, as well as the overbearing Jewish religious leaders, who were twisting the Scriptures for their ill-gotten gains. Jesus made more than 120 references or quotations from the Old Testament Scriptures, to over half of the books of the Hebrew Old Testament, in his three and half year ministry. This may appear to be trivial when you think of a three and half year ministry. However, notice what John says about Jesus, "Now Jesus did many other signs in the presence of the disciples, which are not written in this book." (John 20:30)

John also said, "Now there are also many other things that Jesus did. Were every one of them to be written, I suppose that the world itself could not contain the books that would be written." (John 21:25) Thus, if we take everything Jesus said in the Gospels, it would only amount to 3-4 hours of speaking. Now imagine four speakers at a religious assembly, giving an hour talk each, and each of them referencing or quoting some 30 Scriptures in their allotted hour. These would be considered highly biblical talks. Moreover, Jesus usually never had any scrolls in front of him. Therefore, his quotes and references were from memory. In the famous Sermon on the Mount, he directly or indirectly referenced dozens of Scriptures from memory.

Our Need to Pray

After giving us the complete suit of spiritual armor, Paul goes on to tell us,

Ephesians 6:18 English Standard Version (ESV)

[18] praying at all times in the Spirit, with all prayer and supplication. To that end keep alert with all perseverance, making supplication for all the saints

When we are enticed by our flesh, or come upon a trial, or find ourselves discouraged, prayer can strengthen us immeasurably. (Matthew 26:41) Jesus "offered up prayers and supplications, with loud cries and tears, to him who was able to save him from death, and he was heard because of his reverence."—Hebrews 5:7.

BASIC TEACHING: How Should Christians View Homosexuality and Same Sex Attraction?

You have the only large mainstream church ever to consecrate an openly gay bishop (Gene Robinson), the Episcopal Church in the United States of America. An openly gay Atlanta pastor of Evangelical Lutheran Church in America (Bradley Schmeling) was voted in by a vast majority as the senior pastor at the biggest Lutheran church in Saint Paul, Minn. The Presbyterian Church (U.S.A.) is now allowing openly gay men and women in same-sex relationships to be ordained as clergy.

The issue is so divisive that it has split major denominations in half. Those who see somebody who is sexually involved with members of his or her own sex, as being just an alternative lifestyle, and acceptable as a church member or pastor, while the other side sees it as contrary to nature, and not acceptable for a church member, let alone a pastor, or bishop. Both sides use God's Word as a means of saying that their position is biblical. However, the law of noncontradiction helps us appreciate it is impossible for same sex couples, who are actively in a sexual relationship to be both biblical and not biblical. In other words, someone is wrong in their interpretation of Scripture.

Some who support the right for church members, pastors, and bishops to be actively involved sexually with a person of the same sex, will argue,

"I believe God made us all in His image; He did not make a mistake. We love whom we love, because God wants us to."

In making this comment, the supports are thinking of the following text as their support,

Genesis 1:27 English Standard Version (ESV)

27 So God created man in his own image, in the image of God he created him; male and female he created them.

What does the Bible say about Homosexuality? What does it say about same-sex marriage? Is it a sin to be homosexual active? If it is a sin, then why does homosexuality exist? Is God just being unfair, or is it more complicated than that? Before going on, it might be good to qualify some terms. Many people dealing with same sex attraction find the word homosexual offensive, because to them, it implies one who is sexually active with a person of the same sex. We must admit there are those who struggle with same sex attraction, but realize that the Bible condemns such activity, so they must constantly work to maintain control over themselves.

However, the dictionary defines homosexual as "somebody who is sexually attracted to members of his or her own sex," (Encarta), with no mention of being sexually active. However, dictionaries can be behind in how a word is used and understood. Thus, out of respect for our brothers and sisters, who are struggling with same sex attraction, and find the term homosexual wrong, we will just stick with the phrase same sex attraction, and qualify whether we are referring to sexually active or

139

inactive. Before moving on, let us take a moment to consider how we came to be in this fallen imperfect condition.

Human Rebellion

It was God's intention that his first couple, Adam and Eve, were to procreate, and cultivate the Garden of Eden, until it covered the entire earth, filled with humans worshipping him. —Genesis 1:28

If the first couple had not rebelled, they and their offspring could have lived forever. —Genesis 2:15-17

One of the angels in heaven (who became Satan), abused his free will (James 1:14-15), chose to rebel against God, and he used a lowly serpent to contribute to Adam and Eve abusing their free will, and disobeying God, believing they did not need him, and could walk on their own. —Genesis 3:1-6; Job 1-2.

God removed the rebellious Adam and Eve from the Garden of Eden (Gen 3:23-24) The first human couple had children, but they all grew old and eventually died. (Gen. 3:19; Rom 5:12), just as the animals died. —Ecclesiastes 3:18-20

Genesis 6:5 (AT) tells us just before the flood of Noah, that "the wickedness of man on earth was great, and the whole bent of his thinking was never anything but evil." After the flood, God said of man, the bent of man's mind may be evil from his very youth." (Gen 8:21, AT) Jeremiah 10:23 tells us "that it is not in man who walks to direct his steps." Jeremiah 17:9 tells us that "The heart is deceitful above all things, and desperately sick; who can understand it?" Yes, man was not designed to walk on his own. However, man was also not designed with absolute free will, but free will under the sovereignty of his Creator. Imperfect man is mentally bent toward wickedness, fleshly desires, to which Satan has set it up this world, so it caters to the fallen flesh. "For all that is in the world—the desires of the flesh and the desires of the eyes and pride of life—is not from the Father but is from the world." —1 John 2:16.

Getting back to Genesis 1:27 that says, "God created man in his own image, in the image of God he created him; male and female he created them," which means that man is born with a moral nature, which creates within him a conscience that reflects God's moral values. (Rom 2:14-15) It acts as a moral law within. However, it has an opponent as fallen man also possesses the "law of sin," 'missing the mark of perfection,' the natural desire toward wickedness. Listen to the internal battle of the apostle Paul. (Rom 6:12; 7:22, 23)

Romans 7:21-24 English Standard Version (ESV)

[21] So I find it to be a law that when I want to do right, evil lies close at hand. [22] For I delight in the law of God, in my inner being, [23] but I see in my members another law waging war against the law of my mind and making me captive to the law of sin that dwells in my members. [24] Wretched man that I am! Who will deliver me from this body of death?

However, there is hope,

Romans 7:25 English Standard Version (ESV)

[25] Thanks be to God through Jesus Christ our Lord! So then, I myself serve the law of God with my mind, but with my flesh I serve the law of sin.

From the Old Person to the New Person

The apostle Paul wrote,

1 Corinthians 2:14 English Standard Version (ESV)

14 The natural person does not accept the things of the Spirit of God, for they are folly to him, and he is not able to understand them because they are spiritually discerned.

This does not in and of itself mean, that the unbeliever cannot understand God's Word, as they can, but they see it as foolish, and reject and refuse to apply it. What we are addressing is what Paul meant by natural man. This is one with no spiritual life, in that he follows the desires of his fallen flesh, setting aside God and his Word as mere foolishness. Paul informs us of a hope that these unbelievers fail to find.

Ephesians 4:23 English Standard Version (ESV)

23 and to be renewed in the spirit of your minds,

Colossians 3:9-10 English Standard Version (ESV)

9 Do not lie to one another, seeing that you have put off the old self with its practices **10** and have put on the new self, which is being renewed in knowledge after the image of its creator.

Romans 12:2 English Standard Version (ESV)

2 Do not be conformed to this world, but be transformed by the renewal of your mind, that by testing you may discern what is the will of God, what is good and acceptable and perfect.

In the beginning of a person's introduction to the good news, he will take in knowledge of the Scriptures (1 Tim. 2:3-4), which if his heart is receptive, he will begin to apply them in his life, taking off the old person and putting on the new person. (Eph. 4:22-24) Seeing how the Scriptures have begun to alter his life, he will start to have a genuine faith over the things he has learned (Heb. 11:6), repenting of his sins. (Acts 17:30-31) He will turn around his life, and his sins will be blotted out. (Acts 3:19) At some point, he will go to the Father in prayer, telling him that he is dedicating his life to him, to carry out his will and purposes. (Matt. 16:24; 22:37) This regeneration is the Holy Spirit working in his life, giving him a new nature, placing him on the path to salvation. —2 Corinthians 5:17. (Andrews 2013, 17)

Certainly, you may have thought this long excursion had us off in the weeds. However, it seemed important that the reader understand humanities fall into sin, and exactly what that means, so as to appreciate what is about to be said. Every physical, mental, and emotional issue that has fallen upon man is a direct result of our imperfection. This means mental disorders like depression, bipolar schizophrenia, anxiety disorder, obsessive-compulsive disorder, and so on are a result of inherited imperfection. This would also apply to persons who struggle with same sex attraction.

Some argue that same sex attraction is brought about through socialization. Somebody acquires a personality or traits through their background (nurture), impacted by family, friends, school, work, and so on. Others would argue that same sex attraction is brought about because one is genetically predisposed (nature). I am not going to take on the science of such an issue herein.

Let me just say that it is likely a mixture of both. Let us take a young woman (true story),[46] who was in an abusive marriage, mentally, emotionally and physically. We will call her **Sandy**. She had a very close friend (we will call **Cindy**), who also suffered from the ravages of an abusive husband. One night, after a very trying week, they find themselves alone, sitting on a couch, talking to each other as they watched a movie. Through tears and a broken heart, they unloaded as to just how bad it is. Soon, Sandy goes into an uncontrollable sob, so Cindy holds her in her arms, stroking her hair, comforting her with her soft voice. After a while, the sobbing stops, and Cindy brushes Sandy's tears away. Cindy then leans in and starts kissing Sandy, and Sandy does not pull away.

This begins a five-year same sex relationship, until Sandy starts to feel wrong, and decides to return to her faith. In this true story, Sandy was not actually attracted to women; she did not have same sex attraction (nurture). However, her childhood abuse, coupled with an extremely abusive husband, and a loving and comforting friend, led to her finding comfort in this relationship. Cindy on the other hand, was and is a person that has same sex attraction (nature). She entered the marriage with her husband, because she was trying to avoid the stigma of being of the same sex attraction. She went to the same congregation as Sandy. Here could be a real-life case of one, who was socialized into a same sex relationship, and one that was genetically predisposed into a same sex relationship.

---

[46] The account is true, but the names are changed.

I would argue that the science is irrelevant to the Christian faith. Let us err on the side of those who say that, for some it is genetic and they are predisposed toward same sex attraction. If we concede this, it does nothing to remove the Bible's position on same sex relationships. Remember, the Bible says that we are all mentally bent toward wickedness. What we should understand is that some lean toward different things in this mental bent, and others lean heavenly in other directions. By tentatively erring on this side of some being genetically predisposed, we can better help them, and better understand their struggles. Lastly, because we accept genetic predisposition, this does not exclude their gaining control over their body and mind, as well as their being able to take off the old person and put on the new person. Moreover, it does not exclude that many same sex attraction cases are socialized.

What is the Bible's Viewpoint of Same Sex Attraction?

There is absolutely no ambiguity in the Bible at all. God designed Adam and Eve, to procreate, and sex is to be between a man and a woman. (Gen 1:27, 28; Lev 18:22; Prov 5:18-19) Fornication in Scripture is a reference to sexual sin by homosexual and heterosexual conduct.—Galatians 5:19-21.[47]

However, the Bible does not condone hating those who struggle with same sex attraction, but we are to hate the sin. However, we are to make a stand against sin that is against the moral code of our Creator, and we are **not**

---

[47] Help is available for all who struggle with same sex attraction and those who struggle with intense opposite-sex attraction. http://www.aacc.net/

to cave to public opinion. Our Christian lifestyle is reflective by the moral code within Scripture, and we have a right to our position, by the Creator himself. There is no reason that we should be ashamed of our viewpoint.

1 Peter 2:17 New Living Translation (NLT)

17 Respect everyone, and love your Christian brothers and sisters. Fear God, and respect the king.

Christians should not have an irrational hatred for those that struggle with same sex attraction. We are to respect all people. Anyone spewing hatred, he is not truly acting Christlike. (Matt 7:12) We are to reject same sex relationships, the conduct, not the person. For those that are advocates for gay rights, this is their viewpoint, and we **respectfully** disagree, and **respectfully** articulate as to why.

If some makes the argument that Jesus visited sinners and that he was tolerant of others, this is mixing some truth, but also misleading at the same time. Certainly, Jesus spent time with sinners, but he did not ever condone their sin.

Some may make the point I made in the above, but take it a step further. They may say, "I am born this way, it is not my fault, why should I be punished, or miss out on love, because of inheriting a genetic predisposition?"

You could respond that the Bible does not address the genetic predisposition of same sex attraction, but then again it does not address the mental issues of bipolar either. It is not a science textbook, nor is it a mental health guide. Thus, we should not look for it to resolve the specifics. However, it does address certain thinking and certain actions. Therefore, the Bible might not explicitly address the genetic, but it does address same sex acts.

Some have argued that addictive personalities are genetically predisposed (gambling, drugs, alcohol, intense opposite sex attraction), as well as anger and rage are also viewed as genetic. Giving these ones the same benefit of the doubt as to the leanings being genetic, would we approve of a man that beats his wife, or another man that sexually abuses women, because they may be predisposed to those desires? Certainly not, we would send him to Christian counseling, and expect him to get control over his body and mind, by putting on the mind of Christ. We would acknowledge that he struggles with these desires, and we would expect that he would not put himself in innocent appearing situations.

What the Bible offers is reasonable, and it does not condone homophobic mindsets. The Bible expects those who have same sex attraction to apply the same counsel, as those with intense opposite-sex attraction.

1 Corinthians 6:18 English Standard Version (ESV)

[18] Flee from sexual immorality. Every other sin a person commits is outside the body, but the sexually immoral person sins against his own body.

There are hundreds of thousands, if not millions of men and women, who suffer from intense sexual attraction and addition. The Bible expects them to get control over their body, not give into temptation. The same is expected with those with same sex attraction.

Deuteronomy 30:19 English Standard Version (ESV)

19 I call heaven and earth to witness against you today, that I have set before you life and death, blessing and curse. Therefore choose life, that you and your offspring may live,

Ephesians 4:19 English Standard Version (ESV)

19 They have become callous and have given themselves up to sensuality, greedy to practice every kind of impurity.

Ephesians 5:11 English Standard Version (ESV)

11 Take no part in the unfruitful works of darkness, but instead expose them.

Put to Death What Is Earthly in You

Colossians 3:5 English Standard Version (ESV)

5 Put to death therefore what is earthly in you: sexual immorality, impurity, passion, evil desire, and covetousness, which is idolatry.

One of the greatest mistakes of the Christian and religious leadership is, to be self-righteous in their dealings with those who have same sex attraction, or those that have given into a homosexual lifestyle. The conduct of such ones is n more grievous that the spouse who commits adultery, or the churchgoer who commits fornication, or the churchgoer that finds himself or herself involved in the habit of masturbation or pornography. Sexual sin is sexual sin. There were Christians in the first century who had formerly led a life of homosexuality, who put on the new person as they worked toward becoming a Christian, getting control over themselves, and setting aside their former ways. —1 Corinthians 6:9-11

Does God have the right to set the moral standards of humankind? Yes, he is the Creator of heaven and earth, as well as humans. He designed us to be free moral agents, but under the umbrella of his sovereignty. We were never intended to have absolute freedom, the ability to set our own standards of right and wrong. Moreover, the natural desire is opposite sex attraction. The only reason that same sex attraction exists at present is, our fall into imperfection. It is a symptom of inherited imperfection. Once God has settled the issues raised by Satan and man's rebellion, we will no longer lean toward bad, but will lean toward good. The natural desire for Adam and Eve before the fall was toward good, and to think of or do bad would have been contrary to that nature. After the rebellion and imperfection entered the world, the further removed humans were from Adam and Eve, the more they were and are inclined toward their imperfections, leaning toward bad.

How do we benefit from fighting the desires of the flesh, and obeying God's moral standards, as set out in Scripture? While it may seem unfair now that one cannot act on, nor entertain same sex attraction, even though it may seem natural to him or her, this is a temporary situation. A time is coming when those, who have sided with God and have remained loyal, will receive eternal life. Can you imagine living for hundreds of millions of years, and looking back on that mere 70-80 years of imperfect desires? —John 3:16

God's View Homosexuality

While the liberal religious leaders of the day have watered down the Bible, this does not remove the clear statements from scripture. God created Adam and Eve, man and woman, with the desire, the sexual attraction of man toward woman and woman toward man. God is deeply saddened over the rebellion of Adam and Eve, and the subsequent fall into a sinful depraved world. However, he is correcting the issues that were raised. God condemns all sin, which is all that is anything not in harmony with His personality, standards, ways, will, and purpose.[48]

What if you find yourself having feelings of same sex attraction, does this necessarily mean that you are a homosexual, in the sense that you are not attracted, nor ever will be attracted to the same sex, and that you will fall away into having a sexual relationship with a person of the same sex. No. We do not fully understand our imperfections, and it could be a period of time that you feel this way. However, there is no sense n deceiving ourselves, some will only ever have same sex attraction in this imperfect age that we live in, and they are obligated to have control over themselves, just as the same as any other with inappropriate sexual desires. If one seeks out very good, competent Christian counseling, can they put on the new person and take off the old person, to the point that they find themselves attracted to the opposite sex? Yes, some will be able to, but a few will have to live with and maintain control over their same sex attraction until God brings this imperfect system of things to an end.

---

[48] (See Job 2:10; Psa. 39:1; Lev. 20:20; 2 Cor. 12:21; Pro 21:4; Rom. 3:9-18; 2 Pe 2:12-15; Heb. 3:12, 13, 18, 19)

Just as some mental health professionals, believe that same sex attraction is genetic, and others that it is social, they also believe the same thing about addictive personalities. They also believe the same thing about adults that are sexually attracted to children. We have already agreed in the above that it is likely that it is both. You have a child who grows up in a household where he is sexually abused, and once he is older, the doctors diagnose him as having sexual attractions toward very young children. Now, just because this one has genetic leanings in the direction of young children, and he was socialized in this direction, there is no rational person who would make the argument, "this is who he is, God made him this way, he should be allowed to continue having sexual relations with children." Just because he was born with these leaning and was raised in such an environment that only perpetuated his desires, rational society would expect him to seek professional help. They would expect that he overcome his leanings, and if not, possibly acquire coping skills to maintain control. If he acts out, he would be arrested and locked away. While society has legalized or at least ignored the laws against homosexuality, God has not, and he expects that one get help to overcome, or gain control of the unnatural desires.

Aside from getting professional help from a Christian counselor, what can you do to gain control over your unnatural desires? You can pray to God, really going to him with the issues, opening your heart to him.

Psalm 139:23-24 English Standard Version (ESV)

23 Search me, O God, and know my heart!
   Try me and know my thoughts!
24 And see if there be any grievous way in me,
   and lead me in the way everlasting!

Proverbs 23:7 says, "For as he thinks in his heart, so is he." If we are to get control over our irrational thinking, we do well to fill our mind with good thoughts. (Phil 4:8) This means that we need to be in God's Word daily. The Bible has the power to mold our mind. (Heb. 4:12) Scripture can have a powerful effect on our thinking, if we study it in the appropriate way.

Another measure that needs to be taken is the fleeing from anything that will generate wrong desires, which lead to wrong actions. This means keeping our eyes and ears away from pornography and homosexual advocates. (Col. 3:5) We need to understand that the Bible's moral values are not respected in today's world.

Parents, teachers, couches, and the like influenced the youth of the 1950s and 1960s. Most young people today are very much influenced by hip-hop, rap, and heavy metal music, as well reality television, celebrities, movies, video games, and the Internet, especially social media. Parents are now allowing their children to receive life altering opinions, beliefs, and worldviews from the likes of Snooki, a cast member of the MTV reality show *Jersey Shore*. Kim Kardashian and her family rose to prominence with their reality television series, *Keeping Up with the Kardashians*.

The ABC Family channel (owned by Disney) comes across as a channel that you would want you children watching. However, most of the shows are nothing more than dysfunctional families, promotions of homosexuality as an alternative lifestyle, and young actors and actresses that are playing underage teens in high school, running around killing, causing havoc, and having sexual intercourse with multiple characters on the show. In August 2006, an all-new slogan and visual style premiered on ABC Family: A New Kind of Family. The channel shows such programming as Pretty Little Liars, Twisted, The Fosters, Melissa & Joey, Switched at Birth, The Lying Game, Bunheads and Baby Daddy.

The world has added new words to their vocabulary, like "sexting," which is the act of sending sexually explicit messages and/or photographs, primarily between cellphones. The term was first popularized in 2007. Then, there is "F-Bomb," which we are not going to define fully other than to say that the dictionary considers it "a lighthearted and printable euphemism" for something far more offensive. If all of the above is unfamiliar to you as a parent, and you have a teen or preteen child, you may want to Google the information.

Regardless of the degree of the relationship, these relationships often influence the thinking of a young life. It is important that you do not allow the wrong persons to influence you or your children. The truth is our thinking, and our actions are a direct result of bad associations, be it the wrong friends, music, celebrities, video games, or social media. The same holds true of good associations, like our parents, teachers, coaches, and good friends. Paul warned, "For there are many **rebellious men, empty talkers** and **deceivers**," from whom we should watch out! —Titus 1:10

In the end, with help from God's Word, the Christian congregation, the pastor, family, and Christian counseling, you have a reasonable expectation that you will not act on the same sex desires. Moreover, there is the possibility that you may be one of the few that begins to alter oneself to the point that the desires are no more. If not, self-control will be the way of things until God brings this wicked age to an end. The final warning offered herein is this. Do not allow charismatic religious rhetoric to suggest that the laying on of hands can heal you. This will only leave you vulnerable, as you will then let down your guard, and not seek the help that you need. What they espouse is just not how it works and is unbiblical.

BASIC TEACHING: Are Christians Obligated to Tithe?

Tithe (Old English *teotha*, meaning "a tenth"), generally defined as the tenth part of fruits and profits justly acquired, owed to God in recognition of his supreme dominion, and paid to the ministers of religion. It is an institution of undetermined antiquity, common to many religions. Tithing was adopted in principle by the Christian church from its founding and was subjected eventually to formal legislation by the Synod of Tours (567 ad) and the Synod of Macon (585). The institution was later enforced by civil authority (the late 8th-century Capitularies, or decrees, of Charlemagne), recognized in pre-Norman England, and sanctioned by English statute law in 1285. Tithing has continued in modern times in the established Church of England and the Roman Catholic Church, especially in Austria and Hungary, but elsewhere has been replaced generally by other systems of voluntary support of the clergy.[49]

The first mention of tithing within God's Word was voluntary. Abraham, after his military campaign of rescuing Lot and others, who had been taken captive by Chedorlaomer and his allies, Abram gave the king and priest of Salem[50] a tenth of everything. (Gen. 14:18-20)

---

[49] **Microsoft ® Encarta ® 2006.** © 1993-2005 Microsoft Corporation. All rights reserved.

[50] Salem is an ancient city, whose location would later be the city of Jerusalem.

Some 160 years later, Jacob, the grandson of Abraham made the following vow to God, saying,

Genesis 28:20-22 Updated American Standard Version (UASV)

20 "If God will be with me and will keep me in this way that I go, and will give me bread to eat and clothing to wear, **21** so that I come again to my father's house in peace, then Jehovah will be my God. **22** This stone, which I have set up for a pillar, shall be God's house. And of all that you give me I will give a full tenth to you."

Based on the Scriptural account Abraham's actions of paying the king-priest of Salem, Melchizedek, a tenth of his spoils was not an obligation placed upon the family, namely the descendants of Jacob (Israel's) sons, the Israelites. It would have been unnecessary for Jacob (later named "Israel"), to make the above offer of paying a tenth, if Abraham had obligated them. Likewise, Jacob's vow was not an obligation that his descendants were obligated to carry out either. His vow was specifically meant for himself alone.

Tithing Under the Mosaic Law

On the other hand, God saw fit to incorporate tithing within the Law of Moses. This tithing was designed so that the twelve tribes of Israel could support a thirteenth tribe, the Levites, who served as priests, as they did not receive an inheritance of land. God gave the Levites every tenth in Israel as an inheritance in return for the work they did, the work of the tent of meeting, the initial temporary sacred tabernacle. (Numbers 18:21-24) The Israelites were an agricultural people, every tenth of the land's produce, grain from the soil or fruit from the trees, as well as every tenth animal from the herd or flock belonged to God. Therefore, the tithe was not paid with money. However, if one did wish to pay with money, he would actually have had to pay 20 percent more than those who paid with land and livestock. Leviticus 27:30-33

This obligation to tithe was to be taken very serious, as it was an obligation, a command, not voluntary. If an Israelite was caught giving less, he would then have to pay 20 percent not the ten percent, and offer a guilt sacrifice. (Leviticus 5:14-16) The reason for taking the tithe so serious was the fact that a failure to do so would adversely affect the priesthood, who was supported by it. The tithe was given to serve a need for the ancient people of God, but the question before us is, is it a need that was carried over into Christianity, even today?

Mosaic Law Cancelled

About 16-years after the death/resurrection of Jesus, Gentiles started to come into the Christian congregation. They were not circumcised, so this caused some contention, being that almost all of the Christians at that time were circumcised Jews.

Acts 15:5 English Standard Version (ESV)

5 But some believers who belonged to the party of the Pharisees rose up and said, "It is necessary to circumcise them and to order them to keep the Law of Moses."

Of course, not all agreed with this position, so a letter was written by the apostles and older men of Jerusalem, sharing God's will and purposes on this issue. Were the non-Jews obligated to keep the Mosaic Law? In fact, were the Jews obligated to keep the Law? Keep in mind this also included the law on tithing as well. (Acts 15:6-21) The letter from the Jerusalem council read as follows,

Acts 15:22-29 English Standard Version (ESV)

22 Then it seemed good to the apostles and the elders, with the whole church, to choose men from among them and send them to Antioch with Paul and Barnabas. They sent Judas called Barsabbas, and Silas, leading men among the brothers, **23** with the following letter: "The brothers, both the apostles and the elders, to the brothers who are of the Gentiles in Antioch and Syria and Cilicia, greetings. **24** Since we have heard that some persons have gone out from us and troubled you with words, unsettling your minds, although we gave them no instructions, **25** it has seemed good to us, having come to one accord, to choose men and send them to you with our beloved Barnabas and Paul, **26** men who have risked their lives for the name of our Lord Jesus Christ. **27** We have therefore sent Judas and Silas, who themselves will tell you the same things by word of mouth.**28** For it has seemed good to the Holy Spirit and to us to lay on you no greater burden than these requirements: **29** that you abstain from what has been sacrificed to idols, and from blood, and from what has been strangled, and from sexual immorality. If you keep yourselves from these, you will do well. Farewell."

You will notice that tithing was not listed among "these requirements." In subsequent letters Paul had to deal with the issue of the Mosaic Law with followers elsewhere. He wrote,

Colossians 2:13-14 English Standard Version (ESV)

[13] And you, who were dead in your trespasses and the uncircumcision of your flesh, God made alive together with him, having forgiven us all our trespasses, [14] by canceling the record of debt that stood against us with its legal demands. This he set aside, nailing it to the cross.

Elsewhere Paul wrote,

Romans 10:4 English Standard Version (ESV)

[4] For Christ is the end of the law for righteousness to everyone who believes.

Ephesians 2:13-16 English Standard Version (ESV)

[13] But now in Christ Jesus you who once were far off have been brought near by the blood of Christ. [14] For he himself is our peace, who has made us both one and has broken down in his flesh the dividing wall of hostility [15] by abolishing the law of commandments expressed in ordinances, that he might create in himself one new man in place of the two, so making peace, [16] and might reconcile us both to God in one body through the cross, thereby killing the hostility.

This does not mean that Christians are without a law, as Paul speaks of fulfilling "the law of Christ." (Gal 6:2) He would make the following observation,

Hebrews 7:12 English Standard Version (ESV)

[12] For when there is a change in the priesthood, there is necessarily a change in the law as well.

Few would argue that there is another pastor in the history of Christianity, who has worked and slaved as hard as the apostle Paul. Yet, he never took a tithe, to do the work of an evangelizer. Rather, he got up early and worked as a tent maker, to cover his expenses. (Acts 18:3-

4) Truly, he could say, "You yourselves know that these hands ministered to my necessities and to those who were with me." (Acts 20:34) This is not to suggest that a Christian congregation should not pay pastors, as that is certainly their right to do so. Nevertheless, it is going beyond Scripture, to collect compulsory giving at a certain rate, to pay for congregation expenses, such as a pastor. Thus, in what way are Christians to give to their congregation? How much are they to give?

Christian Giving

Certainly, while Christ was under the Mosaic Law throughout his life and ministry, because he had not offered the sacrifice to remove it yet, we can follow in his principle of, "For with the measure you use it will be measured back to you." (Luke 6:38) Now, are Christians to conclude that if they give to God is a big way; they will receive a return, as though it is an investment in the marketplace. No, absolutely not! The televangelist would love to convince their flock of that, but this is not the case. How are we to understand Jesus' words? The context here is, "the believer's behavior toward others will determine God's behavior toward him or her."[51] In other words, Jesus does not limit our giving of ourselves, our finances, to some specific amount, but that it should be overflowing. This could be even more than ten percent, if it is within the means of the person. (Lu 18:22; Ac 20:35) With someone of far less means, or who is struggling with an expense, such as a medical bill, it may mean their all is 02 percent, because it would be unchristian to take out of their family's necessities. Matthew 15:5-9; 1 Timothy 5:8

---

[51] http://biblia.com/books/nac24/Lk6.38

Unlike the mandatory Mosaic Law, Christian giving is voluntary. Christian giving considers the circumstances of the giver, and that each will differ.

2 Corinthians 8:12 New American Standard Bible (NASB)

¹² For if the readiness is present, it is acceptable according to what *a person* has, not according to what he does not have.

We end up back at the question from the outset of, how much should you give at your church. We cannot resolve that for you, it must come from your heat, from your Christian conscience. It is your heartfelt appreciate from your friendship with God, not some set amount. Simply follow the inspired directive of Paul, without depriving you or your family of the necessities,

2 Corinthians 9:7 English Standard Version (ESV)

⁷ Each one must give as he has decided in his heart, not reluctantly or under compulsion, for God loves a cheerful giver.

BASIC TEACHING: How Does the Bible View Sex Relations?

If we were talking with a Catholic, it would be a reprehensible thought of Mary, having sexual relations with her husband Joseph. Why? Primarily, they view Mary as being a perpetual virgin, never having any children after the miraculous birth of Jesus. However if we look at one of the Catholic Bibles, we find,

Matthew 13:53-56 Jerusalem Bible (JB)

53 When Jesus had finished these parables he left the district; **54** and, coming to his home town, he taught the people in their synagogue in such a way that they were astonished and said, 'Where did the man get this wisdom and these miraculous powers? **55** This is the carpenter's son, surely? Is not his mother the woman called Mary, and his brothers [Greek, *adelphoi*] James and Joseph and Simon and Jude? **56** His sisters [Greek, *adelphai*], too, are they not all here with us?'"

Even so, another reason is, the Catholic Church has had a long standing mindset on sex, which leaves the flocks with the impression that you cannot be a good Catholic, namely be holy, if they have sexual relations, even within the confines of marriage. For the Catholic hierarchy, this is just incompatible. Are marriage relations and holiness incompatible? What does God's Word say on the matter?

In getting the Bible's perspective in the matters of sexual relations, we can go back to the Israelites of the Old Testament. They had a priesthood that God specifically gave them, which God required that they be holy, and we see that marriage was fine for them. (Lev.

162

21:6, 7, 13) Then, we move to the Christian era, and look at the one, whom the Catholic Church views as their first pope,[52] and he too was a married man, as were most of the apostles. (Matt 8:14; 1 Cor. 9:5) If we look at the Catholic *Douay Version* of the Bible, the "overseer," i.e., the "bishop" could be the "husband of one wife." (1 Tim. 3:2) In addition, the "older men" ("priests," in *Douay Version*) could be married. (Titus 1:5-8) Actually, the whole of first century Christians were viewed as "God's chosen ones, holy and beloved," with most of them being married. (Colossians 3:12, 18-21) Were there sexless marriages in the first-century Christian Congregation? Are there to be sexless marriages today? This would be in direct violation of God's Word.

1 Corinthians 7:2-5 English Standard Version (ESV)

[2] But because of the temptation to sexual immorality, each man should have his own wife and each woman her own husband. [3] The husband should give to his wife her conjugal rights, and likewise the wife to her husband. [4] For the wife does not have authority over her own body, but the husband does. Likewise the husband does not have authority over his own body, but the wife does. [5] Do not deprive one another, except perhaps by agreement for a limited time, that you may devote yourselves to prayer; but then come together again, so that Satan may not tempt you because of your lack of self-control.

---

[52] Peter was not the first pope. Peter was not the "rock" that the church was founded on. (Matt 16:18, Jerusalem Bible, JB) Jesus was the "rock" that the church was founded on. (Ac 4:8-11; 1 Pet 2:4-8; Eph. 2:20, JB) The other apostles did not view Peter as having primacy over them (Lu 22:24-26, JB). Considering that Jesus is alive in heaven, and the head of Christianity, there is no need for successors. (Heb. 7:23-25, Rom 6:9; Eph. 5:23, JB)

Therefore, when we investigate the Scriptures, we **do not find** that marriage or sexual relations within a marriage are incompatible. If when God speaks of himself in human, figurative terms, as his relation to Israel, he refers to himself as the "husband." Moreover, Jesus is spoken of figuratively as the "husband" of the Christian congregation. This demonstrates that there is nothing unclean about the marriage relationship, the very relationship that God set in place back in the Garden of Eden. Isaiah 54:5; 62:4, 5; Ephesians 5:23-32; Revelation 19:7; 21:2, 9.

Therefore, we should have absolutely no doubts that after the miraculous birth of Jesus, Mary went on to have normal sexual relations with his wife, which resulted in their having both sons and daughters. (Matthew 1:24, 25; Mark 3:31) This should in no way impede our love and respect for Mary as a holy woman, who was privilege to give birth to the Son of man, Jesus Christ, just as the Jewish people loved and respected Sarah, the woman who miraculously gave birth to Isaac at the age of 90 years old. 1 Peter 3:5-7; Hebrews 11:11-12

The Bible on Divorce and Contraception

When it comes to divorce and abortion, the Catholic Church does well in its discouraging such practices. Nevertheless, the younger Catholic's today, in our progressive world, disagree with the Catholic Church. The Catholic Church does go beyond Scripture when it suggests that there is no reason for a divorce, as well as teaching that "each and every marriage act must remain open to the transmission of life" (Pope Paul VI - Humanae Vitae, Latin, "Human Life").

In the Garden of Eden God initiated marriage between one man and one woman, "For this reason a man shall leave his father and his mother, and be joined[53] to his wife; and they shall become one flesh." (Genesis 2:22-24) Jesus made this clear to the Christian congregation as well, when he stated, "What therefore God has joined together, let not man separate." However, he went on to say, "Whoever divorces his wife, except for sexual immorality, and marries another, commits adultery." Matthew 19:4-6, 9; 5:32

Jesus made it clear that there is but one basis for divorce, which is sexual immorality. When the Catholic Church has raised the bar above the words of Jesus Christ, it has gone beyond Scripture, and made the Word of God invalid, by their man made traditions. History has shown that Catholic Church has long viewed adultery as less severe than divorce itself. The Bible encourages sexual relations between a husband and wife.

Enjoy Marriage

Proverbs 5:15 Lexham English Bible (LEB)

15 Drink water from your *own* cistern
   and flowing waters from inside your own well.

The Bible is not squeamish about sexual relations, and we do well to follow that example, if we are to help, our young ones avoid the pitfalls of this world. The cistern[54] or well is poetic expressions for the wife, who satisfies the desires of the husband. This is considered a

---

[53] The Hebrew word translated "joined" literally means "to cleave, to adhere, specially firmly, as if with glue." (Gesenius' *Hebrew and Chaldee Lexicon to the Old Testament Scriptures*)

[54] A cistern is an underground tank for storing rainwater.

private water source. Having sexual pleasure with one's wife is compared to drinking refreshing water. This comparison may not resonate with many in our modern world, but ancient Palestine had a dry climate that left them waterless at times. Moreover, they had to dig wells to seek out water, so it was a very precious staple of life.

Proverbs 5:16 Lexham English Bible (LEB)

16 Shall your springs be scattered outward?
In the streets, *shall there be* streams of water?

Just as the "cistern" of verse 15 stood for the wife's sexual affections for her husband, the "springs" and "streams of water" of verse 16 is a reference to the husband's sexual affections for his wife. In other words, verse 16a would read something like, 'shall your [the husband's] springs [sexual affections] be scattered outward [someone other than his wife]? Verse 16b would read, 'in the streets [where prostitutes are], shall there be streams of water [the husbands sexual affections]?' Verse 15-16 gives the reader an analogy that the "cistern" [the wife] satisfies the sexual desires of the husband, and the "springs" and "streams of water" [the husband] satisfies the desires of the wife.

Proverbs 5:17 Lexham English Bible (LEB)

17 May they be yours alone,
and not for strangers *who are* with you.

May the sexual desires that the husband receives from his wife, be his alone, never to be shared with another.

Proverbs 5:18 Lexham English Bible (LEB)

18 May your fountain be blessed,
and rejoice in the wife of your youth.

May the husband's sexual desires continue to be quenched by the wife of his youth, not in seeking out a second wife, a mistress, or a prostitute?

Proverbs 5:19-20 Lexham English Bible (LEB)

¹⁹ *She is* a deer of love and a doe of grace;
  may her breasts satisfy you *always*;
  by her love may you be intoxicated continually.
²⁰ Why should you be intoxicated, my child, by a strange woman,
  and embrace the bosom of a foreigner?

To the husband, who has allowed his passions for his wife to continue over the years, she is as desirable and attractive as a female deer, and he is intoxicated with the pleasure she continually brings him, with her body and her love. The husband should reciprocate this to her and her alone. The Hebrew word shaga, which is rendered "intoxicated," is generally used in reference to sin that is committed unintentionally, like our innocent appearing situation that we have spoken about throughout Proverbs chapter five. On reference work reads,

> The primary emphasis in the root [shaga] is on sin done inadvertently. This is indicated in several ways. First, the two derivatives from [saga, shegia, and misgeh] indicate an act perpetrated in ignorance, not willfully. Second, in the ... The Scripture pinpoints at least three causes for such wandering. The first is wine and strong drink (Isa 28:7; Prov 20:1). The second is the seductive strange woman (Prov 5:20, 23) versus the love of one's wife, which ought to

"captivate" one (Prov 5:19). The third is the inability to reject evil instruction (Prov 19:27).[55]

How do we close out this section, by looking at the implications of our day? Why would there be a need for any man or woman for that matter to place themselves in innocent appearing situations by flirting in the workplace because the spouse is not there, by a teenager living a different lifestyle while at school, or by spending time alone with someone of the opposite sex? Why be enticed into sexual affection outside of the marriage?

James 1:14-15 English Standard Version (ESV)

[14] But each person is tempted when he is lured and enticed by his own desire. [15] Then desire when it has conceived gives birth to sin, and sin when it is fully grown brings forth death.

When we consider the Bible's viewpoint on birth control, the Catholic Church has not changed its position since Augustine (354-430 C.E.), who wrote in 419: "I am supposing, then, although you are not lying [with your wife] for the sake of procreating offspring, you are not for the sake of lust obstructing their procreation by an evil prayer or an evil deed. Those who do this, although they are called husband and wife, are not; nor do they retain any reality of marriage, but with a respectable name cover a shame. Sometimes this lustful cruelty, or cruel lust, comes to this, that they even procure poisons of sterility [oral contraceptives]" (*Marriage and Concupiscence* 1:15:17).[56]

---

[55] Victor P. Hamilton, "2325 שָׁגָה", in Theological Wordbook of the Old Testament, ed. R. Laird Harris, Gleason L. Archer, Jr. and Bruce K. Waltke, electronic ed., 904 (Chicago: Moody Press, 1999).

[56] http://www.catholic.com/tracts/birth-control

In 1968, Pope Paul VI issued his landmark encyclical letter Humanae Vitae (Latin, "Human Life"), which reemphasized the Church's constant teaching that it is always intrinsically wrong to use contraception to prevent new human beings from coming into existence.[57]

When we look to the Scriptures, the Bible does not prohibit birth control (contraception). In fact, it does not even mention it, and birth control has been practiced for about 4,000 years among the non-Jewish nations. While the Bible does not condemn birth control, it does condemn abortions, as is clearly stated at Exodus 20:13 and 21:22, 23. Therefore, any birth control, like the "morning after pill," which allows a woman to terminate a pregnancy just by taking a pill, would be biblically condemned. Life begins at conception, and to take a life, would result in the Bible's equation, "a life for a life."

Psalm 139:13-16 English Standard Version (ESV)

[13] For you formed my inward parts;
   you knitted me together in my mother's womb.
[14] I praise you, for I am fearfully and wonderfully made.
Wonderful are your works;
   my soul knows it very well.
[15] My frame was not hidden from you,
when I was being made in secret,
   intricately woven in the depths of the earth.
[16] Your eyes saw my unformed substance;
in your book were written, every one of them,
   the days that were formed for me,
   when as yet there was none of them.

Here again, and method of birth control that is abortive would be biblically wrong, it would be a very

---

[57] http://www.catholic.com/tracts/birth-control

grievous sin. However, what about birth control that is not abortive? There is no command within Scripture to procreate. God specifically told both Adam and Noah, "Be fruitful and multiply and fill the earth." (Genesis 1:28; 9:1) While this is certainly, a command from God, but the context is the extinction of humanity otherwise. If Adam and Eve had chosen to forego having children, there would be no humanity. If Noah and his sons had made the same decision, there would be no humanity. Thus, **it is not** a command in the sense that disallows precautions, but was to get humanity underway. Moreover, there is no such command given to Abraham, or in the Mosaic Law, nor in the New Testament.

Therefore, Married couples can decide for themselves as to whether they want to raise a family, or how many children they want to have, as the Scriptures do not condemn birth control. Thus, according to Scripture, the husband and wife have the right to use non-abortive birth control if they desire. How should other Christians, who choose not to use birth control, view those in the congregation who do?

Romans 14:4 English Standard Version (ESV)

⁴Who are you to pass judgment on the servant of another? It is before his own master that he stands or falls. And he will be upheld, for the Lord is able to make him stand.

Romans 14:10-13 English Standard Version (ESV)

¹⁰Why do you pass judgment on your brother? Or you, why do you despise your brother? For we will all stand before the judgment seat of God;¹¹ for it is written,

"As I live, says the Lord, every knee shall bow to me,
    and every tongue shall confess to God."

12 So then each of us will give an account of himself to God.

13 Therefore let us not pass judgment on one another any longer, but rather decide never to put a stumbling block or hindrance in the way of a brother.

The Bible's View of Celibacy

While the Bible does not demand celibacy from its religious leaders, like the Levitical priesthood of the Old Testament, or congregation overseers within the New Testament, as the Catholic Church maintains, it does speak of *voluntary* singleness. Jesus said,

Matthew 19:12 New American Standard Bible (NASB)

12 For there are eunuchs who were born that way from their mother's womb; and there are eunuchs who were made eunuchs by men; and there are *also* eunuchs who made themselves eunuchs for the sake of the kingdom of heaven. He who is able to accept *this*, let him accept *it*."

As can be seen herein, Jesus never said that any man was to remain celibate. Rather, as was explained in the above, the apostle Peter was married, as were many of the apostles. Mark 1:29, 30; 1 Corinthians 9:5

The apostle Paul covers the subject of voluntary singleness for both men and women as well, when he writes,

1 Corinthians 7:8, 35, 38, 40 New American Standard Bible (NASB)

8 But I say to the unmarried and to widows that it is good for them if they remain even as I. **35** This I say for your own benefit; not to put a restraint upon you, but to promote what is appropriate and *to secure* undistracted devotion to the Lord. **38** So then both he who gives his own virgin *daughter* in marriage does well, and he who does not give her in marriage will do better. **40** But in my opinion she is happier if she remains as she is; and I think that I also have the Spirit of God.

Notice that Paul is speaking of voluntary singleness, not to be distracted from their service to God. Notice that it is that one point, not to be distracted in their service to God. However, a Catholic will add another point that is unbiblical, "to avoid the distraction of *sex*, and *to remain pure*." First, there is more to a marriage than *sex*. If a woman remained single, to better serve God, she would be free from the dozens of hours per week that would have gone into caring for a husband and children. Second, a single person is no more pure than a married person is.

Therefore, singleness is a gift that some Christians have the desire for, which includes both male and female, so that they can devote their lives to serving God. There is no need for some special vow, as this is a personal decision, between God and the one making the commitment, and it is not compulsory. 1 Corinthians 7:28, 36

In fact, anyone religious group suggesting required or obligatory celibacy would be a sign of apostasy,

1 Timothy 4:1-3 New American Standard Bible (NASB)

1 But the Spirit explicitly says that in later times some will fall away from the faith, paying attention to deceitful spirits and doctrines of demons, **2** by means of the hypocrisy of liars seared in their own conscience as with a branding iron, **3** men who forbid marriage *and advocate* abstaining from foods which God has created to be gratefully shared in by those who believe and know the truth.

Maintain the Biblical View

If one were to investigate the Catholic Churches teachings on marriage and sexual relations, it would not find a Scriptural basis, but rather philosophical rather than Biblical, as well as pagan religions. The result is hundreds of millions of Catholics today, who have been shamed into a guilt complex on sexual relations within the marriage, as well as the hardship of forced celibacy on their Catholic priests, nuns and monks.

The Bible views marriage and sexual relations quite different. In the Bible,

Hebrews 13:4 English Standard Version (ESV)

4 Let marriage be held in honor among all, and let the marriage bed be undefiled, for God will judge the sexually immoral and adulterous.

In addition, sexual relations within the marriage do not somehow make these Christians less holy than the one, who have freely chosen to remain single. Moreover, those who do remain single, to serve God, will many times have a closer relationship with God, because they are not sharing themselves with many others, like a spouse and children. Nevertheless, this is no argument toward the idea that they are somehow better in God's eyes. Serious, objective Bible study enables us to uncover teachings that are unbiblical, as opposed to those that are biblical.

John 8:31-32 English Standard Version (ESV)

[31] So Jesus said to the Jews who had believed him, "If you abide in my word, you are truly my disciples, [32] and you will know the truth, and the truth will set you free."

BASIC TEACHING: Is Infant Baptism Biblical?

Before delving into infant Baptism, we will take a moment to look at Baptism. The Greek *baptisma* refers to the method of immersion, including submersion and emergence; it is derived from the verb *bapto*, meaning "dip." (John 13:26) In the Bible, "to baptize" is the same as "to immerse."[58] The Greek *Septuagint* uses a form of the same word for "dip" at Exodus 12:22 and Leviticus 4:6.[59] At the time one is immersed in water, he is for the moment "buried" out of view and then lifted out.

We will look into baptism in the book of Acts, together with related questions: (1) Baptism in the book of Acts, (2) being baptized into Christ, (3) baptism and salvation, and (4) a summary of baptism in the book of Acts. The book of Acts is a historical overview of the Christian congregation from 33 C.E. – 61 C.E. Therefore, the reader will find far more cases of baptism than any of the other New Testament books. The approach herein will be to look at each account in the book of Acts, to offer a summary of whether the account in Acts is descriptive or prescriptive, and an observation as to whether baptism is essential for salvation.

---

[58] Walter A. Elwell and Barry J. Beitzel, Baker Encyclopedia of the Bible (Grand Rapids, Mich.: Baker Book House, 1988), 257.

[59] Robert Laird Harris, Gleason Leonard Archer and Bruce K. Waltke, *Theological Wordbook of the Old Testament*, electronic ed. (Chicago: Moody Press, 1999), 342.

Baptism in the Book of Acts

Christian baptism was a required mark of the Christian community, done in the name if Christ, on the basis of faith in that name, who got baptized in *symbol* of that, and entered into the congregation. (Italics will be added throughout for emphasis)

Acts 1:5; 11:16; Luke 3:16 (English Standard Version)

⁵for John baptized with water, but you will be baptized with the Holy Spirit not many days from now.

¹⁵As I began to speak, the Holy Spirit fell on them just as on us at the beginning. ¹⁶And I remembered the word of the Lord, how he said, 'John baptized with water, but you will be baptized with the Holy Spirit.'

¹⁶ John answered them all, saying, "I baptize you with water, but he who is mightier than I is coming, the strap of whose sandals I am not worthy to untie. He will baptize you with the Holy Spirit and with fire.

In the above Acts 1:5 we have Jesus paraphrasing the Words of John the Baptist as recorded in Luke 3:16, minus the "with fire." There is a contrast going on here, but it is not between water baptism and baptism with the Holy Spirit; no it is between the baptism of John (minus the Holy Spirit) and Jesus' baptism with Holy Spirit. To further this, the reader of acts 1:8 is told that Jesus promised these ones would 'receive power when the Holy Spirit has come upon them.' While waiting for this moment, they were moved to pick a replacement for Judas, and the qualification was that he must who 'have accompanied them during all the time that the Lord Jesus went in and out among them, beginning *from the baptism of John until* the day when he was taken up from them.'[60]

"When the day of Pentecost arrived, they [120 disciples] were all together in one place. And suddenly there came from heaven a sound like a mighty rushing wind, and it filled the entire house where they were sitting. And divided tongues as of fire appeared to them and rested on each one of them. [4]And they were all filled with the Holy Spirit and began to speak in other tongues as the Spirit gave them utterance." On this instance, "those who received his word were baptized, and there were added that day about three thousand souls." It was obvious for those who were in attendance on this day that there was a new way to God; yet the opportunity to the Jewish people throughout the Roman Empire had yet to be completely closed. —Acts 2:1-4, 41.[61]

Acts 2:38, 41 (English Standard Version)

[38]And Peter said to them, "*Repent* and be *baptized* every one of you in the name of Jesus Christ for the *forgiveness* of your sins, and you will receive the gift of the Holy Spirit. [41]So those who received his word were baptized, and there were added that day about three thousand souls.

Those in attendance who has been with Jesus since the days of John the Baptist are certainly taking note of the fact that it was no longer repentance over violations of the Law and the baptism of John, no it was now

---

[60] Darrell L. Bock, *Acts*, Baker exegetical commentary on the New Testament (Grand Rapids, Mich.: Baker Books, 2007), 57-8.
[61] Simon J. Kistemaker and William Hendriksen, vol. 17, *New Testament Commentary: Exposition of the Acts of the Apostles*, New Testament Commentary (Grand Rapids: Baker Book House, 1953-2001), 77.

repentance and baptism *in the name of Jesus Christ* that placed one in a righteous standing before God.[62] It is, in fact, "the blood of Jesus his Son cleanses us from all sin." (1John 1:7) Later, after speaking of Jesus as "the Author of life," Peter said to Jews at the temple: "Repent, therefore, and turn again, that your sins may be blotted out." (Ac 3:15, 19) Here he informed them that they needed to repent from their bad actions against Jesus and "turn again," to accept him, this being what brought forgiveness of sin; there being no mention of baptism at this time.[63]

Acts 8:12-16 (English Standard Version)

[12]But when they believed Philip as he preached good news about the kingdom of God and the name of Jesus Christ, they were baptized, both men and women. [13]Even Simon himself believed, and after being baptized he continued with Philip. And seeing signs and great miracles performed, he was amazed. [14]Now when the apostles at Jerusalem heard that Samaria had received the word of God, they sent to them Peter and John, [15]who came down and prayed for them that they might receive the Holy Spirit, [16]for he had not yet fallen on any of them, but they had only been baptized in the name of the Lord Jesus.

When persecution hit the Judea area, many were inclined to move away with the exception of the apostles. It was at this time that we find Philip in Samaria spreading the gospel message and, with the miraculous power of Holy Spirit, cast out demons and cured the

---

[62] Kenneth O. Gangel, vol. 5, *Acts*, Holman New Testament Commentary; Holman Reference (Nashville, TN: Broadman & Holman Publishers, 1998), 36.

[63] Warren W. Wiersbe, *The Bible Exposition Commentary* (Wheaton, Ill.: Victor Books, 1996), Ac 2:14.

paralyzed and lame. Jubilant, a large number received the message and were baptized, including a certain Simon who had been involved in the magical arts. (Ac 8:4-13) At Samaria when they listened to and believed "good news about the kingdom of God and the name of Jesus Christ, they were baptized." At this juncture the Biblical account spells out that the ones baptized were, not infants, but "both men and women."—Ac 8:12.[64]

There was something distinctive about their receiving Holy Spirit by the laying on of the hands. How? These were actually the first non-Israelites to be added to the church, because the Samaritans were not Jewish proselytes. Moreover, when Philip spread the gospel in Samaria, numerous ones "were baptized, both men and women," but they did not immediately receive the Holy Spirit. (Acts 8:12) Why?

Remember, it was to Peter that Christ Jesus entrusted "the keys of the kingdom"—the privilege of first presenting the opportunity for entry into "the kingdom of the heaven" for different groups of converts. (Matthew 16:19) So it was not until Peter and John went to Samaria and laid their hands on these first non-Jewish disciples that Holy Spirit was poured out on them as a token of their prospective membership in "the kingdom of the heaven."[65]

Acts 8:36, 38 (English Standard Version)

---

[64] Simon J. Kistemaker and William Hendriksen, vol. 17, *New Testament Commentary: Exposition of the Acts of the Apostles*, New Testament Commentary (Grand Rapids: Baker Book House, 1953-2001), 296-98.

[65] Everett Ferguson, *Baptism in the Early Church: History, Theology, and Liturgy in the First Five Centuries* (Grand Rapids, MI.: Eerdmans, 2009), 193-4.

³⁶And as they were going along the road they came to some water, and the eunuch* said, "See, here is water! What prevents me from being baptized?" ³⁸And he commanded the chariot to stop, and they both went down into the water, Philip and the eunuch, and he baptized him.

> * The Ethiopian eunuch was a court official who was in charge of the treasury of the queen of Ethiopia. But since a castrated person was not accepted into the congregation of Israel under the Law, the term *eunoukhos* would apply here not literally but in *its* sense of "court official." (Ac 8:26-39; De 23:1) Ebed-melech, the Ethiopian who rescued the prophet Jeremiah from imprisonment in a cistern, was a eunuch in the court of King Zedekiah.

Was this a hasty act? Not at all! The Ethiopian was a Jewish proselyte.[66] Therefore, he was already a worshiper of the God of the Hebrews with knowledge of the Scriptures, including the Messianic prophecies. However, his knowledge was incomplete. Now that he had received this vital information regarding the role of Jesus Christ, the Ethiopian understood what God required of him and was ready to comply. Baptism was appropriate. (Matthew 28:18-20; 1 Peter 3:21) The Ethiopian eunuch asked to be baptized when they came to "some water." They both "went *down into the water*." Afterward they came "*up out of the water*." (Ac 8:36-40) All these

---

[66] *Proselytes were* non-Israelites who chose to adhere to the Mosaic Law. Leviticus 24:22.

instances imply not a little pool, but a large body of water into and out of which they would have to walk.[67]

Acts 9:17, 18; 22:16 (English Standard Version)

[17]So Ananias departed and entered the house. And laying his hands on him he said, "Brother Saul, the Lord Jesus who appeared to you on the road by which you came has sent me so that you may regain your sight and be filled with the Holy Spirit." [18]And immediately something like scales fell from his eyes, and he regained his sight. Then he rose and was baptized; [16]And now why do you wait? Rise and be baptized and wash away your sins, calling on his name.'

How are sins washed away? Not by mere water immersion, but by calling on his name are sins washed away. Cornelius called on Jesus' name and he accepted Christ and was baptized by Holy Spirit. For this to happen his sins must have been forgiven, yet it was all before he was baptized in water. If one repents and accepts Christ and trusts in His shed blood one's sins can be forgiven. Water immersion in Jesus' name is important, but only as a symbol and public demonstration of repentance of sins and acceptance of Jesus and dedication to do his Father's will faithfully, as Jesus did.[68]

Acts 10:44-48 (English Standard Version)

---

[67] Kenneth O. Gangel, vol. 5, *Acts*, Holman New Testament Commentary; Holman Reference (Nashville, TN: Broadman & Holman Publishers, 1998), 127.

[68] Robert Jamieson, A. R. Fausset, A. R. Fausset et al., *A Commentary, Critical and Explanatory, on the Old and New Testaments* (Oak Harbor, WA: Logos Research Systems, Inc., 1997), Ac 9:17–19.

⁴⁴While Peter was still saying these things, the Holy Spirit fell on all who heard the word. ⁴⁵And the believers from among the circumcised who had come with Peter were amazed, because the gift of the Holy Spirit was poured out even on the Gentiles. ⁴⁶For they were hearing them speaking in tongues and extolling God. Then Peter declared, ⁴⁷ "Can anyone withhold water for baptizing these people, who have received the Holy Spirit just as we have?" ⁴⁸And he commanded them to be baptized in the name of Jesus Christ. Then they asked him to remain for some days.

It is true that the centurion Cornelius was 'a devout and upright man, being well spoken of by the whole Jewish nation and acquainted with the writings of the prophets, who feared God,' who "gave alms generously to the people, and prayed continually to God;" yet he was not a Jewish proselyte as some have suggested. The Biblical record establishes decisively that this army officer was an uncircumcised Gentile in the fullest sense. If Cornelius had been a proselyte, there would have been no reason for Peter to say, "You yourselves know how unlawful it is for a Jew to associate with or to visit anyone of another nation." (Le 19:33, 34; Ac 10:28) Additionally, if he had been a proselyte 'the believers from among the circumcised who had come with Peter would not have been amazed, because the gift of the Holy Spirit was poured out even on the Gentiles.' (Ac 10:45; 11:12) Finally, if he had been a proselyte, why did the "circumcision party, criticized him" over this matter? —Ac 11:2.⁶⁹

In truth, Cornelius was the first of the uncircumcised non-Jews to become a Christian, which demonstrated

---

⁶⁹ Dennis Gaertner, *Acts*, The College Press NIV commentary (Joplin, Mo.: College Press, 1993), Ac 10:48.

that by this time it was unnecessary for Gentiles to get circumcised or become a proselyte, in order to become a member of the Christian congregation. As Peter stated, "God shows no partiality, but in every nation anyone who fears him and does what is right is acceptable to him." (Ac 10:34, 35) It was Peter who opened up The Way to the Jews at Pentecost, to the Samaritans, so to the gospel was now being brought to the uncircumcised Gentiles. In agreement, James replies, "Brothers, listen to me. Simeon has related how God first visited the Gentiles, to take from them a people for his name. —Ac 15:7, 14.

Acts 16:14, 15 (English Standard Version)

¹⁴One who heard us was a woman named Lydia, from the city of Thyatira, a seller of purple goods, who was a worshiper of God. The Lord opened her heart to pay attention to what was said by Paul. ¹⁵ And after she was baptized, and her household as well, she urged us, saying, "If you have judged me to be faithful to the Lord, come to my house and stay." And she prevailed upon us.

Lydia was "a worshiper of God," likely being a proselyte Jew, who was open to the good news of the Christ. As holds true with the other above accounts, baptism always followed the spoken word. (16:13-14) Herein, we find a point that should not escape our notice, this being that "the Lord *opened her heart to pay attention* to what was said by Paul." This evidences that infants were not being baptized in the first-century, as it involved listening to the gospel, accepting it as so and praising God. Being that Lydia's husband is not mentioned, it is likely that she may have been a widow. Conceivably "her household" was made up of relatives, but the expression could also involve servants. Regardless, Lydia obviously went home and shared this good news with her household. As they too accepted the Way, it must have brought her great happiness.[70]

Acts 16:30-33 (English Standard Version)

[30]Then he brought them out and said, "Sirs, what must I do to be saved?" [31]And they said, "Believe in the Lord Jesus, and you will be saved, you and your household." [32]And they spoke the word of the Lord to him and to all who were in his house. [33]And he took them the same hour of the night and washed their wounds; and he was baptized at once, he and all his family.

Again, in the account of the Philippian jailer, you will notice the same two important points: 1) Paul and Silas "spoke the word of the Lord to him and to all who were in his house; and 2) they heard the Word of God, which moved them to baptism. The Philippian jailer did not 'shut off his mind' when the apostle Paul answered his question, "What must I do to be saved?" And Paul and Silas did not mount an 'assault on his emotions' and plead for a large financial contribution. Rather, "spoke the word of the Lord to him." Reasoning with the man, they helped him to come to a clear understanding of God's provisions for salvation. —Acts 16:32.

It must be asked, what is the way to salvation? "The missionaries show the way of salvation to the jailer by coming straight to the point and telling him what he must do: Believe in the Lord Jesus.'" (Acts 16:31) a contrite heart that recognizes the need of the shed blood of Jesus

---

[70] Kenneth O. Gangel, vol. 5, *Acts*, Holman New Testament Commentary; Holman Reference (Nashville, TN: Broadman & Holman Publishers, 1998), 271.

is crucial if we expect to receive salvation. Many offer confusion on the matter by implying intentionally or not that belief in Jesus alone is all that is required. Yet, it seems a bit dogmatic to focus on one facet of Scripture that addresses salvation, while setting the others aside, which is like isolating page three in a business contract, because it says what you want it to say, while ignoring the first two pages.[71]

Acts 19:1-6 (English Standard Version)

[1]And it happened that while Apollos was at Corinth, Paul passed through the inland country and came to Ephesus. There he found some disciples. [2]And he said to them, "Did you receive the Holy Spirit when you believed?" And they said, "No, we have not even heard that there is a Holy Spirit." [3]And he said, "Into what then were you baptized?" They said, "Into John's baptism." [4]And Paul said, "John baptized with the baptism of repentance, telling the people to believe in the one who was to come after him, that is, Jesus." [5]On hearing this, they were baptized in the name of the Lord Jesus. [6]And when Paul had laid his hands on them, the Holy Spirit came on them, and they began speaking in tongues and prophesying.

The baptism of John had reached its course and purpose by 33 C.E., and now Jesus gives the commission to something greater: "Go therefore and make disciples of all nations, baptizing them in the name of the Father and of the Son and of the Holy Spirit." (Matt 28:19) From this point forward, no other baptism had the backing of God. About twenty years later though we find

---

[71] Simon J. Kistemaker and William Hendriksen, vol. 17, *New Testament Commentary: Exposition of the Acts of the Apostles*, New Testament Commentary (Grand Rapids: Baker Book House, 1953-2001), 601-02.

Apollos, a native of Alexandria, who had come to Ephesus; he was an eloquent man, competent in the Scriptures. He spoke and taught accurately the things concerning Jesus, though he knew only the baptism of John.' Apollos was certainly in need of correction, this being the case for the disciples that Paul came into contact with in Ephesus as well. It appears that these men had gotten baptized under the baptism of John after it had been terminated. Therefore, they were baptized in the name of Jesus and received Holy Spirit. —Ac 18:24-26; 19:1-7.

Being Baptized into Christ: (those born again persons, who are anointed with Holy Spirit and become joint heirs with him, are "baptized into *Christ* Jesus.")

At Jesus baptism, he was well aware that he was about to follow a sacrificial course. He knew that "the Son of Man came . . . to give his life as a ransom for many." (Mt 20:28) Jesus understood "that he must go to Jerusalem and suffer many things from the elders and chief priests and scribes, and be [plunged into death], and on the third day be raised." (Mt 16:21) In comparison, he stated: "I have a baptism [death] to be baptized with." (Lu 12:50) Jesus said to his disciples,

Mark 10:38-39

English Standard Version (ESV)

38 "You do not know what you are asking. Are you able to drink the cup that I drink, or to be *baptized with the baptism with which I am baptized?*"**39** And they said to him, "We are able." And Jesus said to them, "The cup that I drink you will drink, and with *the baptism with which I am baptized, you will be baptized*, (italics mine)

Jesus was *completely* baptized into death when he was plunged into death by being executed on Nisan 14.

186

Three days later, his Father completed his baptism as he raised him from the dead. As is clear from the context, Jesus' water baptism that began his ministry was different and separate from this baptism into death. At his water baptism, he simply entered into a life course that would lead to his baptism into death.

While the apostle had been baptized by John (John 1:35-37; 4:1), the baptism with Holy Spirit was yet future, and it would symbolize being baptized into death. (Mr 10:39) Being baptized into Christ's death is far different. Paul made this more explicit in his letter to the Roman congregation, saying: "Do you not know that all of us who have been baptized into Christ Jesus were baptized into his death?"—Rom 6:3.[72]

The path of the Christian who is baptized into Christ Jesus is a way of uprightness in this great test of life in imperfection, which Paul goes on to explain to the congregation of Rome: "We were buried therefore with him by baptism into death, in order that, just as Christ was raised from the dead by the glory of the Father, we too might walk in newness of life. For if we have been united with him in a death like his, we shall certainly be united with him in a resurrection like his."—Ro 6:4, 5; 1Co 15:31-49.

Expounding the subject still more, Paul, in writing to the congregation at Philippi, described his own course as "share his sufferings, becoming like him in his death, that by any means possible I may attain the resurrection from the dead." (Php 3:10, 11) It is God Almighty that competes these ones baptisms. How so? He will raise

---

[72] Robert H. Mounce, vol. 27, *Romans*, electronic ed., Logos Library System; The New American Commentary (Nashville: Broadman & Holman Publishers, 2001), 149-50.

them up out of death and unite them with Christ as immortal spirit persons, who enjoy heavenly life. —1Co 15:53, 54.

Baptism and Salvation

Is water baptism essential to salvation? Salvation was a key question the first-century congregation, because many Judaizers across the Roman Empire argued that the Gentiles could not be saved unless they were circumcised and obeyed the Law. (Acts 15:1-5) However, it is very clear from Scripture that there is only means of salvation, and that is . . .

Ephesians 2:8-9 (English Standard Version)

8For by grace you have been *saved through faith*. And this is not your own doing; it is the gift of God, 9not a result of works, so that no one may boast.

The entire provision for salvation is an expression of God's grace (kindness that is not deserved). There is no way that a descendant of Adam can gain salvation on his own, no matter how noble his works are. Salvation is a gift from God given to those who put faith in the sin-atoning value of the sacrifice of his Son.

Hebrews 5:9 (English Standard Version)

9And being made perfect, he [Jesus] became the source of eternal salvation to all who *obey* him,

Do we have a conflict with what was just stated in Ephesians 2:8-9, that of being *saved through faith*? No, being obedient to God's Word is nothing more than an evident demonstration that a faith is genuine.

James 2:14, 26 (English Standard Version)

[14]What good is it, my brothers, if someone says he has faith but does not have works? Can that faith save him? [26]For as the body apart from the spirit is dead, so also faith apart from works is dead.

A person does not *earn* salvation by his works. But anyone who has genuine faith *will* have works to go with it, works of obedience to the commands of God and Christ, works that demonstrate his faith and love. Without such works, his faith is dead.

Acts 16:30-31 (English Standard Version)

[30]Then he brought them out and said, "Sirs, what must I do to be saved?" [31]And they said, "Believe in the Lord Jesus, and you will be saved, you and your household."

Oversimplification has resulted in many misunderstandings when it comes to God's Word, the Bible. Many have concluded from this that simple mental acceptance of Jesus is therefore all that is required for salvation! This is an oversimplification. True, belief in Jesus as our Ransomer is essential. But it is also necessary to believe what Jesus taught and commanded, to acquire a full understanding of Bible truths. This is shown by the fact that Paul and Silas subsequently "spoke the word of the Lord to him [the jailer] and to all who were in his house." (Acts 16:32) Salvation also involves obedience. As was shown above, Paul showed this when he wrote that Jesus "became the source of eternal salvation to all who *obey* him."—Hebrews 5:9. (Little 2008, 139)

It should be noted that the one being baptized in water enters a special relationship as a servant of Christ, to do His will. The individual does not determine what the will of God is for him, but it is God who makes the decision as to the use of the individual and the placing of such one in the framework of His purposes. There is no place within Scripture that even suggests that baptism is a requirement for salvation. We have already established that salvation is by faith alone, not by works. (Eph. 2:8-9) Being that baptism is a work of righteousness (Matt 3:15), an expression of one dedicating themselves to Christ and his Father; it would negate salvation by faith to say that one must be baptized to ascertain salvation. (Rom 11:16) However, we have also establish that a saved person is not truly such if they have no evident demonstrations of faith. Thus, baptism is just that, an evident demonstration, an outward display of one's faith in Christ Jesus. To obligate it as a means of salvation would be the rejection of Jesus ransom sacrifice. (Hutson 2000, 3-4)

Summary of Baptism in the Book of Acts

In the end of our exploration of Acts, we are now able to offer some conclusions at to what baptism is, what it is not, and the way it was carried out. Although Christian baptism does not wash sins away, it is a symbol of repentance, indicating that the individual being immersed in water has made an unconditional dedication to God through Jesus Christ. (Compare Matthew 16:24.) In view of the fact that hearing the word, believing, and repenting precede water baptism (Ac 2:14, 22, 38, 41) and that baptism requires the individual to make a solemn decision, it is apparent that one must at least be of age to hear, to believe, and to make this decision. From the definition of baptism as stated earlier, it is clear that baptism is complete immersion in water, not a mere pouring. The Bible examples of baptism corroborate this fact.

Infant Baptism

John 3:5 English Standard Version (ESV)

5 Jesus answered, "Truly, truly, I say to you, unless one is born of water and the Spirit, he cannot enter the kingdom of God.

Most who promote infant baptism as being biblical fall back on Jesus' words in the above text. Their view is that since one, who is not "born of water" cannot enter into the kingdom of God,' it follows that logically, infants should be baptized, to avoid the chance of torment and suffering forever in hellfire. While we not discuss it in this chapter, this author does not believe that hellfire is a biblical doctrine (see chapter on Hellfire), but that eternal death is the punishment for sin. Nevertheless, to touch on it briefly, Scripture from the beginning is all too clear,

Genesis 2:17 New American Standard Bible (NASB)

17 but from the tree of the knowledge of good and evil you shall not eat, for in the day that you eat from it **you will surely die**."

Ezekiel 18:4 English Standard Version (ESV)

4 Behold, all souls are mine; the soul of the father as well as the soul of the son is mine: **the soul who sins shall die**.

Romans 6:23 New American Standard Bible (NASB)

23 For the **wages of sin is death**, but the free gift of God is eternal life in Christ Jesus our Lord.

2 Thessalonians 1:7-9 New American Standard Bible (NASB)

⁷ and *to give* relief to you who are afflicted and to us as well when the Lord Jesus will be revealed from heaven with His mighty angels in flaming fire, **⁸** dealing out retribution to those who do not know God and to those who do not obey the gospel of our Lord Jesus. **⁹** These will pay **the penalty of eternal destruction**, away from the presence of the Lord and from the glory of His power

Now, returning to infant baptism, we return to the Book of Acts, where Peter said, "Men of Judah and all you residents of Jerusalem, let me explain this to you and **pay attention** to my words." (2:14) "Men of Israel, **listen** to these words ..." (2:22) "**Repent** and be baptized every one of you in the name of Jesus Christ for the forgiveness of your sins ..." (2:38) "So then, those who had **received his word** were baptized; and that day there were added about three thousand souls." (2:41) We see here that one needs to have the capacity to "pay attention," to 'receive words with understanding,' to 'listen with understanding,' and to "repent." After understanding and accepting what has been heard, they may be baptized. It seems that one would have at least to be at the age of accountability.

Nevertheless, let us look at some texts that use, to suggest that infants were baptized.

Gentile Conversion and Baptism

Acts 10:48 English Standard Version (ESV)

⁴⁸ And he commanded them [Cornelius' household] to be baptized in the name of Jesus Christ. Then they asked him to remain for some days.

Well, some argue that this surely included infants, as they would be part of the household. The thing is, the account does not mention infants. Moreover, the account says, "The Holy Spirit fell on all who heard the word," and they were "speaking in tongues and extolling God," which hardly sounds like infants! (10:44-46)

The Conversion of Lydia

Acts 16:15 English Standard Version (ESV)

¹⁵ And after she [Lydia] was baptized, and her household as well, she urged us, saying, "If you have judged me to be faithful to the Lord, come to my house and stay." And she prevailed upon us.

Again, they would say that there must have been infants in Lydia's household. However, again, not mention of infants, but similarly, it does say in the previous verse, "The Lord opened her heart **to pay attention** to what was said by Paul."

The Philippian Jailer Converted

Acts 16:32-34 English Standard Version (ESV)

³¹ And they said, "Believe in the Lord Jesus, and you will be saved, you and your household." ³² And they spoke the word of the Lord to him and to all who were in his house. ³³ And he took them the same hour of the night and washed their wounds; and he was baptized at once, he and all his family. ³⁴ Then he brought them up into his house and set food before them. And he rejoiced along with his entire household that he had believed in God.

Here there is no mention of infants, but it does mention that the Philippian jailer had to "Believe in the Lord Jesus," which infers that this would be the same obligation for the rest of his family, in order for them to be saved and baptized.

Acts 18:8 English Standard Version (ESV)

⁸ Crispus, the ruler of the synagogue, **believed** in the Lord, **together with his entire household**. And many of the Corinthians hearing Paul believed and were baptized.

We see here that Crispus and his entire household believed in Jesus Christ, a prerequisite to entering the path of salvation, and being baptized as a public display of their accepting Christ. What we have seen from the first-century Christian congregation in the book of Acts is the need to pay attention, to hear, to understand, and to believe in Jesus Christ, before one enters the path of salvation, and was baptized.

Acts 8:12

English Standard Version (ESV)

¹² But when they believed Philip as he preached good news about the kingdom of God and the name of Jesus Christ, they were baptized, both **men and women**.

About Married People

1 Corinthians 7:14 English Standard Version (ESV)

¹⁴ For the unbelieving husband is made holy because of his wife, and the unbelieving wife is made holy because of her husband. Otherwise your children would be unclean, but as it is, they are holy.

Some have suggested that Paul's words to the Corinthians parents, saying the children were "holy" as a result of at least one believing parent, suggests infant baptism. However, this would not, it suggests just the opposite. What it suggests is no need for infant baptism, because any child that is under the age of accountability, would be declared righteous because of at least one believing parent, not because they were baptized as infants. If one pauses to consider, if an infant could be and should be baptized, placing it in the safety of salvation, why would there need to be talk about it receiving merit from at least one believing parent.

Let the Children Come to Me

Matthew 19:13-15 New American Standard Bible (NASB)

[13] Then *some* children were brought to Him so that He might lay His hands on them and pray; and the disciples rebuked them. [14] But Jesus said, "Let the children alone, and do not hinder them from coming to Me; for the kingdom of heaven belongs to such as these."[15] After laying His hands on them, He departed from there.

What the proponents of infant baptism leave out of this account is, the fact that they were not baptized. In addition, his laying hands on them did not serve as some religious ceremony. In fact, the point he was making with children was that whoever humbled themselves like young children was to be "the greatest in the kingdom of heaven." (Matt 18:4; Lu 18:16-17) In fact, Christians are to be,

1 Corinthians 14:20 English Standard Version (ESV)

[20] Brothers, do not be children in your thinking. Be infants in evil, but in your thinking be mature.

Infant Baptism and Circumcision

Genesis 17:12 English Standard Version (ESV)

[12] He who is eight days old among you shall be circumcised. Every male throughout your generations, whether born in your house or bought with your money from any foreigner who is not of your offspring,

Those who are advocates of infant baptism, go back to the Israelite his, and point to eight day old infants being circumcised, trying to find a correlation. They say that baptism of infants was simply a replacement of circumcision. Is this the case? No.

Circumcision was not a public display that one was now on the path to salvation, but rather was to 'be a sign of the covenant between God and Abraham.' (Gen 17:11) Moreover, females were not circumcised. If it were true that infant baptism was a replacement for circumcision; then, infant girls would not be baptized. Obviously, the supposed correspondence is not valid. Moreover, under the Mosaic Law, it was the parents, who carried out circumcision on their son. This, if there was some parallel, it would be the parents who baptized their infant son, which one would think, would have been mentioned in the New Testament.

The Great Commission

Matthew 28:19 English Standard Version (ESV)

[19] Go therefore and make disciples of all nations, baptizing them in the name of the Father and of the Son and of the Holy Spirit, [20] teaching them to observe all that I have commanded you. And behold, I am with you always, to the end of the age."

Disciples are taught ones, who then are obligated to turn around and teach others. This would hardly apply to infants. Christian disciples, as parents are looking to bring their children up in the discipline and instruction of the Lord, not baptize them as infants. Ephesians 6:4

BASIC TEACHING: Who is the Antichrist?

If one were to ask different Christians what they believe about the antichrist, there would be different views on the subject. "Dispensationalists look for a future Roman ruler who will appear during the tribulation and will rule over the earth. Those in the amillennialist school interpret the term symbolically."[73] It is more than these two choices though, as some feel the antichrist is one person, while others feels that it is a group of people, who are in opposition to Christ, while others feel it is anyone that is "anti" Christ." Powerful people of the past have been labeled the antichrist, such as the Roman Emperor Nero, Adolf Hitler, the German philosopher Friedrich Nietzsche, and more recently, radical Islam.[74] However, others are looking for a powerful world leader to come or that is hear, but has not stepped out of the shadows, who will rule the world. For theses ones, they point to Revelation chapter 13 as referring to the antichrist,

What About Revelation Chapter 13

Revelation 13:18 American Standard Version (ASV)

18 Here is wisdom. He that has understanding let him count the number of the beast, for it is the number of a man **[the antichrist]**: and his number is Six hundred and sixty and six **[666]**.

---

[73] http://biblia.com/books/hlmnillbbldict/Page.p_75

[74] The Islamic Antichrist: The Shocking Truth about the Real Nature of the Beast by Richardson, Joel (Jul 28, 2009)

Before delving into what the Bible specifically says about the antichrist, let us deal with Revelation chapter 13. In order for this chapter of Revelation alone to apply, the antichrist must just be one person, and we will soon discover that this just is not the case. Let us look at Revelation 13:2, "And the beast that I saw was like a leopard; its feet were like a bear's, and its mouth was like a lion's mouth. And to it the dragon gave his power and his throne and great authority." What do these features denote?

The body parts of this brute are a composite of three of the four creatures of Daniel 7:1–6, but in reverse order: body of **a leopard**, feet of **a bear**, and mouth of **a lion. In** Daniel's vision, these represented historical empires that opposed Judah, such as Babylon and Persia. Here they are all combined into one monster—raw political-military power.

The Christians of John's day immediately grasped that the form of the monster current in their day was imperial Rome. Where did Rome's power come from? **The dragon gave the beast his power and his throne and great authority**. Although God has ordained that government be used for good (Rom. 13:1–7), clearly the devil has mastered the art of twisting what God means for good and turning it to evil.[75]

Revelation 13:1 American Standard Version (ASV)

¹ and he stood upon the sand of the sea. And I saw a beast coming up out of the sea, having ten horns, and seven heads, and on his horns ten diadems, and upon his heads names of blasphemy.

---

[75] Kendell H. Easley, *Revelation*, *vol. 12*, *Holman New Testament Commentary* (Nashville, TN: Broadman & Holman Publishers, 1998), 227.

What or who do these seven heads represent. The seven heads are seven world empires throughout Bible history that have had some kind of impact on God's people, five of which were before John's day: Egypt Assyria, Babylon, Medo-Persia, and Greece. The sixth of those world empires was in existence during John's day, Rome, with the seventh world empire yet to come. Look at John's reference again in the same book.

Revelation 17:9-10 American Standard Version (ASV)

9 Here is the mind that has wisdom. The seven heads are seven mountains, on which the woman sits:

10 and they are seven kings; the five are fallen **[Egypt, Assyrian, Babylon, Medo-Persia, and Greece]**, the one is **[Rome]**, the other is not yet come **[?]**; and when he comets he must continue a little while.

We can conclude that the first wild beast from the sea (vss. 1-10) and the second wild beast from the earth (vss. 11-18) of Revelation 13 represent two governmental powers. The first wild beast "the dragon **[Satan, Rev. 12:3, 9]** gave it his power and his throne and great authority." The second wild beast "exercises all the authority of the first beast on his behalf and compels the earth and those who live on it to worship the first beast." Therefore, these beasts or governmental powers are against Christ, consequently, they are antichrists.

Antichrist Defined and Explained

We can now define antichrist as anyone, any group, any organization, or any government that is *against* or *instead of* Christ, or who mistreat his people. Thus, we are not just looking for one person, one group, one organization, or one power. The Bible does not refer to just one antichrist.

1 John 2:18 American Standard Version (ASV)

¹⁸ Children, it is the last hour **[John is the last of the 12 apostle and is almost a hundred, close to death]**; and as you have heard that antichrist coming, even now <u>many antichrists</u> have appeared; whereby we know that it is the last hour **[of John's protection (the apostolic period), as he dies shortly thereafter]**.

2 John 1:7 American Standard Version (ASV)

⁷ For many deceivers are gone forth into the world, those who do not confess the coming of Jesus Christ in the flesh. This is the deceiver and the antichrist.

We notice from 1 John 2:18 that it is "the last hour." It is the last hour, because John is almost one hundred years old, and he is the last of the twelve apostles, of the apostolic period, who could protect the Christians from the great apostasy that was coming. We also notice that John says there are "many antichrists." John refers to these collectively as "the antichrist" here in 2 John 1:7. Should Christians be looking for some future time, to identify some specific antichrist?

1 John 4:3 American Standard Version (ASV)

³ and every spirit that does not confess Jesus is not from God. This is the spirit of the antichrist, which you heard was coming and now is in the world already.

First John was written in the last years of the first century, about 98 C.E., and yet John says that there were antichrists already in the world during his day. It is the signs of antichrists in John's day, which let him, know it was the last hour. What characteristics do the antichrists have?

1 John 2:22 American Standard Version (ASV)

²² Who is the liar but he that denies that Jesus is the Christ? This is the antichrist, even he that denies the Father and the Son.

1 John 2:18-19 American Standard Version (ASV)

¹⁸ ... now many antichrists have appeared ... ¹⁹ They went out from us, but they were not of us; for if they had been of us, they would have continued with us: but they went out, that they might be made manifest that they all are not of us.

John 15:20-21 American Standard Version (ASV)

²⁰ Remember the word that I said unto you; 'A servant is not greater than his master.' If they persecuted me, they will also persecute you; if they kept my word, they will keep yours also. ²¹ But all these things will they do to you for my name's sake, because they know not him that sent me.

Psalm 2:2 American Standard Version (ASV)

² The kings of the earth take their stand And the rulers take counsel together, Against Jehovah, and against his anointed [Messiah, or Christ), saying,

Matthew 24:24 American Standard Version (ASV)

²⁴ For there shall arise false Christs, and false prophets, and shall show great signs and wonders; so as to lead astray, if possible, even the elect.

Thus, it would be any person, group, organization, or power, who

(1) The antichrist denies that Jesus is the Christ,

(2) The antichrist denies the Father and the Son,

(3) Some of the antichrist have abandoned the Christian faith, and thereafter work in opposition to Christ,

(4) The antichrist is anti-Christian

BASIC TEACHING: Is Hell a Place of Eternal Torment?

Hundreds of millions of both Catholic and Protest Christians have long held that hell is a place of eternal torment for the damned. According to the Encarta *Encyclopedia*, "Hell, in theology, any place or state of punishment and privation for human souls after death. More strictly, the term is applied to the place or state of eternal punishment of the damned, whether angels or human beings. The doctrine of the existence of hell is derived from the principle of the necessity for vindication of divine justice, combined with the human experience that evildoers do not always appear to be punished adequately in their lifetime. Belief in a hell was widespread in antiquity and is found in most religions of the world today."

However, it would seem that hellfire and brimstone has lost its spark. The same encyclopedia goes on to say, "In modern times the belief in physical punishment after death and the endless duration of this punishment has been rejected by many. The question about the nature of the punishment of hell is equally controversial. Opinions range from holding the pains of hell to be no more than the remorse of conscience to the traditional belief that the "pain of loss" (the consciousness of having forfeited the vision of God and the happiness of heaven) is

combined with the "pain of sense" (actual physical torment).[76]

Probably the most famous hellfire and brimstone preacher was Jonathan Edwards (1703-1758), used to put the fear of God into the hearts and minds of the 18th-century Colonial Americans with detail, explicit, lifelike, word pictures of hell

"Sinners in the Hands of an Angry God" Known for his fiery sermons, clergyman Jonathan Edwards helped start the Great Awakening, an American religious revival of the 1740s.

> The God that holds you over the pit of hell, much as one holds a spider, or some loathsome insect over the fire, abhors you, and is dreadfully provoked: his wrath towards you burns like fire; he looks upon you as worthy of nothing else, but to be cast into the fire; he is of purer eyes than to bear to have you in his sight; you are ten thousand times more abominable in his eyes, than the most hateful venomous serpent is in ours. You have offended him infinitely more than ever a stubborn rebel did his prince; and yet it is nothing but his hand that holds you from falling into the fire every moment.

> O sinner! Consider the fearful danger you are in: it is a great furnace of wrath, a wide and bottomless pit, full of the fire of wrath, that you are held over in the hand of that God, whose wrath is provoked and incensed as much against you, as against many of the damned in

[76] Microsoft ® Encarta ® 2006. © 1993-2005 Microsoft Corporation. All rights reserved.

hell. You hang by a slender thread, with the flames of divine wrath flashing about it, and ready every moment to singe it, and burn it asunder;[77]

Like Edwards, many other Catholic and Protestant preachers, say that God has this eternal place in the offing for the wicked. However, what does the Bible really teach?

Hell

Without being bogged down in doctrinal issues, let us just deal with the facts. "Hell" is the English translation for the Hebrew word Sheol and the Greek word Hades. Therefore, we need not ask, what Hell is. However, what did the word mean when it was first placed in English translations? Webster's Eleventh New International Dictionary, under "Hell" says: [Middle English, from Old English; akin to Old English *helan* to conceal, Old High German *helan*, Latin *celare*, Greek *kalyptein*] before 12th century"[78] The word "hell" meant to 'cover' over or 'conceal,' so it would have meant a place 'covered' or 'concealed,' such as a grave.

Sheol

Webster's dictionary, "[Hebrew Shě'ōl] 1597: the abode of the dead in early Hebrew thought"[79] *Collier's Encyclopedia* (1986, Vol. 12, p. 28) says: "Since Sheol in

---

[77] Edwards, Jonathan (2010-05-20). Sinners In The Hands Of An Angry God (Kindle Locations 151-152). Old Land Mark Publishing. Kindle Edition.

[78] http://biblia.com/books/mwdict11/word/hell

[79] http://biblia.com/books/mwdict11/word/sheol

Old Testament times referred simply to the abode of the dead and suggested no moral distinctions, the word 'hell,' as understood today, is not a happy translation." Some translations choose to use a transliteration, Sheol, as opposed to the English hell, *AT, RSV, ESV, LEB, HCSB, and NASB.*

Hades

Everyone knows that Hades was "the underground abode of the dead in Greek mythology."[80] However, as far as early Christianity, the Greek translation of the Old Testament, the Septuagint, uses the word Hades 73 times, employing it 60 times to translate the Hebrew word Sheol. Luke at Acts 2:27 write, "For you will not abandon my soul to **Hades**, or let your Holy One see corruption." Luke was quoting Psalm 16:10, which reads, "For you will not abandon my soul to **Sheol**, or let your holy one see corruption." Notice that Luke used Hades in place of Sheol. Therefore, Hades is the Greek equivalent of Sheol, as far as Christians and the Greek New Testament is concerned. In other words, Hades is also the abode of the dead in early Christian thought. Some translations choose to use a transliteration, Hades, as opposed to the English hell, *ASV, AT, RSV, ESV, LEB, HCSB, and NASB.*

Gehenna

Gehenna Hebrew *Ge' Hinnom*, literally, valley of Hinnom appears 12 times in the Greek New Testament books, and many translators render it by the word "hell." Most translations **have chosen poorly not to** use a

---

[80] http://biblia.com/books/mwdict11/word/hades

transliteration, *Gehenna* or *Geenna*, as opposed to the English hell, *ASV, AT, RSV, ESV, LEB, HCSB, and NASB.* There is little doubt that the New Testament writers and Jesus used "Gehenna" to speak of the place of final punishment. What was Gehenna?

According to the Holman Illustrated Bible Dictionary (p. 632), Gehenna or the Valley of Hinnom was "the valley south of Jerusalem now called the Wadi er-Rababi (Josh. 15:8; 18:16; 2 Chron. 33:6; Jer. 32:35) became the place of child sacrifice to foreign gods. The Jews later used the valley for the dumping of refuse, the dead bodies of animals, and executed criminals."[81] We would disagree with the other comments by the Holman Illustrated Dictionary, "The continuing fires in the valley (to consume the refuse and dead bodies) apparently led the people to transfer the name to the place where the wicked dead suffer." This just is not the case.

In the Old Testament, the Israelites did burn sons in the fires as part of a sacrifice to false gods, but not for the purpose of punishment, or torture. By the time of the New Testament period, hundreds of years later, the only thing thrown in Gehenna was trash and the dead bodies of executed criminals. For what purpose were these thrown into Gehenna? It was used as an incinerator, a furnace for destroying things by burning them. Notice that any bodies thrown in Gehenna during the New Testament period were already dead. Thus, if anything, these people saw Gehenna as a place where they destroyed their trash and the bodies of dead criminals. Thus, if Jesus used this to illustrate as the place of the wicked, it would have represented destruction as the punishment.

---

[81] http://biblia.com/books/hlmnillbbldict/Page.p_632

How are we to understand the "Fire"?

Mark 9:43-48 English Standard Version (ESV)

43 And if your hand causes you to sin, cut it off. It is better for you to enter life crippled than with two hands to go to hell, to the unquenchable fire. **45** And if your foot causes you to sin, cut it off. It is better for you to enter life lame than with two feet to be thrown into hell. **47** And if your eye causes you to sin, tear it out. It is better for you to enter the kingdom of God with one eye than with two eyes to be thrown into hell, **48** 'where their worm does not die and the fire is not quenched.'

Matthew 13:42 English Standard Version (ESV)

42 and throw them into the fiery furnace. In that place there will be weeping and gnashing of teeth.

Here is why we should use the transliteration as opposed to the English "hell." Jesus did not use the word "Hades" in the above texts, the equivalent of Sheol, but rather Gehenna. Jesus used comparisons in his teaching, using things that his listeners could relate. As we learned in the above Gehenna was a garbage dump that was used as an incinerator, to destroy whatever was thrown in, and only bodies of criminal were thrown in, after they were already dead. In other words, the fire was used as a symbol, not of torment, but rather of being destroyed, complete destruction, namely annihilation by fire.

What did Jesus mean by "there will be weeping and gnashing of teeth"? We can look at what he said about those, who believed they were on the right path,

Matthew 7:21-23 English Standard Version (ESV)

²¹ "Not everyone who says to me, 'Lord, Lord,' will enter the kingdom of heaven, but the one who does the will of my Father who is in heaven.²² On that day many will say to me, 'Lord, Lord, did we not prophesy in your name, and cast out demons in your name, and do many mighty works in your name?'²³ And then will I declare to them, 'I never knew you; depart from me, you workers of lawlessness.'

In other words, those who will be weeping and gnashing of teeth" are those who believed they had the truth, but did not. Can you imagine giving your whole life to what you believe to be the correct path, only to get to the edge and discover, you are on the wrong path, because you chose to do your will, not the will of the Father? Now then, what about what John penned in the book of Revelation?

Revelation 21:8 English Standard Version (ESV)

⁸ But as for the cowardly, the faithless, the detestable, as for murderers, the sexually immoral, sorcerers, idolaters, and all liars, their portion will be in the lake that burns with fire and sulfur, which is the second death."

John speaks of a "lake that burns with

fire and sulfur," where the wicked are thrown. It would seem that if hellfire were truth, this would be the place. However, we are simple told by John, this is "the second death." Moreover, he had told his readers earlier,

Revelation 20:13-14 English Standard Version (ESV)

[13] And the sea gave up the dead who were in it, Death and Hades gave up the dead who were in them, and they were judged, each one of them, according to what they had done. [14] Then Death and Hades were thrown into the lake of fire. This is the second death, the lake of fire.

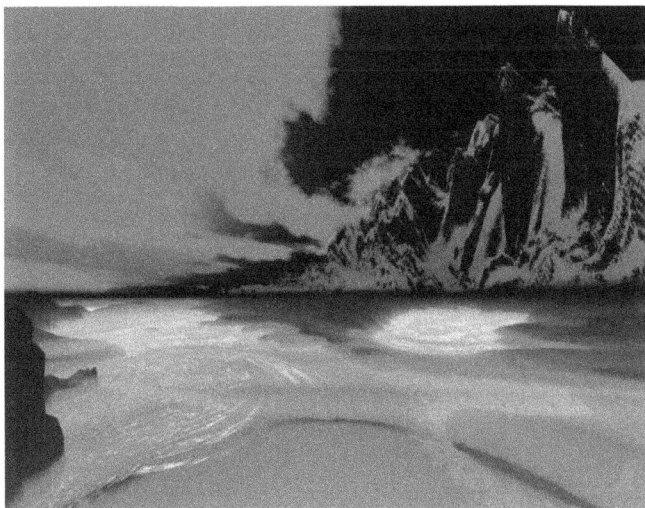

Notice that death, which is what we inherited from our first parents Adam and Eve, as well as Hades (gravedom), is going to be "thrown into the lake of fire." Is not death and Hades abstract, are they able to be tormented and suffer forever. No. However, the fire does picture their eternal destruction, which will take place once they 'give up the dead who were in them.' Note that Paul clearly said, "The last enemy to be destroyed is death." (1 Corinthians 15:26)

The fire and burning with in Scripture are simply representing annihilation, or eternal destruction. Therefore, there is no eternal torment in Sheol (gravedom), Hades (equivalent of Sheol) hell (English translation), Gehenna (symbol of destruction), or the lake of fire (symbol of destruction). What about the parable of the sheep (righteous) and the goats (wicked), which has the goats, or the wicked going away into eternal punishment?

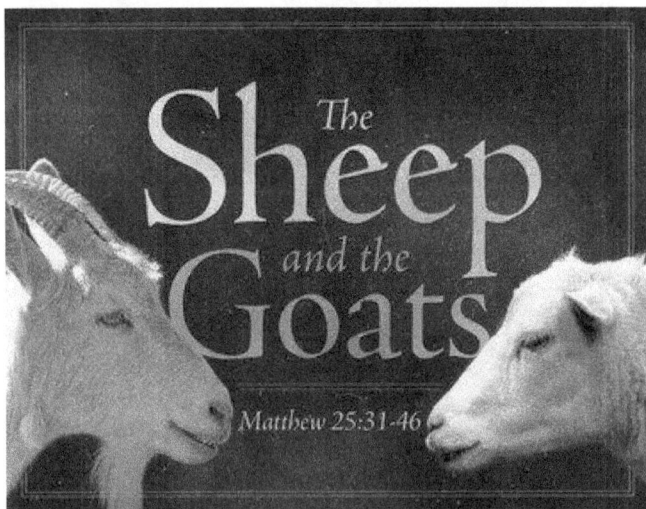

The
Sheep
and the
Goats
Matthew 25:31-46

Matthew 25:46 English Standard Version (ESV)

⁴⁶ And these will go away into eternal punishment [*Kolasin*], but the righteous into eternal life."

Kolasin "akin to *kolazoo*"[82] "This means 'to cut short,' 'to lop,' 'to trim,' and figuratively a. 'to impede,' 'restrain,' and b. 'to punish,' and in the passive 'to suffer loss.'[83] The first part of the sentence is only in harmony with the second part of the sentence, if the eternal punishment is eternal death. The wicked receive eternal death and the righteous eternal life. We might at that Matthews Gospel was primarily for the Jewish Christians, and under the Mosaic Law, God would punish those who violated the law, saying they "shall be cut off [penalty of death] from Israel." (Ex 12:15; Lev 20:2-3) We need further to consider,

2 Thessalonians 1:8-9 English Standard Version (ESV)

⁸ in flaming fire, inflicting vengeance on those who do not know God and on those who do not obey the gospel of our Lord Jesus. ⁹ They will suffer the punishment of eternal destruction, away from the presence of the Lord and from the glory of his might

Notice that Paul says too that the punishment for the wicked is "eternal destruction." Many times in talking with those that support the position of eternal torment in some hellfire, they will add a word to Matthew 25:46 in their paraphrase of the verse, '*conscious* eternal punishment.' However, Jesus does not tell us what the eternal punishment is, just that it is a punishment and it is eternal. Therefore, those who support eternal conscious fiery torment will read the verse to mean just that, while

---

[82] W. E. Vine, Merrill F. Unger, and William White Jr., *Vine's Complete Expository Dictionary of Old and New Testament Words* (Nashville, TN: T. Nelson, 1996), 498.

[83] Gerhard Kittel, Gerhard Friedrich, and Geoffrey William Bromiley, *Theological Dictionary of the New Testament* (Grand Rapids, MI: W.B. Eerdmans, 1985), 451.

those, who hold to the position of eternal destruction, will take Matthew 25:46 to mean that. Considering that Jesus does not define what the eternal punishment is, this verse is not a proof text for either side of the argument. Does Jesus' parable, The Rich Man and Lazarus, not support the hellfire doctrine? (Luke 16:19-31)

Jesus gave us some 40 parables or illustrations, filling them with symbols and images that represented a message he was trying to share. Now, we get to this one, and we want to take it literal? Robert H. Stein writes,

> Similarly, the parable of the rich man and Lazarus (Luke 16:19–31) is to be interpreted as a parable, and thus according to the rules governing the interpretation of parables. It is not to be interpreted as a historical account. (Luke reveals this by the introduction "A certain man …" which is used in the Gospel to introduce parables [cf. Luke 10:30; 14:16; 15:11;

16:1; 19:12]. This is clearer in the Greek text than in most translations, but it is fairly obvious in the NASB.)[84]

In discussing interpretation rules, stein goes on to say,

> In a similar way there are different "game" rules involved in the interpretation of the different kinds of biblical literature. The author has played his "game," has sought to convey his meaning, under the rules covering the particular literary form he used. Unless we know those rules, we will almost certainly misinterpret his meaning. If we interpret a parable (Luke 16:19–31) as if it were narrative, or if we interpret poetry (Judg. 5) as if it were narrative, we will err. Similarly, if we interpret a narrative such as the resurrection of Jesus (Matt. 28:1–10) as a parable, we will also err (1 Cor. 15:12–19).[85]

Step One in Understanding Parables

Read the context of the parable. You need to find out the setting of the parable, looking for the conditions and the circumstances. Why was the parable told? What prompted its being told?

Step Two in Understanding Parables

Consider the cultural backgrounds, such as the laws and customs of the setting, as well as the idioms that were spoken of earlier.

---

[84] Robert H. Stein, *A Basic Guide to Interpreting the Bible: Playing by the Rules* (Grand Rapids, MI: Baker Books, 1994), 30.
[85] IBID., 76.

Step Three in Understanding Parables

This is a two-point step. The first point is to **look to the author of the parable for the upcoming meaning of the parable**. An interpreter of a parable by Jesus would see what he meant in the context it was spoken, and then consider his teaching as a whole. The second point is, **do not assign subjective meanings to the elements of a parable**. Generally, a parable teaches one basic point.

Stage One: Discovering the Main Characters

In any given parable, it is highly important to find the main 2–3 characters.

Stage Two: Looking to the End

As is true with any kind of story, the end of the story carries the weight of importance. This is no different with parables. The ending is where the answers lie.

Stage Three: Who Carries the Conversation

Which character carries the conversation?

Stage Four: Who Gets the Most Press

Generally, whoever gets the most coverage in a story is the primary character, followed by the secondary person that must exist to facilitate the story and its main point.[86]

The setting of the parable of *The rich man and Lazarus* (Lu 16:19-31) is Jesus speaking, with the Pharisees listening in, who were well known as one who hungered for riches. What was Jesus teaching by this parable?

---

[86] Edward D. Andrews, *A Concise Guide to Biblical Interpretation: The Quest for Meaning* (Cambridge, OH: Edward Andrews, 2012), 120–127.

It had nothing to do with punishment for sin. It had to do with two different groups of people, the rich man (Jewish religious leaders) and the beggar Lazarus (poor Jewish people), as there was about to be a drastic change in their privileged and lowly positions. The Rich man, the Jewish religious leaders opposed Jesus and the Good News of the Kingdom that he brought, because he was busy sharing it with the common Jewish people. This, in fact, tormented the Jewish religious leaders to no end, to the point of their seeking to kill him. (Luke 20:19, 20, 46, 47) Conversely, the beggar Lazarus represents, the poor, common Jewish people, who were looked upon with disdain, like beggars by the Jewish religious leaders, were being given the privilege position of becoming disciples of Jesus, and the first to enter into the kingdom. —1 Cor. 1:26-29.

What is the meaning of the "tormented with fire and sulfur" in Revelation 14:9-11?

Revelation 14:9-11 English Standard Version (ESV)

9 And another angel, a third, followed them, saying with a loud voice, "If anyone worships the beast and its image and receives a mark on his forehead or on his hand, **10** he also will drink the wine of God's wrath, poured full strength into the cup of his anger, and he will be tormented with fire and sulfur in the presence of the holy angels and in the presence of the Lamb.**11** And the smoke of their torment goes up forever and ever, and they have no rest, day or night, these worshipers of the beast and its image, and whoever receives the mark of its name."

In the above text, those who worshipping the symbolic "beast and its image," they will be "tormented with fire and sulfur." The context here is not what happens after these one's deaths, but rather what happens to them while they are alive. What is it that torments these ones while they are alive? It is the proclamations of Christians that worshipers of the "beast and its image" will experience, to such a level that it is referred to as "tormented with fire and sulfur." Looking at the context of 14:11, it is **not** the torment that lasts forever; it is '**the smoke** of their torment that goes up forever and ever.' What is smoke is a signal of their symbolic burning that will rise forever, because the lesson learned will never be forgotten. Is there yet another example of this in Scripture? Yes.

The Judgment of Edom

Isaiah 34:9-12 English Standard Version (ESV)

⁹ And the streams of Edom shall be turned **into pitch**,
   and her soil **into sulfur**;
   her land shall become **burning pitch**.
¹⁰ Night and day it **shall not be quenched**;
   its smoke shall go up forever.
From generation to generation it shall lie waste;
   none shall pass through it forever and ever.
¹¹ But the hawk and the porcupine shall possess it,
   the owl and the raven shall dwell in it.
He shall stretch the line of confusion over it,
   and the plumb line of emptiness.
¹² Its nobles—there is no one there to call it a kingdom,
   and all its princes shall be nothing.

Was Edom thrown into some literal hellfire to burn forever? No. The Edomite nation, an enemy of God's people was removed, which is described in the above in poetic terms, highly symbolic language. It was as though Edom were consumed by fire and sulfur. If we were to go to the geographical location of ancient Edom, would we see smoke still rising? No. The smoke was and still is today, a signal of a lesson learned from the destruction that Edom faced. This smoke filled lesson will rise forever, in that the lesson learned will live on forever through the Word of God. After Jesus destroys the last enemy death, is it believed that the Bible will no longer be needed? The Bible is a book that will stand forever, as a signal of what humanity already experienced. Let us take this one step further as we look at our next text that is often drawn on to support hellfire doctrine.

Revelation 20:10 English Standard Version (ESV)

[10] and the devil who had deceived them was thrown into the lake of fire and sulfur where the beast and the false prophet were, and they will be tormented (Greek, *basanos*) day and night forever and ever.

The Greek word used here for "torment," *basanizo*, primarily means "to test by rubbing on the touchstone" (*basanos*, "a touchstone"), then, "to question by applying torture."[87] The Bible is our case law (law established on the basis of previous verdicts), which will serve as a touchstone[88] (a standard by which something is judged) that humans were never designed to walk on their own, but to live under the sovereignty of their Creator. The issues raised by Satan will have been settled by humanities walking through thousands of years of an object lesson, for which the Bible is the case law, the touchstone, which will be around forever, as a reminder of the issues raised and settled.

---

[87] W. E. Vine, Merrill F. Unger, and William White Jr., *Vine's Complete Expository Dictionary of Old and New Testament Words* (Nashville, TN: T. Nelson, 1996), 176.

[88] A touchstone is a hard black stone formerly used to test the purity of gold and silver according to the color of the streak left when the metal was rubbed against it.

The Moral Test

We know that man and woman were created in the image of God, and so when we hear of people who have tortured criminals, we call that inhumane. Would we expect that the One, whose image we are made in would see the eternal torment of sinners as humane? This would be incompatible with the very person of God. How are we to know how God views justice?

(Exodus 21:23-24) But if there is harm, then you shall pay life for life, eye for eye, tooth for tooth, hand for hand, foot for foot,

(Leviticus 24:20) fracture for fracture, eye for eye, tooth for tooth; whatever injury he has given a person shall be given to him.

(Deuteronomy 19:21) Your eye shall not pity. It shall be life for life, eye for eye, tooth for tooth, hand for hand, foot for foot.

(Judges 1:7) And Adoni-bezek said, "Seventy kings with their thumbs and their big toes cut off used to pick up scraps under my table. As I have done, so God has repaid me." And they brought him to Jerusalem, and he died there.

(Matthew 5:38-42) "You have heard that it was said, 'An eye for an eye and a tooth for a tooth.' But I say to you, Do not resist the one who is evil. But if anyone slaps you on the right cheek, turn to him the other also. And if anyone would sue you and take your tunic, let him have your cloak as well. And if anyone forces you to go one mile, go with him two miles. Give to the one who begs from you, and do not refuse the one who would borrow from you."

The above texts are but a few of how God views justice, and it is all too clear that he sees it as the punishment needs to be proportionate, to be the best response to crime. In other words, if an Israelite were to steal his neighbor's cow, he would have to replace it with the cow, and any financial loss he suffered, even some extra as punitive damages. However, would God expect that thief to have to work as a slave to his neighbor for the rest of his life, and his children and grand children's lives as well? Not that punishment would be way out of proportion to the crime.

Now, let us look at the punishment that God gave Adam and Eve, if they were to sinfully rebel, rejecting him and his sovereignty, by choosing to eat from the Tree he had commended them not to eat from.

Genesis 2:17 English Standard Version (ESV)

[17] but of the tree of the knowledge of good and evil you shall not eat, for in the day that you eat of it you shall surely die."

Eat from the tree (i.e., reject God as sovereign) = death. The punishment for sin was death. Please go back and look at Genesis 2:17 in your Bible and as many other translations as you can. Did you notice some footnote from God that said, "And 4,000 years from now, when Jesus arrives, I am going to change the sentence from death to eternal torment in some literal lake of fire?"

Imagine you live in some small American town. You get your driver's licenses. Then, one day, you are pulled over for going 35-Miles Per Hour (MPH) in a 25 MPH zone. The police officer writes you a ticket, and tells you to appear in court the following month, where the judge will fine you $50.00. You arrive at court the following month, and are in front of the judge, and he just found

221

you guilty, and sentences you not to a $50.00 fine, but to be taken outside of the courthouse and shot to death by a firing squad. Would anyone suggest that the punishment of a death sentence was proportionate to the crime of a speeding ticket? Would anyone find justice in the law enforcement officer saying the penalty was a mere $50.00 fine, and then the judge later raising the penalty to such an extreme level of the death penalty? God gave Adam the penalty of death, for committing the greatest sin of any human in history, as he had rejected God in perfection, and sentencing billions to death along with him. Would it then be justice, for God to raise the punishment bar to eternal torment in the Lake of Fire? Let us now look at imperfect humanity.

(Romans 3:23) for all have sinned and fall short of the glory of God,

(Romans 5:12) therefore, just as sin came into the world through one man, and death through sin, and so death spread to all men because all sinned

(Romans 6:7) For one who has died has been set free from sin.

(Romans 6:23) For the wages of sin is death, but the free gift of God is eternal life in Christ Jesus our Lord.

If Adam commits the great sin a human could commit and he gets death, how is it justice that imperfect humans supposedly getting eternal torment in a Lake of Fire?

There are five factors to imperfect humans being even less culpable (Guilty) than Adam was. **(1)** We are imperfect and live in an imperfect world, compounded with the fact that God's Word says we are mentally bent and lean toward doing bad. We read, "When the LORD saw that the wickedness of man on the earth was great, and that the whole bent of his thinking was never anything but evil, the LORD regretted that he had ever made man on the earth." (Gen. 6:5, AT) **(2)** We have a wicked spirit creature, Satan the Devil, who is misleading the entire world of humankind. We read, "Be sober-minded; be watchful. Your adversary the devil prowls around like a roaring lion, seeking someone to devour." (1 Pet 5:8, ESV) **(3)** We live in a world that caters to the imperfect flesh. We read, "For all that is in the world, the desires of the flesh and the desires of the eyes and pride in possessions, is not from the Father but is from the world. And the world is passing away along with its desires, but whoever does the will of God abides forever." (1 John 2:16-17) **(4)** We are unable to understand our inner person, which the Bible informs us is wicked: "The heart is deceitful above all things, and desperately sick; who can understand it?" (Jeremiah 17:9) (5) In imperfection, man is unable of directing his own step. Jeremiah 10:23

Unlike Adam, we are imperfect from the start, and Adam received death for sin. **Adam was** perfect, with the natural desire to do good, he was mentally perfect, and he lived in a paradise, in direct communication with God. **We are** born mentally bent toward sin, have Satan and demons after us, naturally desire to do bad, have an imperfect fallen world that surrounds us, which caters to our flesh desires, have heart (inner person) is deceitful and desperately sick, and are unable to walk on our own. Thus, it is right and just that imperfect humans are to receive eternal torment in some literal Lake of Fire. If one who dies, is freed from sin, by having paid the wages of sin paid for through death (Rom 6:23), not the ransom of Christ, why should he then suffer eternally in some fiery torment?

BASIC TEACHING: Are the Genesis Creative Days Literally Only 24 Hours Long?

There are over a dozen different interpretations concerning the creative days of Genesis. Herein we will consider the main four in an effort to make our point. First, there is the *young earth view* that asserts that all physical creation was produced in just six literal 24-hour days sometime between 6,000 and 10,000 years ago. Second, there is the *day-age view* that asserts that each creative day is to be understood figuratively as creative periods of unknown durations of time. According to this view the earth is millions of years old, and the universe is billions of years old. Third, there is the *restoration view* (gap theory) that asserts that there is a large gap of time between Genesis 1:1 and 1:2. Fourth, there is the *literary framework view* that asserts that God was not having Moses address how He created the world, nor the length of time in which to do such. This view holds that this account in Genesis one is merely a literary outline that summarizes a theology of creation. This so-called "seven day framework" is not to be understood in a literal sense of order and chronology, but is a literary device expressing God's involvement in creation and the Sabbath. All four of these views are held by different Evangelical Christian scholars, but the authors of this book set aside three of these as being contrary to Scripture and science. We will discuss the first two views listed above in more detail below. [89]

---

89. For a more in-depth understanding of these for creative views, see Gregory A. Boyd and Paul R. Eddy, *Across the Spectrum* (Grand Rapids, Baker Academic, 2002), 50–73.

We do not believe those who hold to the young-earth view of creationism have the evidence to support their case. Actually, we do not believe they even speak in terms of evidence. Why? Most of the young-earth commentators attempt to disprove the day-age view by using many words like "possibly," "could be," "may be," and so on. Also, we do not believe they look at the evidence without theological bias. Professor Kirk Wise writes:

> I am a young-age creationist because that is my understanding of the Scripture. As I shared with my professors years ago when I was in college, if all the evidence in the universe turns against creationism, I would be the first to admit it, but I would still be a creationist because that is what the Word of God seems to indicate. Here I must stand. (Ashton, 2001)[90]

It shows theological bias when he states that no evidence will change his mind. Just as in the case of Galileo, theologians cast doubt on the Bible by ignoring scientific evidence. The Bible was not out of harmony with the truth that the earth revolves around the sun and not the other way. God's Word needed no revision. It was the Catholic Church's misinterpretation of the Bible that caused the problem. As one grows in understanding of physics, biology, and chemistry (as is also true with history, ancient languages, and manuscripts), one may need to revise conclusions derived from previous knowledge. When knowledge increases, it calls for humility to make adjustments in ones thinking.

---

90. http://richarddawkins.net/articles/115.

To suggest, as do many conservative Christians, that one needs to read the Bible in a plain way (*sensus plenoir*) is quite misleading, as though one would never consider otherwise. Galileo's own words to a pupil said it well: "Even though Scripture cannot err, its interpreters and expositors can, in various ways. One of these, very serious and very frequent, would be when they always want to stop at the purely literal sense."[91] The professor argues that because Genesis chapter one was written as historical narrative, it disallows an interpretation that has millions of years involved. This is hardly the case, for he goes on to admit that other historical narratives contain imbedded material that is not to be taken literally. Moreover, it is implied that one who accepts long creative periods must also believe the Big Bang theory, and believe that fossils are millions of years old, and believe in other facets of Evolution. This is simply untrue.

Simply put, Genesis 1:1 says: "In the beginning God created the heavens and the earth." (*ESV*) This would include our home, the earth, and our solar system and galaxy that King David referred to when he looked into the night sky and wrote: "When I look at your heavens, the work of your fingers, the moon and the stars, which you have set in place, what is man that you are mindful of him, and the son of man that you care for him?" (Psalm 8:3, 4, *ESV*) It would also include all the billions of universes that David was unable to see with his naked eye. Therefore, all this came *before* the first day of creative preparation for life on the earth that starts in Genesis 1:3, as would also be the case with the description of the earth as found in verse 2. It is not until we get to Genesis 1:3–5 that Moses starts to expound on

---

91. Letter from Galileo to Benedetto Castelli, December 21, 1613.

the first day of creation specifically in respect to the earth.

What does this mean? It means that regardless of how long you may feel the creative days were, verses 1 and 2 are covering things that existed prior to the start of the events described in the successive creative days. Therefore, it takes nothing away from the Bible when geologists state that the earth is four billion years old, or astronomers who have calculated the age of the universe say it is at least 14–20 billion years old. For the Christian to argue with science is only history repeating itself, as you will see before this chapter closes. Again, Genesis chapter one, verses 1, 2, are outside the events of the creative days, which are simply a summary of the steps taken to transform the condition of verse 2 into the habitable earth in which the animals and Adam and Eve were created.

Now that we have settled the controversy between science and the *erroneous* interpretations of man's tradition that the universe and earth were created in only six literal days, we should clear the air over the age and origin of the sedimentary geological strata. Many have postulated that it was formed at the time of the flood of Noah. This answer is not to be found in God's Word. Those who hold to the young-earth view (6,000–10,000 years old), work very hard to try to reconcile the geologic column and the fossils of dinosaurs and such, in which they try to overcome evidence that shows the earth is millions of years old. What is now known and acknowledged by science is that the geological record does *not* contain a series of gradual and progressive stages of fossils from one species to another. Actually, the fossil record supports the creation account in that new species appear suddenly on the scene within this geological column, having absolutely no connection with any other species. The problem with young-earth proponents is that they are unable to use this information because it will not fit with their belief that all land and sea animals were created in two 24-hour days. This is not to say that this publication accepts the idea that the sea and land animals have existed for untold hundreds of millions of years, but it does not negate that the fifth and sixth creative days were possibly many thousands of years long, having flying and sea creatures, and land animals being created throughout, as well as dinosaurs.

What exactly does the Bible reveal? It says plainly that Jehovah God is the "fountain of life." (Psalm 36:9) In other words, life did not come from nothing, and then develop gradually in some evolutionary process over billions of years. Additionally, God's Word says that everything was created according to its kind. (Genesis 1:11, 21, 24) And finally, the Bible does provide the time period of man's creation, some 6,000 years ago. On this, both archaeology and Biblical chronology are not far off from each other. Creation is clearly stated within God's Word, and can be understood in relation to the correct study and interpretation of its texts, in light of factual science, astronomy, physics, chemistry, geology, and biology. The evolutionary theory stands in opposition to the Bible and to the facts of paleontology and biology. The ideas of young-earth creationists are not supported by God's Word either, conflicting with astronomy, physics, and geology.

Back in the seventeenth century, the world-renowned scientist Galileo proved beyond any doubt that the earth was not the center of the universe, nor did the sun orbit the earth. In fact, he proved it to be the other way around (no pun intended), with the earth revolving around the sun. However, he was brought up on charges of heresy by the Catholic Church and ordered to recant his position. Why? From the viewpoint of the Catholic Church, Galileo was contradicting God's Word, the Bible. As it turned out, Galileo and science were correct and the Church was wrong, for which it issued a formal apology in 1992. However, the point we wish to make here is that in all the controversy, the Bible was never in the wrong. It was a misinterpretation on the part of the Catholic Church, and not a fault with the Bible. One will find no place in the Bible that claims the sun orbits the earth. So where would the Church get such an idea? From Ptolemy (b. about 85 C.E.), an ancient astronomer, who argued for such an idea.

A geocentric model that the earth is the center of the universe was long held by Ptolemy's predecessors like Aristotle and most of the ancient Greek philosophers. The idea of the earth being the center of the universe was held on to by the fact that the observer with his naked eye saw both the sun and moon appear to revolve around the earth each day, while the earth appeared to stand still. Now consider that the church fathers of the third to the fifth centuries C.E. were inundated by Greek thought, believing philosophical thinking was a means of interpreting God's Word. Commenting on such ones, Douglas T. Holden[92] stated, "Christian theology has become so fused with Greek philosophy that it has reared individuals who are a mixture of nine parts Greek thought to one part Christian thought." Couple this with a literal reading of some texts that should be understood figuratively and you have the makings for a conflict between the Church and the scientific world.

In interpretation, you may find one verse that appears to be in direct conflict with another (such as, the

---

92. Douglas T. Holden, *Death Shall Have no Dominion: A New Testament Study* (Bloomington: Bethany Press, 1971), 14.

earth will be destroyed by fire, or, the earth will last forever). We do not automatically assume that God's original Word is wrong. We must do some investigative work: (1) Is there a scribal error? (2) Is there an error in translation? (3) Is this a case of one verse using "earth" in a literal sense, while another is using figurative language, speaking of mankind as the "earth?" This can be the case with science as well. One does not let the scientific world dictate our understanding of Scripture, but we should not be so dogmatic in the face of scientific facts that we will, like Professor Kirk Wise, set aside "all the evidence in the universe [that] turns against creationism," while still holding onto erroneous, unreasonable, and unscriptural interpretations.

We have many of conservative scholarship who still argues that the earth and all life on it were created in six literal 24-hour days. As you may know, this flatly contradicts modern-day science. Do we have another Galileo moment in time? Who is correct here, the scholars or science? One thing is for certain, there is no fault to be found in God's Word. The Bible does not explicitly say these creative days were literal 24-hour days. What many are failing to realize and quite a few refuse to accept is that, in both the Hebrew and the Greek Scriptures, the word for "day" (Heb., yohm; Gr., hēmera) is used both in a literal and in a figurative sense. Moreover, this is not a case of inerrancy. In other words, if one does not accept six literal 24 hour days, he has abandoned inerrancy. True inerrancy does not consider whether they are literal or figurative creative days, but rather is your interpretation in harmony with what the author meant by the words that he used.

These six creative days are representative of being like six successive days of a week. If we look at most modern translations, they read, "**the** first day," "**the** second day," "**the** third day," and so on. This is an error in translation and should read. "And there was evening and there was morning, **a** first day." (Gen. 1:5) There is no definite article in the Hebrew of these six creative days. It is the translators that choose to add it into their translations. (ESV, LEB, HCSB, NIV, etc.) However, the American Standard Version and the New American Standard Bible read, "And there was evening and there was morning, one day." (1:5) If we were talking about a definite period of time, generally there should be a definite article in the Hebrew, because it is written in the prose genre. It is only in Hebrew poetry that the definite article could be omitted. What we are looking at with these six creative days is simply a sequential pattern, as oppose to six literal units of definite time.

SIX CREATIVE DAYS		
DAY	**WORKS**	**GENESIS**
1	Light gradually came to be;[93] a separation between day and night	1:3–5
2	Expanse, a separation between the waters below from the waters above	1:6–8
3	Dry land appears; produces vegetation	1:9–13

---

93. Many believe that God said: "Let there be light" and it immediately appeared. No, this was a gradual process, taking such an enormous amount of time that speculation would be the result of any guess. J. W. Watt's translation reflects this gradual process: "And gradually light came into existence." (*A Distinctive Translation of Genesis*) This light from our sun was spread through the dark overcast, to the point that it was not at first observable but gradually became observable through time.

4	Sources of light now become visible from earth [94]	1:14–19
5	Aquatic souls and flying creatures	1:20–23
6	Land animals; man and woman created	1:24–31

While the word "day" in Hebrew can mean a 24-hour period, clearly *yohm* and context allows for the creative days to be understood as a period of time, an age, or an era. For example, immediately after he mentions the six creative days, Moses uses the same word for "day" in a more general way, lumping *all six creative days together as one day*:

Genesis 2:4: These are the generations of the heavens and of the earth when they were created, in the day that Jehovah God made earth and heaven.

Here we are given the context of just how Moses is using *yohm*, which in this verse is referring to all six creative periods as "in the day." With this alone, it is difficult to argue that in chapter one *yohm* was being used to refer literally to a 24-hour period. Below are a few other examples where *yohm* is being used in the sense of an extended period of time, age, or era:

Proverbs 25:13 (ASV): As the cold of snow *in the time* ["day" *yohm*] of harvest, So is a faithful messenger to them that send him; For he refreshes the soul of his masters.

---

94. And God said, "Let there be light," and there was light, the first day. Hebrew has different words that distinguish their source and their quality. The Hebrew word used in verse one for "light" is *ohr*, which carries the general sense. However, by the fourth "day," or creative period, the Hebrew word changes to *maohr*, which is now referring to the source of the light.

Isaiah 4:2 (ASV): *In that day* [*yohm*] shall the branch of Jehovah be beautiful and glorious, and the fruit of the land shall be excellent and comely for them that are escaped of Israel.

Zechariah 14:1 (ASV): Behold, *a day* [*yohm*] *of* Jehovah cometh, when thy spoil shall be divided in the midst of thee.

You will have those who cling to the 24-hour creative day by informing you that *yohm*, "day, " is used 410 times outside of Genesis with a day and number and in all cases it is to be taken literally, meaning an ordinary day. First, let us point out that there is no absolute grammatical rule in Hebrew that would make this mandatory in every case. Young-earth proponents must support their proposition with their circular argument. For the sake of an argument, let us say that their claim is true. To have "day" used with an ordinal number in 410 places outside of Genesis chapter one would not negate *yohm* being used in a different setting (like creation) with ordinal numbers and still be referring to periods of time (epochs). One must keep in mind that those uses of a *yohm* outside the creation account are used in reference to humans and a human day. Because Genesis is the only place in Scripture where periods of time can be used with ordinal numbers, there is no problem with it being the exception to the rule. No other book has the setting of the creation of heaven and earth, so to equate uses of *yohm* in totally different settings with its use in Genesis is circular reasoning, as if to say: "*Yohm* is used with ordinals in 410 occurrences outside of Genesis and they are literal, so *yohm* must be literal in Genesis because it is used with ordinal numbers." You might as well say that "*yohm* is literal with ordinal numbers because *yohm* should be literal with ordinal numbers." The young-earth proponent's argument is circular by supporting a premise with a premise instead of a conclusion.

Exodus 20:11: For in six days Jehovah made heaven and earth, the sea, and all that in them is, and rested the seventh day: wherefore Jehovah blessed the sabbath day, and hallowed it.

Is Moses, the writer of Genesis, making reference here at Exodus 20:11 to the six creative days as a representative for the weekly Sabbath, thus suggesting that the six creative days were literal 24-hour days? No, this is not so. At Genesis 2:4, the same writer uses *yohm*, "day," figuratively to refer to the six creative days of Genesis chapter one and Exodus 20:11 as a whole, starting from the gradual appearance of light on the first day (Genesis 1:3, as it would appear to an earthly observer), but does not include the earth as it lay in its prior existence, in which it is described as being "without form and void, and darkness was over the face of the deep. And the Spirit of God was hovering over the face of the waters."

Another stumbling block for those who wish to take the creation account in a literal sense of 24-hour periods is that the context is really presented as events that take long periods of time to accomplish.

Genesis 1:11, 12: And God said, Let the earth put forth grass, herbs yielding seed, and fruit-trees bearing fruit after their kind, wherein is the seed thereof, upon the earth: and it was so. [Resulting in] And the earth brought forth grass, herbs yielding seed after their kind, and trees bearing fruit, wherein is the seed thereof, after their kind: and God saw that it was good.

Obviously we are dealing with far more time than one 24-hour day would allow when speaking of grass, herbs, and fruit trees sprouting *and* growing to maturity *and* producing seed and fruit.

Genesis 2:18–20: And Jehovah God said, It is not good *that the man should be alone;* I will make him a help meet for him. And out of the ground Jehovah God formed every beast of the field, and every bird of the heavens; and brought them unto the man to see what he would call them: and whatsoever the man called every living creature, that was the name thereof. And the man gave names to all cattle, and to the birds of the heavens, and to every beast of the field; but for man there was not found a help meet for him.

At this point in the creation account it was still the sixth creative day. However as verse 27 of chapter 1 shows, it is the close of the sixth creation day. After all else had been created, after the animals had been fashioned, just before sundown of that day, "God created man in his own image, in the image of God he created him; male and female he created them." Taken literally, this means that Adam and Eve were created in the last hour of the sixth day. The question here is, if the sixth "day" was only going to be 24 hours, why would Adam be lonely? God would have known he was creating his helper in that sixth "day." Why the concern for loneliness if it were only moments before Eve was to be created? For this reader, the implication is that the sixth day is a long creative period.

Even more activity would be impossibly crammed into the sixth creative day if it were only a 24-hour period. Adam is assigned the task of naming the different kinds of animals. This is not a simple task of just picking a name randomly. In the ancient culture, names carried even more meaning than in our modern Western culture. Names were chosen to be descriptive, to reflect something about the person, animal, or thing. From the descriptive forms of the names Adam chose, it is obvious that it took some time, for the account literally reads, "whatever the man called *every living creature*, that was its name."[95] (Genesis 2:19) For example, the Hebrew word for the "ass" refers to the usual reddened color. The Hebrew word for stork is the feminine form of the word meaning "loyal one."[96] This name is certainly a perfect fit, as the stork is known for the loving care it gives its young, and the loyalty of staying with its mate for life, something that would have been impossible to observe within a mere 24-hour day.

Regardless, it has been estimated, even if Adam has taken just one minute to name each pair, it would have taken 40 days with no sleep. It was only after Adam completed this task that Eve was created. Yet, even conceding the possibility that the process of naming the animals went quicker, because Adam named only the basic kinds of animals, like what went in Noah's ark at the time of the flood, which did not involve thousands of creatures, it would have taken weeks, possibly months, not a literal 24-hour day. It is during the process of Adam's naming the animals that it is discovered that "for the man no helper was found who was like him." (Genesis 2:20) Thus, we now see where the concern from Genesis 2:18 comes from, with God's reference to Adam's getting lonely. If it took weeks, months, or decades for Adam to complete his assignment of naming the animals, he would have had the time to grow lonely, but not in a couple hours as would be the case with a 24-hour day.

95. Walter A. Elwell and Barry J Beitzel, *Baker Encyclopedia of the Bible* (Grand Rapids, Mich.: Baker Book House, 1988), S. 93.

96. *Enhanced Brown-Driver-Briggs Hebrew and English Lexicon.* electronic ed. (Oak Harbor, WA : Logos Research Systems, 2000), S. 339.

Thus, the context here is that over a long period of time of naming the animals, Adam took note that he was alone while all the animals had mates. Let us take an extensive look at this again with the leading Hebrew language scholar of the 20th century, Dr. Gleason L. Archer.

It thus becomes clear in this present case, as we study the text of Genesis 1, that we must not short-circuit our responsibility of careful exegesis in order to ascertain as clearly as possible what the divine author meant by the language His inspired prophet (in this case probably Moses) was guided to employ. Is the true purpose of Genesis 1 to teach that all creation began just six twenty-four-hour days before Adam was "born"? Or is this just a mistaken inference that overlooks other biblical data having a direct bearing on this passage? To answer this question we must take careful note of what is said in Genesis 1:27 concerning the creation of man as the closing act of the sixth creative day. There it is stated that on that sixth day (apparently toward the end of the day, after all the animals had been fashioned and placed on the earth—therefore not long before sundown at the end of that same day), "God created man in His own image; He created them male and female." This can only mean that Eve was created in the closing hour of Day Six, along with Adam.

As we turn to Genesis 2, however, we find that a considerable interval of time must have intervened between the creation of Adam and the creation of Eve. In Gen. 2:15 we are told that Yahweh Elohim (i.e., the LORD God) put

Adam in the garden of Eden as the idle environment for his development, and there he was to cultivate and keep the enormous park, with all its goodly trees, abundant fruit crop, and four mighty rivers that flowed from Eden to other regions of the Near East. In Gen 2:18 we read, "Then the LORD God said, 'It is not good for the man to be alone; I will make him a helper suitable for him.' " This statement clearly implies that Adam had been diligently occupied in his responsible task of pruning, harvesting fruit, and keeping the ground free of brush and undergrowth for a long enough period to lose his initial excitement and sense of thrill at this wonderful occupation in the beautiful paradise of Eden. He had begun to feel a certain lonesomeness and inward dissatisfaction.

In order to compensate for this lonesomeness, God then gave Adam a major assignment in natural history. He was to classify every species of animal and bird found in the preserve. With its five mighty rivers and broad expanse, the garden must have had hundreds of species of mammal, reptile, insect, and bird, to say nothing of the flying insects that also are indicated by the basic Hebrew term ʿ ôp̱ ("bird") (2:19). It took the Swedish scientist Linnaeus several decades to classify all the species known to European scientists in the eighteenth century. Doubtless there were considerably more by that time than in Adam's day; and, of course, the range of fauna in Eden may have been more limited than those available to Linnaeus. But at the same time it must have taken a good deal of study for Adam to examine each specimen and decide on an appropriate name for it, especially in view of the fact that he had absolutely no human tradition behind him, so far as nomenclature was concerned. It must have required some years, or, at the very least, a considerable number of months for him to complete this comprehensive inventory of all the birds, beasts, and insects that populated the Garden of Eden.

Finally, after this assignment with all its absorbing interest had been completed, Adam felt a renewed sense of emptiness. Genesis 2:20 ends with the words "but for Adam no suitable helper was found." After this long and unsatisfying experience as a lonely bachelor, God saw that Adam was emotionally prepared for a wife—a "suitable helper." God, therefore, subjected him to a deep sleep, removed from his body the bone that was closest to his heart, and from that physical core of man fashioned the first woman. Finally God presented woman to Adam in all her fresh, unspoiled beauty, and Adam was ecstatic with joy.

As we have compared Scripture with Scripture (Gen. 1:27 with 2:15–22), it has become very apparent that Genesis 1 was never intended to teach that the sixth creative day, when Adam and Eve were both created, lasted a mere twenty-four hours. In view of the long interval of time between these two, it would seem to border on sheer irrationality to insist that all of Adam's experiences in Genesis 2:15–22 could have been crowded into the last hour or two of a literal twenty-four-hour day. The only reasonable conclusion to draw is that the purpose of Genesis 1 is not to tell how fast God performed His work of creation (though, of course, some of His acts, such as the creation of light on the first day, must have been instantaneous). Rather, its true purpose was to reveal that the Lord God who had revealed Himself to the Hebrew race and entered into personal covenant relationship with them was indeed the only true God, the Creator of all things that are. This stood in direct opposition to the religious notions of the heathen around them, who assumed the emergence of pantheon of gods in successive stages out of preexistent matter of unknown origin, actuated by forces for which there was no accounting.[97]

Below, we see more examples of accounts within creation that are not instantaneous.

Genesis 2:8-9 American Standard Version (ASV)

[8] And Jehovah God planted a garden in Eden, in the East, and there he put the man whom he had formed. [9] And **out of the ground made Jehovah God to grow every tree** that is pleasant to the sight, and good for food; the tree of life also in the midst of the garden, and the tree of the knowledge of good and evil.

The straightforward reading of this text is that it is not an instantaneous creation. It is that Jehovah God planted the trees, and they grew, as we understand trees grow, in a normal fashion.

---

[97] Gleason L. Archer, New International Encyclopedia of Bible Difficulties, Zondervan's Understand the Bible Reference Series, 59-60 (Grand Rapids, MI: Zondervan Publishing House, 1982).

Genesis 1:11-12 English Standard Version (ESV)

11 And God said, "Let the earth sprout vegetation, plants yielding seed, and fruit trees bearing fruit in which is their seed, each according to its kind, on the earth." And it was so. **12** The earth **brought forth vegetation**, plants yielding seed according to their own kinds, and trees bearing fruit in which is their seed, each according to its kind. And God saw that it was good.

Here again, the straightforward reading, we are seeing the natural process of all vegetation, as opposed to it being created instantly.

In addition, it should be noted that God's Word explicitly helps man to appreciate that a "day" to Jehovah God is not measured in the same way as man.

Psalm 90:4: For in Your sight a thousand years are like yesterday that passes by, like a few hours of the night.

2 Peter 3:8: Dear friends, don't let this one thing escape you: with the Lord one day is like 1,000 years, and 1,000 years like one day.

2 Peter 3:10: But the Day of the Lord will come like a thief; on that [day] the heavens will pass away with a loud noise, the elements will burn and be dissolved, and the earth and the works on it will be disclosed.

Going Back to the Beginning

Genesis 1:1 English Standard Version (ESV)

¹ **In the beginning**, God created the heavens and the earth.

What do we learn from this one little phrase? **First**, the universe had a beginning. **Second**, since Jehovah God is the Creator of the Universe, then his existence is outside of creation. In other words, God is existing outside the material universe and so not limited by it. He is beyond, outside of his creation. **Third**, prior to the creation account of the universe, there was no matter and energy. Rather, the universe was created from nothing. **Fourth**, before Genesis 1:1 activity, there was no time as we know it. **Fifth**, God is the sovereign of the universe, and it is him alone that sets the laws and standards that exist under the umbrella of that sovereignty. The 24 elders on the Revelation of John proclaim, "Worthy are you, our Lord and God, to receive glory and honor and power, for you created all things, and by your will they existed and were created." (Rev. 4:11) It is beyond science as to how matter and energy came into existence, because what they do know by natural law (thermodynamics), 'energy cannot be created or destroyed.' All science can do is accept the matter and energy are givens. On the other hand, God's Word is clear that he supernaturally created matter, energy, space, and time as well as the laws that govern them.

Genesis 1:2 English Standard Version (ESV)

² The earth was without form and void, and darkness was over the face of the deep. And the Spirit of God was hovering over the face of the waters.

In order to deal with the scientific view that the universe is 20 billion years old, they would postulate that that time is to be found between Genesis 1:1 and 1:2. This is why in some translations, you find a space between verse 1 and verse 2, which is known as the Gap Theory (or Restitution Theory).[98] There is no reason to suggest such an idea, it is simply that God by way of his human author, Moses, informed the readers of the creation of the universe, followed by the condition of the earth, before God turn his attention to carrying out acts of creation on the earth, to prepare it for human habitation. According to verses 1 and 2, the universe, which includes the earth was in existence for an unknown period of time before God began the creative days.

First Day: Light (1:3–5)

Genesis 1:3-5 Updated American Standard Version (UASV)

3And God proceeded to say, "Let light come to be, and there came to be light. 4 And God saw that the light was good. And God divided the light from the darkness. 5 God began calling the light Day, and the darkness he called Night. And there came to be evening and there came to be morning, one day.

There are many different interpretations about how long the Genesis creation days were. We are only going to concern ourselves with two, because one is the orthodox position, the other is the second most common position and the position of the author. For a discussion of the length of the Genesis day, please see the first difficulty in the Bible Difficulties in Genesis, Genesis 1:1 Is the earth only 6,000 to 10,000 years old? Are the

---

[98] This is "as if some great catastrophe (presumably the fall of Satan and his banishment to Earth) befell Earth after its original perfect and complete creation. On this view the six days of creation actually represent the re-creation of the world after its original demise. This view is not widely supported today because it is neither consistent with the grammar of the text nor supportable from the scientific evidence. Nonetheless, it is impossible to know how much (if any) time elapsed between verses 1 and 2." (Whorton 2008)

creative days literally, only 24 hours long? Keep in mind that a different interpretation of this does not alter the inerrancy of Scripture, because it is an interpretation of Scripture, not an error in Scripture. Also, you can listen to the evidence, and make the decision for yourself.

When we look at verses 2-5 of Genesis chapter 1, we need to appreciate that this is not the birth of the sun and the moon; they were there in outer space long before that first creative day. However, they would not have been visible until this time, if one were on the earth. Now, on this first creative day, light evidently punched through the expanse that surrounded the earth, so that it would have been visible to an earthly observer, had there been one. Thus, there was now an evening and there was morning, the first day, because of the rotating earth.

Second Day: The Expanse (1:6–8)

Genesis 1:6-8 English Standard Version (ESV)

6 And God said, "Let there be an expanse in the midst of the waters, and let it separate the waters from the waters." **7** And God made the expanse and separated the waters that were under the expanse from the waters that were above the expanse. And it was so. **8** And God called the expanse Heaven. And there was evening and there was morning, the second day.

Some older translations like the King James Version and the American Standard Version read, "let there be a firmament." Modern translations read like the ESV above, "let there be an expanse." Bible critics tried to use the rendering "firmament" to say that the Bible writers borrowed from the creation myths, as some are picture with this "firmament" as a metal dome. However, even within the King James Version, the marginal reading is "firmament." The Hebrew word, raqia, for "expanse" means "to spread out, stamp, or expand."

We do not understand how the Almighty God brought this separation about, pushing the waters up from the earth, until "waters that were above the expanse" surrounded the circle of the earth. Genesis 1:20 reads "let birds fly above the earth across the expanse of the heavens."

What took place on the second "day"? How have Bible critics tried to us the poor translation of the Hebrew word for "expanse"? What picture can you draw in your mind as God accomplished the separation of the waters from the waters?

Third Day (a): Land (1:9–10)

Genesis 1:9-10 English Standard Version (ESV)

9 And God said, "Let the waters under the heavens be gathered together into one place, and let the dry land appear." And it was so. **10** God called the dry land Earth, and the waters that were gathered together he called Seas. And God saw that it was good.

Again, we should not expect Moses to disclose explicit detail as to how this was accomplished. However, we can see the exercise of great power on the part of God, as we are being informed about incredible earth movements in the formation of land areas. The geologist, who studies the structure of the earth, would see verses 9-10 as a series of sudden violent catastrophes. Moses, on the other hand, indicates clear direction and control by our Creator, as he formed the earth to be inhabited.

In the book of Job, He questions God. Therefore, God takes Job to task over the creation account, by asking Job numerous questions that emphasizes the greatness of God over against man. Where was Job when the earth was created? Can job measure the earth? How is it that the earth just hangs in the sky?

Job 38:3-6 English Standard Version (ESV)

³ Dress for action like a man;
 I will question you, and you make it known to me.

⁴ "Where were you when I laid the foundation of the earth?
 Tell me, if you have understanding.
⁵ Who determined its measurements—surely you know!
 Or who stretched the line upon it?
⁶ On what were its bases sunk,
 or who laid its cornerstone,

Third Day (b): Vegetation (1:11-13)

Genesis 1:11 English Standard Version (ESV)

¹¹ And God said, "Let the earth sprout vegetation, plants yielding seed, and fruit trees bearing fruit in which is their seed, each according to its kind, on the earth." And it was so.

The light from the sun was now coming through the expanse much stronger by this time, to the point of photosynthesis, which is an absolute need to green plants. This is the process by which green plants and other organisms turn carbon dioxide and water into carbohydrates and oxygen, using light energy trapped by chlorophyll.

Fourth Day: Sun, Moon, and Stars, (1:14–19)

Genesis 1:3, 5 English Standard Version (ESV)

³And God said, "**Let there be light**," and there was light. ⁵And there was evening and there was morning, **the first day**.

Genesis 1:16, 19 English Standard Version (ESV)

¹⁶And **God made the two great lights**—the greater light to rule the day and the lesser light to rule the night—and the stars. ¹⁹And there was evening and there was morning**, the fourth day**.

In the above there appears to be a Bible difficulty, in that Genesis 1:3, 5 informs the reader that God brought about light during the first creation day, when he said: "'Let there be light,' and there was light." Then, Genesis 1:16, 19 informs the reader that "God made the two great lights" during the fourth creation day. Hence, did God create or make light on the first or fourth creation day? Before we begin to answer this difficulty, we must bear in mind that Genesis was written from a human perspective, as an earthly observer, as if he were there; not from a heavenly observation.

In looking at the fourth creation day first, we see that the "greater light" for ruling the day is our sun, and the "lesser light" for ruling the night is our moon. A further explanation of this is found at Psalm 136:7-9 (ASV): "To him that made great lights; for his loving-kindness endures forever: The sun to rule by day; for his loving-kindness endures forever; the moon and stars to rule by night; for his loving-kindness endures forever."

Returning to the first creation day, we find the expression: "let there be light." *Ohr* is the Hebrew word for light, which conveys the idea of light in a broad sense. However, for the fourth creation day, a different word is chosen, *maohr*, which refers to a source of light. Rotherham, in a footnote on "Luminaries" in the *Emphasised Bible*, says: "In ver. 3, *'ôr* [*ohr*], light diffused." Then he goes on to show that the Hebrew word *maohr* in verse 14 has the sense of something "affording light." In other words, on the first creation day *ohr* (light) was spread throughout the earth's atmosphere (being diffused). To an earthly observer, had he been there: he would have not been able to discern the source of light. However, by the fourth creation day, the observer would have been able to see the *maohr* (source) of that light, as the atmosphere would have changed.

It should also be noted that Genesis 1:16 does not use the Hebrew verb bara, meaning, "create." Instead, the Hebrew verb asah is used, meaning, "make." The reason being, Genesis 1:1 informs us "God created the heavens (which would include sun, moon and stars) and the earth." In other words, the "greater light" (sun) and the "lesser light" (moon) were created long before the fourth creation day. What we have on the fourth creation day is Jehovah God "making" the "greater light" and the "lesser light" to exist in a new way with the surface of the earth and the expanse that had now dissipated even further, allowing the source of light to be seen from earth. God said, "Let there be lights in the expanse of the heavens . . ." (Gen 1:14). This being a further indication of their discernibleness. In addition, they were "to separate the day from the night. And let them be for signs and for seasons, and for days and years." These were to evidence the existence of God and draw attention to His great power, as well as lead man in numerous ways.

Those who steadfastly argue for the young earth view in light of all the evidence against this, here again, this creates a problem, because they also argue that the earth's sun was not created until the fourth day, it literally did not exist until the fourth day. Some suggest that the light from the first creation day was not from our sun but from another source, maybe a temporary light source, or the illumination of God himself. The problem with this, there literal 24 hour days for the first three days had solar days, because they see the text "there was evening and there was morning" as literal. How do you have solar days for three creation days, without our sun? If these three creative days are not defined by our sun, then the length of those days are unclear. As you can see, this is just another monumental difficulty for those that would take the creation account to be literal, when it was not meant to be taken that way.

Fifth Day: Sea Animals and Birds, (1:20–25)

Genesis 1:20-21 English Standard Version (ESV)

20 And God said, "Let the waters swarm with swarms of living creatures [souls],[99] and let birds fly above the earth across the expanse of the heavens." **21** So God created the great sea creatures and every living creature [soul] that moves, with which the waters swarm, according to their kinds, and every winged bird according to its kind. And God saw that it was good.

---

[99] Heb., nephesh chaiyah, singular, "living soul"

The literal translations here decided to be a little more dynamic equivalent in their rendering of the Hebrew nephesh chaiyah, living soul. The term applies to the creatures in the sea, as well as the birds 'flying above the earth across the expanse of the heavens.' This would also apply to the fossil remains of sea monsters that have been discovered in recent times. If we are to fully understand the soul, it would be best to render the Hebrew nephesh (soul) and the Greek Psyche (soul) literally.

Sixth Day: Land Animals and Man, (1:24–31)

Genesis 1:24-31 Lexham English Bible (LEB)

[24] And God said, "Let the earth bring forth living creatures according to their kind: cattle and moving things, and wild animals according to their kind." And it was so. [25] So God made wild animals according to their kind and the cattle according to their kind, and every creeping thing of the earth according to its kind. And God saw that *it was* good.

[26] And God said, "Let us make humankind in our image and according to our likeness, and let them rule over the fish of the sea, and over the birds of heaven, and over the cattle, and over all the earth, and over every moving thing that moves upon the earth." [27] So God created humankind in his image, in the likeness of God he created him, male and female he created them. [28] And God blessed them, and God said to them, "Be fruitful and multiply, and fill the earth and subdue it, and rule over the fish of the sea and the birds of heaven, and over every animal that moves upon the earth."

[29] And God said, "Look—I am giving to you every plant *that* bears seed which *is* on the face of the whole

earth, and every kind of tree *that bears fruit*. They shall be yours as food." ³⁰ And to every kind of animal of the earth and to every bird of heaven, and to everything that moves upon the earth in which *there is* life *I am giving* every green plant as food." And it was so. ³¹ And God saw everything that he had made and, behold, *it was* very good. And there was evening, and there was morning, a sixth day.

As you can see on the sixth creation day we are introduced to the creation of both domestic and wild animals, these being in relation to what man could tame and use domestically, as opposed to what remain wild. Within this creation period was also the greatest of all creation, the creation of both man and woman. It with the creation of humans alone that it was said they were 'created in the image of God.'

Then there is the problem of the seventh day, as far as the young earth view is concerned: it never ended. There was no opening and closing, as occurred with the preceding six days; it is still in progress from the close of the sixth day, more than 6,000 years ago.

Hebrews 4:4, 5, 9–11: For somewhere He has spoken about the seventh day in this way: And on the seventh day God rested from all His works. Again, in that passage [He says], They will never enter My rest. A Sabbath rest remains, therefore, for God's people. For the person who has entered His rest has rested from his own works, just as God did from His. Let us then make every effort to enter that rest, so that no one will fall into the same pattern of disobedience.

Clearly, the context of God's Word as a whole shows the earth to be much older than 6,000+ years.

Habakkuk 3:6: He stood, and measured the earth; He beheld, and drove asunder the nations; And the *eternal mountains* were scattered; The *everlasting hills* did bow; His goings were as of old.

Micah 6:2: Hear, O ye mountains, Jehovah's controversy, and ye *enduring foundations of the earth*; for Jehovah hath a controversy with his people, and he will contend with Israel.

Proverbs 8:22-23 (ASV): Jehovah possessed me in the beginning of his way, Before his works of old. I was set up from everlasting, from the beginning, Before the earth was.

The writer of Proverbs is using the age of the earth to emphasize that wisdom is much older. But if one accepts the young-earth theory (4004 B.C.E. for the creation of man),[100] when Solomon, who died shortly after 1000 B.C.E., wrote this, the earth would have been only about 3,000 years old—so not much of an emphasis.

Science has established that light travels at 186,282 miles per second. We know that it takes 100,000 years for light to cross our galaxy. We also know that it has taken hundreds of millions of years for the light of the stars we now see to reach the earth. Let us not repeat the Galileo history once more. It takes humility to learn from past experience. The Galileo conflict between science and the Church should at the very least help Christendom to avoid taking "day" as a literal 24-hour day when Scripture itself allows for another understanding; context weighs in that direction and science has established that the earth and the universe are far older than 6,000–

---

100. Archbishop James Usher (1581–1656) developed a chronology of the Bible, and dated creation at 4004 B.C.E.

10,000 years. Regardless of whether some scholars will concede to the correct understanding, this would in no way put the Bible in the wrong, for it is its interpreters who have misunderstood it. We must keep in mind that science (or the scientist) has no quarrel with the Bible: the quarrel would be with the misinterpretation of the teachers of Christendom, orthodox Jews, and others.

The website ChristianAnswers.Net concludes: "The lesson to be learned from Galileo, it appears, is not that the Church held too tightly to biblical truths; but rather that it did not hold tightly enough. It allowed Greek philosophy to influence its theology and held to tradition rather than to the teachings of the Bible. We must hold strongly to Biblical doctrine, which has been achieved through sure methods of exegesis. We must never be satisfied with dogmas built upon philosophic traditions."[101] However, it is also true that science alone should not determine our interpretation, but it is to be used in a balanced way, as another source to consider.

The theologians of the Inquisition and Pope Urban VIII in fact, condemned the Copernican theory. They argued that it contradicted the Bible: to be specific, Joshua's statement: "O sun, stand still . . . So the sun stood still, and the moon stopped." (Joshua 10:12, *ESV*) Of course, this is not meant to be taken literally. There are several reasonable explanations, one of which, I will give you here. Verse 13 says that "the sun stopped in the midst of heaven and did not hurry to set for about a whole day." This could simply allow for a slower movement of the earth, giving the appearance to an earthly observer that the sun and moon had stood still. As for another reasonable explanation, one Bible

---

101.   http://www.christiananswers.net/q-eden/edn-c007.html. (Accessed January 28, 2010.)

encyclopedia comments: "While this could mean a stopping of earth's rotation, it could have been accomplished by other means, such as a refraction of solar and lunar light rays to produce the same effect." Therefore, once more, it becomes obvious that the Bible does not contradict itself.

In Summary

- The Hebrew word for day that was used for the creation days of Genesis chapter 1 is the same word used at Genesis 2:4 as a reference to the whole of the creative period, six days, "in the day that . . ."
- The Bible uses the word for "day" as longer periods than a 24-hour day "one day is as a thousand years." (2 Peter 3:8; Psalm 90:4)
- There are indicators within the first two chapters that we are dealing with periods longer than 24-hour days.
- (1) **Third Day**: At Genesis 1:11-12, we find that trees grew from seeds to maturity, and produced seeds of their kind. This takes months, even years.
- (2) **Sixth day**: We find Adam was created, went to sleep, named thousands of animals (names that indicate observation of the animals), grew lonely (looking for a helper), went to sleep, Eve was produced out of Adam's rib. This is obviously longer than 24 hours.
- (3) **Seventh Day**: Genesis 2:2 informs us that God "proceeded to rest."[102] The reader will note that Hebrews 4:4 shows that God is still in his rest from the ending of the six creative days. Therefore, the seventh day has been running for thousands of years

---

[102] Why do I have it rendered as a continuous, "proceeded to rest", when most translations read "he rested"? Heb., waiyishboth (imperfect sequential): The verb is in the imperfect state denoting incomplete or continuous action, or action in progress.

thus far, which allows the other creative days to be thousands of years long.

As it usually turns out, the so-called contradiction between science and God's Word lies at the feet of those who are interpreting Scripture incorrectly. To repeat the sentiments of Galileo when writing to a pupil—Galileo expressed the same sentiments: "Even though Scripture cannot err, its interpreters and expositors can, in various ways. One of these, very serious and very frequent, would be when they always want to stop at the purely literal sense."[103] I believe that today's scholars, in hindsight, would have no problem agreeing.

---

103. Letter from Galileo to Benedetto Castelli, December 21, 1613.

BASIC TEACHING: Who Is the Avenging Messenger that Destroys the Wicked Ones?

Herein we will discuss Ezekiel 9:1-11 verse-by-verse, where God sends six executioners and man with inkhorn, to execute all, who were committing detestable things, but to spare those who had a mark on their foreheads because they had been sighing and groaning over the gross sin in Jerusalem. What did this mean for Jerusalem at the time, and what does it mean for us today?

Blessed are Those Who Hear the Word of God and Keep It

Luke 11:28 English Standard Version (ESV)

28 But he [Jesus] said, "Blessed rather are those who hear the word of God and keep it!"

> True blessing comes to those who hear and obey God's Word (see 8:1–21). Dedication to Jesus involves more than saying good things about him. Dedication to Jesus means listening and obeying. (Buter 2000, 187)

God has always worked toward bringing happiness to his human creation in the most loving way. In the beginning, he made our first parents Adam and Eve perfect, placing them in a paradise garden, likely the size of the state of Rhode Island. He gave them the opportunity at everlasting life here on earth, which they would cultivate into a global paradise, having a beautiful animal kingdom and a loving relationship with their Creator. Even when Adam and Eve rejected God's sovereignty, he moved to offer his Son as a seed, who would offer his own life as a ransom.

Death Came through Adam but Life Comes through Christ

John 3:16 New American Standard Bible (NASB)

[16] "For God so loved the world, that He gave His only begotten Son, that whoever believes in Him shall not perish, but have eternal life.

Matthew 20:28 English Standard Version (ESV)

[28] even as the Son of Man came not to be served but to serve, and to give his life as a ransom for many."

Romans 5:12 English Standard Version (ESV)

[12] Therefore, just as sin came into the world through one man, and death through sin, and so death spread to all men because all sinned

Certainly, few would deny that world conditions today are filled with wickedness at every turn. Most of the world is living in poverty to the point of starvation. Terrorism has had the world in its grips since 9/11, 2001. There seems to be one natural disaster after another, taking hundreds of thousands of lives the world over. Cruel crimes like murder, kidnapping, and rape are so common; it no longer seems to shock us. The world seems to be heading from socialism, to outright communism, with few citizens even noticing until it is too late.

Godlessness in the Last Days

Revelation 12:9-12 New American Standard Bible (NASB)

⁹ And the great dragon was thrown down, the serpent of old who is called the devil and Satan, who deceives the whole world; he was thrown down to the earth, and his angels were thrown down with him. … ¹² For this reason, rejoice, O heavens and you who dwell in them. Woe to the earth and the sea, because the devil has come down to you, having great wrath, knowing that he has *only* a short time."

2 Timothy 3:1-5 English Standard Version (ESV)

¹ But understand this, that in the last days there will come times of difficulty. ² For people will be lovers of self, lovers of money, proud, arrogant, abusive, disobedient to their parents, ungrateful, unholy, ³ heartless, unappeasable, slanderous, without self-control, brutal, not loving good, ⁴ treacherous, reckless, swollen with conceit, lovers of pleasure rather than lovers of God, ⁵ having the appearance of godliness, but denying its power. Avoid such people.

Therefore, the need has grown so great for the people to hear,

Matthew 24:14 Holman Christian Standard Bible (HCSB)

¹⁴ This good news of the kingdom will be proclaimed in all the world as a testimony to all nations. And then the end will come.

Vision of Abominations in Jerusalem

Ezekiel 8:1-18: In the sixth year, in the sixth month, on the fifth day of the month, **Ezekiel had a vision**, in which he was carried several hundred miles back to Jerusalem by. There he is shown disgusting things that are taking place in the temple of Jehovah. Ezekiel was first brought to the entrance of the north gate of the Temple's inside court, and just north of the entrance loomed the altar of the sex goddess, Asherah. He was then brought me to the door of the Temple court. I looked and saw a gaping hole in the wall. Engraved all around the wall was every form of detestable thing, crawling creatures and beasts, as well as all the idols of the house of Israel. Ezekiel saw Seventy elders from the house of Israel worshiping before the wall. They try to offer excuses, "Jehovah does not see us. Jehovah has abandoned the land." (8:12) Ezekiel was then taken to the entrance at the north gate of the Temple of God. He saw women sitting there, weeping for Tammuz, the Babylonian fertility god. Finally, he Ezekiel was taken to the inside court of the Temple of God. There between the porch and the altar were about twenty-five men. Their backs were to God's Temple. They were facing east, bowing in worship to the sun. What was Jehovah God's reaction?

Ezekiel 8:18 Updated American Standard Version (UASV)

[18] Therefore, I [Jehovah] will act in wrath. My eye will not spare, nor will I have pity. And though they cry in my ears with a loud voice, I will not hear them."

The Vision of Slaughter

Ezekiel 9:1-2 Updated American Standard Version (UASV)

1 Then he [Jehovah] cried in my ears with a loud voice, saying, "Come near, O executioners of the city, each with his smashing (destroying) weapon in his hand!" **2** And behold, six men came from the way of the upper gate, which faces toward the north, each man with his slaughter weapon in his hand; and one man in the midst of them clothed in linen, with a writer's inkhorn[104] at his waist, and they went in, and stood beside the bronze altar.

The vision of the defiled temple from chapter 8 remained over Ezekiel. In the above verse 1, Ezekiel begins to inform us of what took place next, as Jehovah God began to call out into his ear with a loud voice. Those being called were executioners, with their

---

104

If like inkhorns of recent antiquity, the writing kit or inkhorn consisted of two parts, a receptacle for the pens and a box for the ink. Sometimes it was made of ebony or some other hard wood, but generally of metal: bronze, copper, or silver; often highly polished and of exquisite workmanship. It was about nine or ten inches long, one and a half or two inches wide, and about half an inch deep. The hollow shaft contained pens of reed and a penknife and had a lid. The inkhorn was usually carried in the belt or suspended by cords. -- James M. Freeman and Harold J. Chadwick, *Manners & Customs of the Bible* (North Brunswick, NJ: Bridge-Logos Publishers, 1998), 380.

weapons of destruction in hand, being brought in to destroy the inhabitants. Who were they? It says that they were "executioners." Most have suggested these to be guards, saying that the word $p^equddot$ can mean, "To be in charge of appointments and administration of punishment."[105] The ESV, NRSV, HCSB and the NASB translate it "executioners" here, with the NIV (2011) spelling it out more clearly, "Bring near those who are appointed to execute judgment on the city." Most commentaries refer to these ones as 'city guards,' while going on to say that they are also angels. However, the suggestion that they are city guards does not seem to be the case.

In verse 2 they are referred to as "men," which would seem to bolster the idea of their being guards of the city. However, the context of this chapter demonstrates that they were more than human, and angels were often referred to as men, when they were sent to earth as messengers. (See, e.g., Gen 18:2; 32:24; Dan 10:5) Angels have the power to materialize in human form. Therefore, the "six men" in Ezekiel's vision were evidently materialized angelic messengers, who were sent to hand out judgment on the inhabitants, who lacked remorse and repentance over the abominations within the city. There were seven, if we count the one, who was clothed in linen; therefore, this could stand for completeness as to the actions they were about to take.[106] Verse 2 singled out the man in linen by his clothing, and the fact that he was sent ahead of the others. It may also be that this, "one man in the midst of

---

[105] Fisch, *Ezekiel*, 47; Taylor, *Ezekiel*, 101.

[106] Seven was the number symbolic of completeness in Jewish apocalyptic and suggested that their actions would be conclusive. -- Lamar Eugene Cooper, *Ezekiel*, vol. 17, The New American Commentary (Nashville: Broadman & Holman Publishers, 1994), 127.

them clothed in linen, with a writer's inkhorn," was of a higher rank, i.e., a higher position.

In Ezekiel's vision, what is the assignment of this 'one man clothed in linen'? This was/is cleared up for the reader as God lays out his commission. Listen,

Ezekiel 9:3-4 Updated American Standard Version (UASV)

³ Then the glory of the God of Israel had gone up from the cherub on which it rested to the threshold of the house. And he called to the man clothed in linen, who had the writer's inkhorn by his waist. ⁴ And Jehovah said to him, "Pass through the midst of the city, through the midst of Jerusalem, and put a mark on the foreheads of the men who sigh and groan over all the abominations that are committed in it."

The man in linen is being sent on a mission of mercy, to help save the lives of the righteous ones within Jerusalem. In verse 3, we are told, "the glory of the God of Israel had gone up from the cherub on which it rested to the threshold of the house."[107] This is fittingly, the innermost compartment of the temple, namely, the threshold of the Holy of Holies, where the Ark of the Covent was located. 'The mercy seat [atonement cover] was on the ark of the testimony, from between the two cherubim.' Between the two cherubs was the Shekinah[108]

---

[107] "The use of the singular [keruv] instead of the plural is unusual, but the reference is doubtless to the two [keruvim] that sat atop the ark and formed the mercy seat." (Zimmerli 1979, 254)

[108] **SHEKINAH** (Shě kī' nah) Transliteration of Hebrew word not found in the Bible but used in many of the Jewish writings to speak of God's presence. The term means "that which dwells," and is implied throughout the Bible whenever it refers to God's nearness either in a person, object, or His glory. (Brand, Draper and Archie 2003, 1480)

appeared, which was a symbol of God's presence in the Most Holy. (Numbers 7:89) It is from here that God handed down his orders to the man clothed in linen, to go through Jerusalem ahead of the other "six men," using his pen and ink to place a mark on the foreheads of all who were groaning and sighing over the detestable things being done in Jerusalem.

Everyone in Jerusalem was in grave danger, as his or her lives were uncertain, because God was about act in wrath. His eye was not going to spare, nor was he going to have pity. Even though these ones would surely cry in his ears with a loud voice, he was not going to hear them. (8:18) These sentiments are not necessarily all encompassing, as he is a God of justice, who will not destroy the righteous with the unrighteous. Well, then upon whom was the wrath of God to be felt? It would be those, who were involved in the detestable things mentioned in Ezekiel chapter 8. Those who survived would be those who viewed these actions as an abomination.

The man with the inkhorn was to pass through the midst of the city, placing a mark on the foreheads of the righteous ones, where it would be visible to all, including the six men, who were to follow. "The 'mark' was therefore to distinguish the righteous from the guilty."[109] This would require the man with the inkhorn to travel the entire Jerusalem community, including the gates, where people did business, and from house to house, to carry out his mission of locating and marking those that were rightly disposed for life. These ones were offended daily over the false worship, the setting aside the only true God, for idol worship, for false gods like Tammuz,

---

[109] Lamar Eugene Cooper, *Ezekiel*, vol. 17, The New American Commentary (Nashville: Broadman & Holman Publishers, 1994), 127.

and sun worship, among other things. This mark would serve to identify these ones as true worshipers. How important was the work of the man with the inkhorn? This becomes apparent from what Ezekiel tells his listeners next,

Ezekiel 9:5-6 Updated American Standard Version (UASV)

⁵ And to the others he said in my hearing, "Pass through the city after him, and strike. Your eye shall not spare, and you shall show no pity. ⁶ slay utterly the old man, the young man and the virgin and little children and women; but come not near any man upon whom is the mark. And begin at my sanctuary." So they started with the elders who *were* before the house.

Yes, the divine directions, these six angelic men were to pass by all Israelites, who had their foreheads marked, as they went about killing the inhabitants of Jerusalem. The instruments for smashing obviously were meant for smashing the skulls of those, who were worthy of being executed. Therefore, it seems quite appropriate that the foreheads of true worshipers were to be marked for survival. No one was to be spared, be it they elderly, or the weaker vessel of women, or even young children, unless they had a mark. Therefore, children would be marked as well. God's foreknowledge would allow him to be well aware of the actions of the young children in the years to come, when

Adolf Hitler as an Infant April 20, 1889 – April 30, 1945)

they were at the age of accountability and older.

Small Excursion

If anyone of us had the ability perfectly to foresee the future of anyone, and we lived in the small town of Sulzberger Vorstadt, Germany in 1890, when Adolf Hitler was but an infant, we would not lose one night's sleep over executing him as an infant. Let us take a more Sci-Fi (syfy) look at the above idea. Suppose we could currently travel back in time, and was able to go back to 1890, to execute infant Adolf Hitler, no one would likely see a problem with this, knowing that he would slaughter six million Jews some 40-years later. Therefore, considering God's foreknowledge of the future, and that the man with the inkhorn was an angelic representative, as were the six other men, so they could perfectly carry out his commission to cleanse Jerusalem of its wicked element. This is a total cleansing, even of those, who were yet to commit the disgusting abominations.

Counterfactuals are conditional statements in the subjunctive mood: for example, "If I were rich, I would buy a Mercedes"; "If Barry Goldwater had been elected president, he would have won the Vietnam War"; and "If you were to ask her, she would say yes." Counterfactuals are so called because the antecedent or consequent clauses are typically contrary to fact: I am not rich, Goldwater was not elected president, and the U.S. did not win the Vietnam War. Nevertheless, sometimes the antecedent and/or consequent is true. For example, your friend wants to ask the girl of his dreams for a date and, emboldened by your reassurance that "If you were to ask her, she would say yes," does ask her and she does say

265

yes. One of the leading apologists of the 20th century and now the 21st century, William Lane Craig writes

Counterfactual statements make up an enormous and significant part of our ordinary language and are an indispensable part of our decision making: For example, "If I pulled out into traffic now, I wouldn't make it"; "If I were to ask J. B. for a raise with his mood, he'd tear my head off"; "If we sent the Third Army around the enemy's right flank, we would prevail." Clearly life-and-death decisions are made daily on the basis of the presumed truth of counterfactual statements.

Christian theologians have typically affirmed that in virtue of his omniscience, God possesses counterfactual knowledge. He knows, for example, what would have happened if he had spared the Canaanites from destruction, what Napoleon would have done had he won the Battle of Waterloo, and how Jones would respond if I were to share the gospel with him.[110]

_____

[110] James K. Beilby;Paul R. Eddy. *Divine Foreknowledge: Four Views* (p. 120). Kindle Edition.

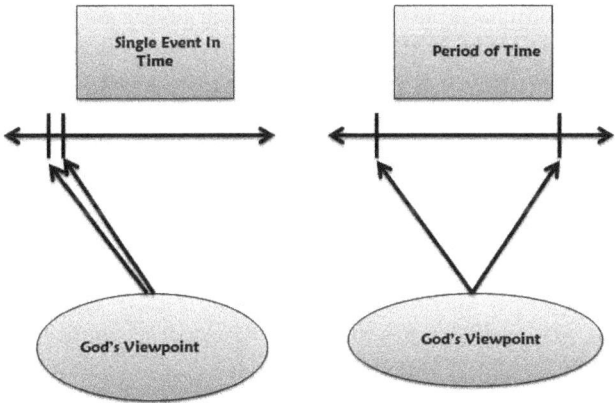

Image 2 Foreknowledge of God

I spent some time reading an article from Craig, where he used 2,523 words rationalizing how God could command someone, be it human soldiers or angelic representatives, to execute young children, even infants.[111] Personally, I feel that he dodged the obvious, God has the foreknowledge to see what one will do, and if we believe in an Almighty God, this is not as objectionable as it might seem. Nevertheless, he is responding to atheists, skeptics, and Bible critics, so he is trying to find a rational reason for such a command, as their preunderstanding is that the miraculous is impossible. Nevertheless, let us say that God is cleansing an evil, wickedness in the Bible, he is able to see, just like in image 2 above, because he is outside of time, and can look at the timeline of any event.

Before God carried out his very first creative act, there was no time, as we humans know it. Once the universe(s) were created, the sun and the moon have

---

[111] http://www.reasonablefaith.org/slaughter-of-the-canaanites

served humans as a timepiece for determining the seasons, days, and years. (Gen 1:14-18) Before the creation, there was no time for God to be outside of, as time did not exist. After creation God was still outside of the universe(s), his creation, in his heavenly home, meaning that, in essence, he was/is still outside of time. However, he is very much involved in his creations and is quite aware of everything that happens within his creation, as he personally involves himself, even directly at times. (1Ki 18:18-29) Therefore, on some occasions he does do a cleansing within the imperfect condition that humanity finds itself in, because it fits within the outworking of his will and purposes.

End of Excursion

Where was this judgment to begin? The six men were to begin at God's sanctuary." Therefore, they started with the elders who were before the house. Those idolaters may have felt protected within the temple, because they knew that dead bodies would defile the temple, but they were sadly mistaken. In fact, Ezekiel makes it clear that God wants to defile the temple with these idolaters.

Ezekiel 9:7 Updated American Standard Version (UASV)

7 And he said to them, "Defile the house, and fill the courtyards with the slain." Go out!" Thus, they went out and struck down *the people* in the city.

In the end, the temple did not serve these ones as some sort of place of protection, because they were the ones violating the owner of the house. The temple was no sanctuary or place of refuge from being executed for their wicked ways. Jaazaniah was the son of Shaphan; the individual in Ezekiel's vision of the 70 men who offered incense before carved idolatrous symbols in the temple at Jerusalem. (Ezekiel 8:7-11) These were the ones were first, who 'faced the executioners of the city, each with his smashing (destroying) weapon in their hand!' Then, there were the women weeping for Tammuz, the Babylonian and Sumerian god. "Twenty-five men, with their backs to the temple of Jehovah, and their faces toward the east, worshiping the sun toward the east," followed them. (Ezekiel 8:14-16) After the judgment of these ones, who one might expect to be the survivors, the house was defiled, and the courtyards were filled with slain ones.

Ezekiel was now alone; possibly feeling that if there are no survivors in the temple, what hope is there for the rest in and around the city. Ezekiel now informs his readers of his reaction to the gore before his eyes,

Ezekiel 9:8 Updated American Standard Version (UASV)

8 And while they were striking, and I was left alone, I fell upon my face, and cried, "Ah, O Lord Jehovah! Will you destroy all the remnant of Israel in the outpouring of your wrath on Jerusalem?"

Ezekiel's concern fell to the preservation of his people, hoping the whole nation was not facing extinction. This is especially true, because there were only a "remnant of Israel" left after Assyria had conquered the northern ten tribes of Israel, deporting any survivors throughout the Assyrian Empire, and brining in other conquered peoples to live in the North. Then the Babylonian Empire destroyed the Assyrian Empire; thereafter, laying siege to Jerusalem, taking King Jehoiachin and his family, along thousands of others captive to Babylon, including Ezekiel. Knowing that the promise given to Abraham was in jeopardy, or at least so it seemed, Ezekiel became frightened for what this vision portended for the future of his people and the promised seed. Ezekiel now informs his readers of Jehovah's response,

Ezekiel 9:9-10 Updated American Standard Version (UASV)

⁹ Then he said to me, "The iniquity (serious sin) of the house of Israel and Judah *is exceedingly* great, and the land is filled with blood, and the city is full of injustice. For they say Jehovah abandoned the land, and *Jehovah does not see.* ¹⁰ But as for me also, my eye will have neither pity nor will I spare, but I will bring their deeds upon their head.

Closing out this vision of the prophet Ezekiel, the reader sees that the one man with the inkhorn carrying out this work of saving lives as he was commanded, to completion.

Ezekiel 9:11 Updated American Standard Version (UASV)

¹¹ And behold, the man clothed in linen, who had the inkhorn at his waist, reported the matter, saying, "I have done as you commanded me."

God, like a loving Father had watched as his child nation, the Israelites, had delved into serious sin repeatedly for almost a thousand years. Time after time, he saved them from their false worship, their rebellion, their extreme immorality, their sacrificing their own children in the fires, to false gods. He was grief-stricken and compassionate as he sent numerous judges (Ehud, Barak, Gideon, Samson, and others) to rescue them after they failed to heed his advice, rejecting God for false gods, and not thoroughly cleansing the Promise Land. He then sent one prophet after the other, trying to steer them back on course to pure worship. Many times, they killed the very messengers God had sent.

How does this vision play out in the history of the Israelite nation? In just a few short years after his vision, the Babylonians destroyed the city of Jerusalem and the temple. Of course, in that destruction, were the "the old man, the young man and the virgin and little children and women." The Babylonians were not a nation to show pity on the people that they conquered. There was no one in any favored position that was spared Jehovah's wrath. (Ezekiel 9:6) The rulers and religious leaders were given a very violent death for their corruption and idolatrous worship. However, a remnant did survive, being taken captive to Babylon for seventy-years.

2 Kings 25:18-21 Updated American Standard Version (UASV)

¹⁸ And the captain of the guard took Seraiah the chief priest, and Zephaniah the second priest, and the three keepers of the threshold (doorkeepers, officers of the temple). ¹⁹ And out of the city he took an officer that was set over the men of war, and five men of them that saw the king's face (king's council or advisors) who were found in the city; and the scribe (secretary), the captain of the army, who mustered the people of the land; and sixty men of the people of the land, who were found in the city. ²⁰ And Nebuzaradan the captain of the guard took them and brought them to the king of Babylon at Riblah. ²¹ And the king of Babylon struck them down and put them to death at Riblah in the land of Hamath. So Judah was taken into exile out of its land.

We must understand that we are not to carry out an allegorical interpretation of every aspect of prophetic visions. It is best to see the main point, with a few likenesses that can be applicable in later times. The vision of a prophet has an overall picture with aspects that fit the historical events. For example, the above aspects fit the vision, but there were no angelic messengers that passed through the city, placing literal marks on the foreheads of the people, who were to survive. Nevertheless, these marks represent, a symbolic work, the fact that a remnant was to survive, and it would be those who had been faithful to pure worship. This is the case, a remnant did survive, and they were the ones that God selected, like Baruch the secretary of Jeremiah, and Ebed-melech the Ethiopian and the Rechabites. (Jeremiah 45:1-5; 39:15-18; 35:1-19)

Excursion on Interpreting Prophecy

We are to follow the normal grammatical-historical interpretation. By this, we mean the historical aspect would be the historical setting of the prophet. The prophecy usually has some application to their generation, or something in the near future. We have done that in the above. However, some prophecies also deal with the arrival of Christ in the first century (between 02 B.C.E. and 100 C.E.), as well as prophecies that are **farther along in time** than the end of the apostolic era, **what is known as the** "last days," "end times," or the Day of Jehovah." (Isaiah 2:2 and Micah 4:1) Then, there is "the last day," not to be confused with "last days." (John 6:39-40, 44; 11:24; 12:48) While some prophecies were pointing to a very distant future, it must be remembered that they were very applicable to the prophet's historical setting.

For example, even though Paul spoke of a coming resurrection (1 Thessalonians 4:15-17), these verses still had meaning for those in the congregation at Thessalonica. The same holds true, when Paul writes his second letter to the Thessalonians, informing them that they were in error for seeing the "day of the Lord" as coming in the first century. "For that day will not come unless the apostasy comes first and the man of lawlessness is revealed, the son of destruction." (2 Thessalonians 2:1-3) The Apostle John wrote the book of Revelation, which has apocalyptic prophecies for what we call the end times, but it was meaningful for a Christianity suffering under the persecution of Roman Emperor Domitian (51-96 C.E.), as it offered hope to circumstances that seemed hopeless. (Revelation 20:4-6, 12)

Then, we must turn our attention to the grammatical aspects of our prophetic verses. Again, we must never assume that the words and the sentences that hold them are to be treated differently in this genre. The norms of grammatical interpretation are to be applied here as well. We have done that in the above. True, there are symbolic and figurative expressions within prophecy, but this does not lesson our need to interpret them literally. How do we do that? We ascertain what the symbolic or figurative language stands for, and this is what we take literally. Isaiah says that we will live beyond 100 years of age during the millennium, and we now live 2,700 years after Isaiah and counting, still awaiting that millennium.

Well, the righteous spoken of in Isaiah 65:20 will live forever, not just longer than one hundred years. However, this statement was made at a time when the life expectancy was in the thirties. Therefore, to say the righteous will celebrate their one-hundredth birthday as a norm, was to make the point of a very long life. The point of a very long life is what we trust to become true and take literally. Additionally, just because symbolic and figurative language is found in prophecy, this does not mean that all prophecy is to be taken figuratively and symbolically. When we look at the next verse in Isaiah, which applies to the millennium, we do not take these words figuratively, "They shall build houses and inhabit them; they shall plant vineyards and eat their fruit." (Zuck 1991, 241-243) The question now is how we might apply Ezekiel's words at Isaiah 9:1-11 to our time.

What about the "one man in the midst of them clothed in linen, with a writer's inkhorn," who was to "Pass through the midst of the city, through the midst of Jerusalem, and put a mark on the foreheads of the men who sigh and groan over all the abominations that are committed in it"? Is this one symbolic of someone in our day? Who are the ones today, who are sighing and groaning over the detestable things being done in the antitypical Jerusalem? Here we look to the interpretation of the Bible Knowledge Commentary.

God told the scribe dressed **in linen, Go throughout ... Jerusalem and put a mark on the foreheads of those who grieve and lament over the detestable things** in **the city**. God knew those who had remained faithful to Him, and would spare them in His judgment (cf. God's marking of the 144,000 for preservation during the Tribulation, Rev. 7:3–4).

God then told the guards to **follow** the scribe **through the city and kill, without showing pity**. Those not receiving **the mark** were to be destroyed. There was to be no distinction by age or sex; the judgment would come on the **old** and **young**, on **men ... women, and children**.

Then God ordered the guards, **Begin at** the **sanctuary**. Significantly the judgment first began in the house of God (cf. 1 Peter 4:17). Since the evil had spread from the temple throughout the land (Ezek. 8), the judgment would follow the same course. So the guards **began with the elders**, the priests whose backs were turned to God (8:16). Their slaughter would **defile the temple and fill the courts with the slain**, but the temple had already been defiled with their idolatrous practices. The historical fulfillment of this is seen in 2 Chronicles 36:17–19.[112]

In finding any corresponding implications for our day, or during the future Tribulation, there must be the same pattern of meaning. What are the basic points of Ezekiel 9:1-11?

- God poured out his wrath on his chosen people, the Israelites, who were deeply involved in unclean worship.
- However, God sent someone to mark those fit for survival. What were the criteria for receiving this mark?
- They were sighing and groaning over the detestable unclean worship.
- Six other men were order to execute those involved in unclean worship. Where were they to start?
- Judgment was to start at the sanctuary, i.e., the religious leaders.
- A remnant survived this judgment because of the mark that they possessed.

---

[112] Charles H. Dyer, "Ezekiel," ed. J. F. Walvoord and R. B. Zuck, *The Bible Knowledge Commentary: An Exposition of the Scriptures* (Wheaton, IL: Victor Books, 1985), 1245.

Without getting into the specifics of who is who and what role each party plays, let us first talk about what we have today.

We have a Christianity that is divided into 41,000 denominations. We have liberal Christianity (false Christianity), who make up about eighty-five percent of those 41,000 denominations, and have abandoned pure worship, for unclean worship. We have moderate Christianity, who makes up about ten percent of the 41,000 denominations, while trying to walk the line of unclean and clean worship, which they do by **not** taking a stand for clean worship. We have a remnant of five percent, who are solidly on the clean worship side of the line, but who are still failing to carry out the Great Commission assigned them.

I would emphasize that, we are to evangelize, so as to make disciples, which is more involved that simply sharing the Gospel. Paul summarizes the most basic elements of the gospel message, that is, the death, burial, resurrection, and appearances of the resurrected Christ. (1 Cor. 18:1-8) Therefore, the Gospel explained in detail or simply stated as Paul has put it, will not be enough to convert many unbelievers to the faith. Therefore, it is best to understand our responsibility as evangelist, in the sense of being able to proclaim or explain our Christian teachings both offensively and defensively: to **(1)** defend God's Word, **(2)** defend the faith, **(3)** pull some who doubt back from the fire (marking them), and **(4)** most importantly, to help the lost find salvation.

Excursions on How All Christians are to be Evangelizers

We live in a world today where Genesis 6:5 and 8:21 is magnified a thousand fold.

Genesis 6:5 Updated American Standard Version (UASV)

5 Jehovah saw that the wickedness of man was great in the earth, and that every inclination of the thoughts of his heart was only evil continually.

Genesis 8:21 Updated American Standard Version (UASV)

21 And when Jehovah smelled the pleasing aroma, and Jehovah said in his heart, "I will never again curse the ground because of man, for the inclination of man's heart is evil from his youth. Neither will I ever again strike down every living thing as I have done.

Jesus said of 'what will be the sign of his coming and of the end of the age?' (Matt 24:23)

Matthew 24:14 English Standard Version (ESV)

14 And this gospel [good news] of the kingdom will be proclaimed throughout the whole world as a testimony to all nations, and then the end will come.

With much of what we see today, one wonders what the goods news could be.

Isaiah 52:7 English Standard Version (ESV)

7 How beautiful upon the mountains
   are the feet of him who brings good news,
who publishes peace, who brings good news of happiness,
   who publishes salvation,
   who says to Zion, "Your God reigns."

Nahum 1:15 English Standard Version (ESV)

15 Behold, upon the mountains, the feet of him
who brings good news,
who publishes peace!
Keep your feasts, O Judah;
fulfill your vows,
for never again shall the worthless pass through you;
he is utterly cut off.

Romans 10:15 English Standard Version (ESV)

15 And how are they to preach unless they are sent?
As it is written, "How beautiful are the feet of those who
preach the good news!"[113]

Christianity today, has sadly, fallen away from the
evangelism that they had been assigned, the preaching
and teaching of the Good News, the making of disciples.
(Matt 24:14; 28:19-20) The first-century Christians were
very zealous when it came to sharing the Good News,
biblical truths with others. In fact, the newly interested
ones were taught the basics of the faith, before they were
baptized. Once they were baptized, they were
immediately involved in spreading these same biblical
truths to others. This is why just seventy years after the
sacrificial death of Jesus Christ; there were more than a
million Christians spread all throughout the then known
world of the Roman Empire. Christians today, should
have this same zeal, because Jesus gave only one
command that was to be carried out after his departure,
the making of disciples.

Sadly, our work as evangelists has taken on a
completely new meaning these days. Why? First, we have
to share biblical truths with unbelievers. Second, we must
also pull some Christians who doubt back from the fire.
Third, we must help the liberal and moderate Christian

---

[113] Romans 10:15 : Cited from Isa. 52:7; [Nah. 1:15; Eph. 6:15]

back to the right side of the fence (symbolically marking them on the head for survival), to get some back on the path of salvation. There are two billion Christians in this world and only five percent are of the truly conservative mindset for such a work. However, they are not even engaged in this work, as they ought to be. Therefore, the question that continues to go unanswered comes from Jesus himself,

Luke 18:8 English Standard Version (ESV)

[8] I tell you, he will give justice to them speedily. Nevertheless, when the Son of Man comes, will he find faith on earth?"

One thing is for certain, Jesus is not going to feel any sympathy for those that have abandoned clean worship for unclean worship. These liberal and moderate Christians have abandoned biblical truths for modern day political correctness, to fit in with a world of humanity that has rejected the biblical truths we were sent to deliver. Even moderate Christians, who try to call themselves conservatives, defenders of the Word of God and defenders of the faith, have abandoned that Word of God. It does not matter how desperately these groups feel that they are doing the right things, because Jesus has had one message they have failed to appreciate.

Matthew 7:21-23 English Standard Version (ESV)

I Never Knew You

[21] "Not everyone who says to me, 'Lord, Lord,' will enter the kingdom of heaven, but **the one who does the will of my Father** who is in heaven. [22] On that day many will say to me, 'Lord, Lord, did we not prophesy in your name, and cast out demons in your name, and do many mighty works in your name?' [23] And

then will I declare to them, 'I never knew you; depart from me, you workers of lawlessness.'

In the end, the truly conservative Christians (the man with the inkhorn), are doing the will of the Father, namely carrying out the Great Commission on the unbelievers, but who are also marking the unclean worshipers, the ones sighing and groaning over the detestable things being done in the name of God today, by pseudo-Christianity. I think we can all figure out who the executioners are, the six, who are carrying the clubs to execute those who were unwilling to see the light.

Matthew 25:31-34 English Standard Version (ESV)

The Final Judgment

[31] "When the Son of Man comes in his glory, and all the angels with him, then he will sit on his glorious throne.[32] Before him will be gathered all the nations, and he will separate people one from another as a shepherd separates the sheep from the goats. [33] And he will place the sheep on his right, but the goats on the left. [34] Then the King will say to those on his right, 'Come, you who are blessed by my Father, inherit the kingdom prepared for you from the foundation of the world.

Bibliography

Akin, Daniel L. *The New American Commentary: 1, 2, 3 John*. Nashville, TN: Broadman & Holman , 2001.

Alden, Robert L. *Job, The New American Commentary, vol. 11* . Nashville: Broadman & Holman Publishers, 2001.

Anders, Max. *Holman New Testament Commentary: vol. 8, Galatians-Colossians* . Nashville, TN: Broadman & Holman Publishers, 1999.

Andrews, Edward D. *AN INTRODUCTION TO BIBLE DIFFICULTIES So-Called Errors and Contradictions*. Cambridge: Christian Publishing House, 2011.

—. *An Introduction to Bible Difficulties: So-called Errors and Contradictions*. Cambridge, OH: Christian Publlishing House, 2012.

—. *BOOKS OF 2 JOHN 3 JOHN and JUDE CPH New Testament Commentary*. Cambridge: Christian Publishing House, 2013.

Archer, Gleason L. *Encyclopedia of Bible Difficulties*. Grand Rapids: Zondervan, 1982.

Arnold, Clinton E. *Zondervan Illustrated Bible Backgrounds Commentary Volume 2: John, Acts.* . Grand Rapids, MI: Zondervan, 2002.

—. *Zondervan Illustrated Bible Backgrounds Commentary Volume 3: Romans to Philemon*. Grand Rapids: Zondervan, 2002.

—. *Zondervan Illustrated Bible Backgrounds Commentary Volume 4: Hebrews to Revelation.* Grand Rapids, MI: Zondervan, 2002.

—. *Zondervan Illustrated Bible Backgrounds Commentary: Matthew, Mark, Luke, vol. 1.* Grand Rapids, MI: Zondervan, 2002.

Bercot, David W. *A Dictionary of Early Christian Beliefs.* Peabody: Hendrickson, 1998.

Blomberg, Craig. *The New American Commentary: Matthew .* Nashville, TN : Broadman & Holman Publishers, 2001.

Boa, Kenneth, and Kruidenier. *Holman New Testament Commentary: Romans.* Nashville: Broadman & Holman, 2000.

Borchert, Gerald L. *The New American Commentary: John 1-11 .* Nashville, TN: Broadman & Holman Publishers, 2001.

Borchert, Gerald L. *The New American Commentary vol. 25B, John 12–21.* Nashville: Broadman & Holman Publishers, 2002.

Brand, Chad, Charles Draper, and England Archie. *Holman Illustrated Bible Dictionary: Revised, Updated and Expanded.* Nashville, TN: Holman, 2003.

Bromiley, Geoffrey W., and Gerhard Friedrich. *Theological Dictionary of the New Testament, ed. Gerhard Kittel, vol. 4.* Grand Rapids, MI: Eerdmans, 1964-.

Buter, Trent C. *Holman New Testament Commentary: Luke.* Nashville, TN: Broadman & Holman Publishers, 2000.

Cooper, Lamar Eugene. *The New American Commentary, Ezekiel, vol. 17.* Nashville, TN: Broadman & Holman Publishers, 1994.

Easley, Kendell H. *Holman New Testament Commentary, vol. 12, Revelation.* (Nashville, TN: Broadman & Holman Publishers, 1998.

Elwell, Walter A. *Evangelical Dictionary of Theology (Second Edition).* Grand Rapids: Baker Academic, 2001.

Gangel, Kenneth O. *Holman New Testament Commentary: Acts.* Nashville, TN: Broadman & Holman Publishers, 1998.

Gangel, Kenneth O. *Holman New Testament Commentary, vol. 4, John* . Nashville, TN: Broadman & Holman Publishers, 2000.

Geisler, Norman L., and Thomas Howe. *The Big Book of Bible Difficulties.* Grand Rapids: Baker Books, 1992.

George, Timothy. *The New American Commentary: Galatians* . Nashville, TN: Broadman & Holman Publishers, 2001.

Hill, Jonathan. *Zondervan Handbook to the History of Christianity.* Oxford: Lion, 2006.

Keener, Craig S. *The IVP Bible Background Commentary: New Testament.* Downer Groves, IL: InterVarsity Press, 1993.

Kenneth, Boa., and Kruidenier. *Holman New Testament Commentary: Romans, Vol. 6.* Nashville, TN: Broadman & Holman, 2000.

Larson, Knute. *Holman New Testament Commentary, vol. 9, I & II Thessalonians, I & II Timothy, Titus,*

Philemon. Nashville, TN: Broadman & Holman Publishers, 2000.

Lea, Thomas D. *Holman New Testament Commentary: Vol. 10, Hebrews, James*. Nashville, TN: Broadman & Holman Publishers, 1999.

Lea, Thomas D., and Hayne P. Griffin. *The New American Commentary, vol. 34, 1, 2 Timothy, Titus*. Nashville: Broadman & Holman Publishers, 1992.

Martin, D Michael. *The New American Commentary 33 1, 2 Thessalonians* . Nashville, TN: Broadman & Holman, 2001, c1995 .

Mathews, K. A. *The New American Commentary vol. 1A, Genesis 1-11:26* . Nashville: Broadman & Holman Publishers, 2001.

Matthews, K. A. *The New American Commentary Vol. 1B, Genesis 11:27-50:26*. Nashville: Broadman and Holman Publishers, 2001.

Melick, Richard R. *The New American Commentary: vol. 32, Philippians, Colissians, Philemon*. Nashville, TN : Broadman & Holman Publishers, 2001.

Mirriam-Webster, Inc. *Mirriam-Webster's Collegiate Dictionary. Eleventh Edition*. Springfield: Mirriam-Webster, Inc., 2003.

Mounce, William D. *Mounce's Complete Expository Dictionary of Old & New Testament Words*. Grand Rapids, MI: Zondervan, 2006.

Myers, Allen C. *The Eerdmans Bible Dictionary* . Grand Rapids, Mich: Eerdmans, 1987.

Polhill, John B. *The New American Commentary 26: Acts*. Nashville: Broadman & Holman Publishers, 2001.

Pratt Jr, Richard L. *I & II Corinthians, vol. 7, Holman New Testament Commentary* . Nashville, TN: , 2000: Broadman & Holman Publishers, 2000.

Smith, Gary. *The New American Commentary: Isaiah 1-39, Vol. 15a.* Nashville, TN: B & H Publishing Group, 2007.

—. *The New American Commentary: Isaiah 40-66, Vol. 15b.* Nashville, TN: B&H Publishing, 2009.

Stein, Robert H. *A Basic Guide to Interpreting the Bible: Playing by the Rules.* Grand Rapids: Baker Books, 1994.

—. *The New American Commentary: Luke.* Nashville, TN: Broadman & Holman , 2001, c1992.

Torrey, Reuben A., and Edward D. Andrews. *DIFFICULTIES IN THE BIBLE Alleged Errors and Contradictions: Updated and Expanded Edition.* Cambridge: Christian Publishing House, 2012.

Vine, W E. *Vine's Expository Dictionary of Old and New Testament Words.* Nashville: Thomas Nelson, 1996.

Walls, David, and Max Anders. *Holman New Testament Commentary: I & II Peter, I, II & III John, Jude.* Nashville: Broadman & Holman Publishers, 1996.

Walton, John H. *Zondervan Illustrated Bible Backgrounds Commentary (Old Testament) Volume 1: Genesis, Exodus, Leviticus, Numbers, Deuteronomy.* Grand Rapids, MI: Zondervan, 2009.

—. *Zondervan Illustrated Bible Backgrounds Commentary (Old Testament) Volume 5: The Minor Prophets, Job, Psalms, Proverbs, Ecclesiastes, Song of Songs.* Grand Rapids, M: Zondervan, 2009.

Walton, John H., Victor H. Matthews, and Mark W
      Chavalas. *The IVP Bible Background
      Commentary: Old Testament*. Downers Grove:
      IVP Academic, 2000.

Weber, Stuart K. *Holman New Testament Commentary,
      vol. 1, Matthew*. Nashville, TN: Broadman &
      Holman Publishers, 2000.

Wood, D R W. *New Bible Dictionary (Third Edition)*.
      Downers Grove: InterVarsity Press, 1996.

Zuck, Roy B. *Basic Bible Interpretation: A Prafctical Guide
      to Discovering Biblical Truth*. Colorado Springs:
      David C. Cook, 1991.

Other Books Authored by Edward D. Andrews

WALK HUMBLY WITH YOUR GOD: Putting God's Purpose First in Your Life

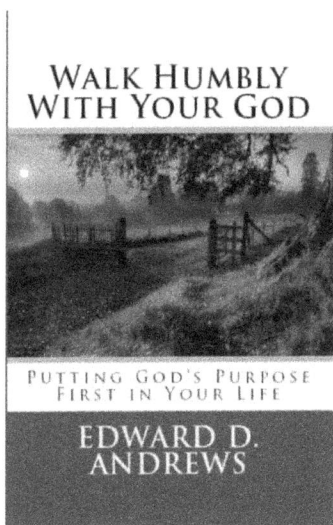

The purpose of this book is to serve as a guide to all Christians, who are interested in walking with God, living a good and productive Christian life, carrying ourselves rightly in the love of God. What does this involve? We must visit the words of Jesus Christ, as he similarly says, "If you keep my commandments, you will abide in my love, just as I have kept my Father's commandments and abide in his love." (John 15:10) To evidence the love of God in our lives, we need to apply the Word of God in everyday life. Jesus also said, "If you know these things, happy you are if you do them."—John 13:17.

It is my genuine expectation that this publication will help you to more fully evidence the love of God in your life and thus can fulfill the wishes of the Creator himself, "Be wise, my son, and make my heart glad, that I may answer him who reproaches me."—Proverbs 27:11.

APPLYING GOD'S WORD MORE FULLY IN YOUR LIFE: How to Broaden and Deepen Your Understanding of God's Word[114]

APPLYING GOD'S
WORD MORE FULLY
IN YOUR LIFE

HOW TO BROADEN AND DEEPEN YOUR
UNDERSTANDING OF GOD'S WORD

EDWARD D.
ANDREWS

Hundreds of millions of Christians around the world are lacking the basic knowledge of the Bible's teachings. Moreover, they are therefore, unable to take advantage of the full happiness of partaking in joint worship of God; they need to have their powers of discernment trained by constant practice to distinguish good from evil, they need to leave the elementary doctrine of Christ and move on to maturity. This book has been penned for that very purpose, to help all Christians to increase and expand their understanding of God's Word and to apply it more fully in their lives. Be aware that this book will ask questions that are designed, to help us investigate our inner-self.

---

[114] https://www.createspace.com/3829757

MISREPRESENTING JESUS: Debunking Bart D. Ehrman's Misquoting Jesus[115]

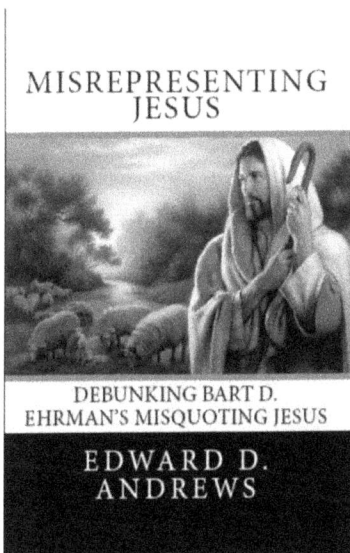

MISREPRESENTING
JESUS

DEBUNKING BART D.
EHRMAN'S MISQUOTING JESUS

EDWARD D.
ANDREWS

Edward Andrews boldly answers the challenges Bart D. Ehrman puts against the divine inspiration and authority of the Bible. By glimpsing into the life of Bart D. Ehrman and following along his course of academic studies, Andrews helps the reader to understand the biases, assumptions, and shortcomings supporting Ehrman's arguments. Using sound logic, technical exegesis, and conservative interpretation, Andrews helps scholars overcome the teachings of biblical errancy that Ehrman propagates.

"A sometimes complex area has been made very palatable and enjoyable to read. Dare I say--even quite exciting!" —Online reviewer

---

[115] https://www.createspace.com/3759006

THE TEXT OF THE NEW TESTAMENT: A Beginner's Guide to New Testament Textual Criticism[116]

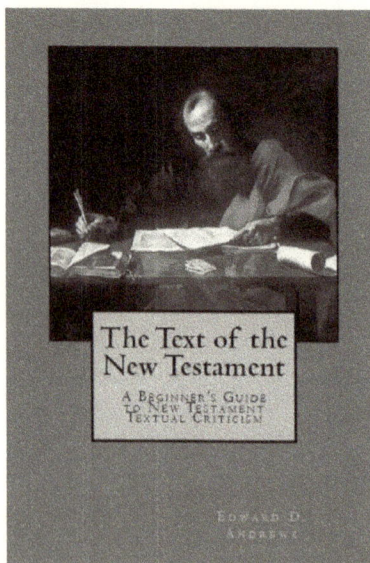

Many critics of the Bible say that we cannot know what was said, because we do not have the originals. This is a false claim, because we can get back to the originals by restoring what was there through the science of textual criticism, and a restored text, is the same as the originals, minus being on the same original papyrus.

Starting with the basics, Edward D. Andrews guides you through New Testament textual criticism. Starting with the threat to the authority and authenticity of the New Testament text (Bible critics), The Text of the New Testament leads you through each aspect of textual studies to prepare you for studying the Bible as a student of the textual history. Even more importantly, Andrews presents arguments to defend the Bible's authority and accuracy against the latest onslaught of atheist and agnostic scholarship undermining the Bible as divinely inspired, inerrant and irrefutable. Andrews gives the student the history of the text, explaining the

---

[116] https://www.createspace.com/3789167

art and science of textual criticism, offering the reader a word picture of the ancient books, as well as the basics of paleography (dating manuscripts). In addition, he explains how we can restore what the original text said, the different methods of textual criticism, taking the reader through the process of publishing the original New Testament books, along with the 1,400-year period of corruption by copyists, culminating with the 400 years of restoration, and so much more. This will enable the Bible student to defend himself against those who wish to cast doubt on the trustworthiness of our Greek New Testament text.

THE COMPLETE GUIDE TO BIBLE TRANSLATION: Bible Translation Choices and Translation Principles[117]

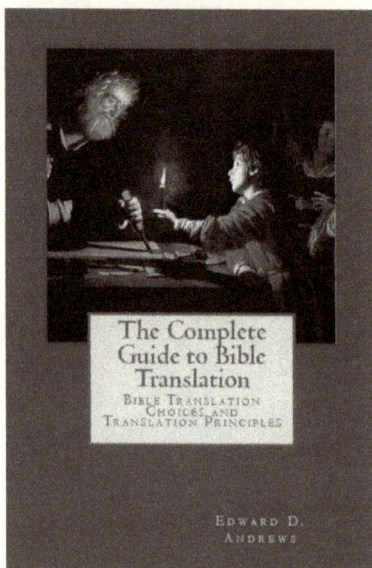

It is a daunting task for the new Bible student to walk into a store for the purpose of purchasing a Bible. Immediately, he is met with shelves upon shelves of more than 100 different English translation choices: AMP, AT, ASV, BLE, CEB, CEV, ERV, ESV, HCSB, IB, ISV, JB, KJ21, LB, MLB, NAB, NASB, NCV, NEB, NET, NJB, NIV, NIVI, NIRV, NKJV, NLT, NLV, NRSV, REB, RSV, RVB, SEB, TEV, TNIV, WE and on and on. He is even further bewildered when he realizes that, in addition to the standard format, there are different formats within each translation: a reference Bible, a study Bible, a life application Bible, an archaeology Bible. He further notices that some translations claim to be Essentially Literal, while others claim to be Dynamic Equivalent (thought for thought), which only serves to increase his confusion.

The goal of THE COMPLETE GUIDE TO BIBLE TRANSLATION is to offer those new to the subject an

---

[117] https://www.createspace.com/3771321

overview of the history and methods, aims and results of the Bible translation process.

In addition, the reader will gain an appreciation of the work and lifetime efforts of hundreds of Bible scholars over the past 450-years, who have labored, so that we can say that we have many very good translations that are a mirror like reflection of the original, in translation. The reader will also find that he or she has a renewed confidence in the reliability of the Bible. Finally, the reader will be able to determine for himself or herself, which translations are the best for study and research.

YOUR GUIDE FOR DEFENDING THE BIBLE: Self-Education of the Bible Made Easy[118]

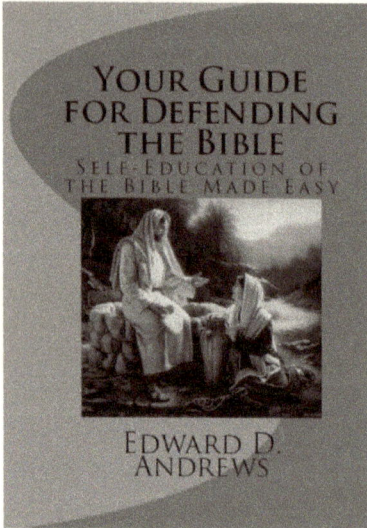

LET ME ASK YOU SOME QUESTIONS:

(1) Do you want to waste your hard-earned money by buying the wrong books?

(2) Do have some basic Bible knowledge, and would love to have more?

(3) Do you wish that you could be better at sharing your faith, defending what you know to be true?

(4) Do you fear those tough Bible questions?

(5) Do you want to be able to defend God's Word as true, inerrant and inspired?

(6) Are you tired of the Bible scholars having all the knowledge?

(7) Do you want to have confidence when you are talking to others about the Bible?

---

[118] https://www.createspace.com/3764440

(8) Do you want to learn how to study better, and more efficiently?

(9) Do you want to accomplish these things in the most productive way possible?

If one were to go on any discussion board on the worldwide Internet, he or she would find hundreds of millions in ongoing, unending debates on countless websites about God's Word and its reliability and inspiration. In other words, 'is the Bible the Word of God?' Sadly, the reader of this book will find many people today, who are losing faith in the belief that the Bible is the inspired, inerrant Word of God. Why?

Liberal-progressive Christianity has overtaken conservative Christianity in the last 70-years. These are the ones, who claim that the Bible is a book by man alone, not inspired; being subject to errors, contradictions, and "unscientific." Other critics argue that the Bible is nothing more than a collection of myths and legends. Still, others argue that archaeology and Biblical chronology cannot be harmonized. Other critics claim that the Gospels of Mathew, Mark, Luke and John are not historically accurate. Others still, argue that Jesus was not divine, claiming he was merely a traveling sage.

Your Guide for Defending the Bible offers the Bible student an introduction to many different subject areas that will help him or her to follow the following biblical counsel:

BE PREPARED TO MAKE A DEFENSE
1 Peter 3:15 English Standard Version (ESV)

But in your hearts honor Christ the Lord as holy, always being prepared to make a defense to anyone who asks you for a reason for the hope that is in you

CONTEND FOR THE FAITH

Jude 1:3 English Standard Version (ESV)

Beloved, although I was very eager to write to you about our common salvation, I found it necessary to write appealing to you to contend for the faith that was once for all delivered to the saints.

HELP THOSE WHO DOUBT

Jude 1:22-23 English Standard Version (ESV)

And have mercy on those who doubt; save others by snatching them out of the fire;

AN INTRODUCTION TO BIBLE DIFFICULTIES: So-called Errors and Contradictions[119]

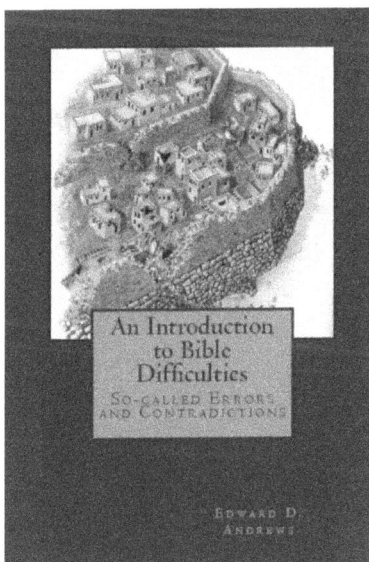

The Bible is loaded with thousands of difficult, challenging passages- many of which become obstacles in the development of our faith. These difficulties arise out of differences in culture, language, needs, religious and political organization, not to mention between 2,000 and 3,500 years of separation. Calling attention to these difficulties and sifting out the misconceptions, Edward Andrews defends the inerrancy of the Bible, clarifies apparent contradictions, and arms you with what you need to defend your faith in the Bible.

---

www.ingramcontent.com/pod-product-compliance
Lightning Source LLC
Chambersburg PA
CBHW031827090426
42741CB00005B/161